FRITZI KALLOP'S BIRTH BOOK

FRITZI KALLOP'S BIRTH BOOK

Fritzi Farber Kallop, R.N., B.S.,
Certified ASPO Childbirth Educator

with *Julie Houston*

VINTAGE BOOKS

A DIVISION OF RANDOM HOUSE

NEW YORK

A VINTAGE ORIGINAL, July 1988
FIRST EDITION

Grateful acknowledgment is made to the following for permission to reprint previously published illustrations:

Illustrations on pages 100 (first figure), 154, 164, 179, 235, 260, and 261 are adapted from illustrations by Childbirth Graphics Ltd., Rochester, New York. Illustrations on pages 12, 29, and 181 (second figure) are adapted from illustrations in *The Complete Book of Pregnancy and Childbirth* by Sheila Kitzinger. Copyright © 1980 by Dorling Kindersley Ltd., London. Used with permission of Alfred A. Knopf, Inc. Illustrations on page 41 are adapted from illustrations by Jan Ruby Baird, based on drawings by Eva Schuchardt. © Maternity Center Association. Illustrations on pages 7, 8, 9, 30, 100 (second figure), 208, 233, 285, and 292 are adapted with permission of Ross Laboratories, Columbus, OH 43216, from illustrations in *Clinical Education Aid,* volume nos. 18, 13, 13, 12, 18, 17, 17, 10, and 10, © 1978, 1979, 1980 Ross Laboratories. Illustrations on pages 46, 74, 158, 159, and 181 (first figure) are adapted from illustrations in *Dr. Miriam Stoppard's Pregnancy and Birth Book* by Dr. Miriam Stoppard. Copyright © 1986 by Dorling Kindersley Ltd., London. Used with permission of Villard Books, a division of Random House, Inc. Birth series photographs © Mary Motley Kalergis.

Library of Congress Cataloging-in-Publication Data
Kallop, Fritzi.
Fritzi Kallop's birth book.
1. Pregnancy. 2. Childbirth. 3. Infants—Care.
I. Houston, Julie. II. Title. III. Title: Birth
book. [DNLM: 1. Labor—popular works.
2. Neonatology—popular works.
3. Pregnancy—popular works. WQ 150 K14b]
RG525.K246 1987   618.2   86-29680
ISBN 0-394-75345-3 (pbk.)

Book design by Tasha Hall

Manufactured in the United States of America
10 9 8 7 6 5 4 3 2 1

This book is dedicated to my parents,
husband and children, who gave me
my roots, and to Elisabeth Bing,
who gave me my wings.

Preface

When I graduated from nursing school in 1968 and needed to choose a specialty, I chose labor and delivery for some very superficial reasons. Every nurse had to rotate shifts, which I could do easily because I was single and had no family responsibilities, and newborns had a certain appeal. I had no inkling of what frantic, pain-ridden women I was to encounter when I had virtually no appropriate skills to assist them. Nor were local anesthetics available at The New York Hospital at the time, so heavy medication was the only route to pain relief in labor. Fortunately, the groundswell of interest in Lamaze preparation was just beginning, and when the chance came for me to take a class from Elisabeth Bing, a founder of Lamaze in the United States, I quickly signed up, not because it would certify me to become a Lamaze instructor but because it seemed to offer a way to help those suffering women I worked with. After I completed the course, Mrs. Bing invited me to be her assistant. Intrigued and flattered, I took the job; meanwhile, I continued to work full time in labor and delivery.

Lamaze wasn't difficult to teach, as I had feared it would be, probably because our students were so highly motivated and receptive to every bit of information we gave them. The true test began when I assisted in labor the same couples we had taught in class. It was a revelation to see how much they benefited from what they'd been taught. Soon I was teaching my own classes and deluged by students.

How could I have *so* underestimated a specialty area! Childbirth was not just a physical process to be endured, but a challenge that could be taken on with enthusiasm and prepared for with hard work. Fears, old wives' tales, and misconceptions could be addressed, techniques of relaxation and breathing to cope with pain could be taught. Assisting couples to learn how to work together became my goal. Fortunately, local anesthetics were also becoming available to allow couples who experienced a difficult labor or delivery to continue to participate fully in the birth of their infant.

The purpose of this book is not only to give you information and to teach you techniques to use but also to share with you some of the wonderful, warm moments that I have experienced over my almost twenty years of teaching and assisting more than five thousand couples in giving birth. If you are pregnant, capitalize on this special time in your life, and prepare for probably the greatest event you and your spouse have yet encountered together.

Good luck, and may your child's wondrous birth mark the beginning of a terrific new life as a parent.

FRITZI KALLOP

Contents

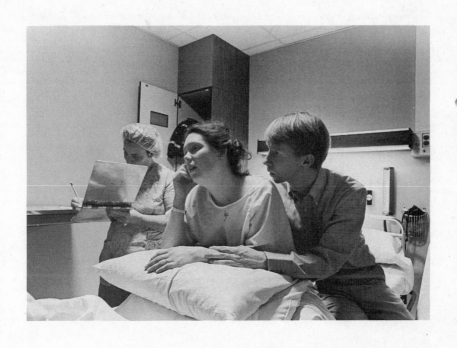

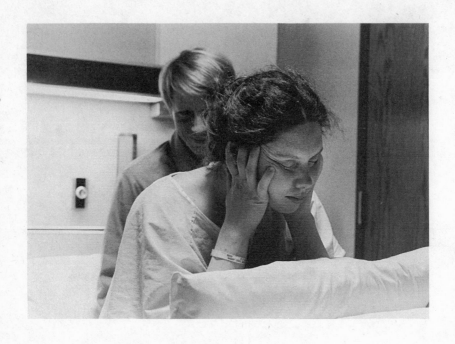

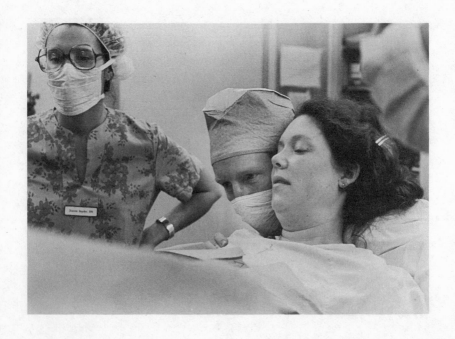

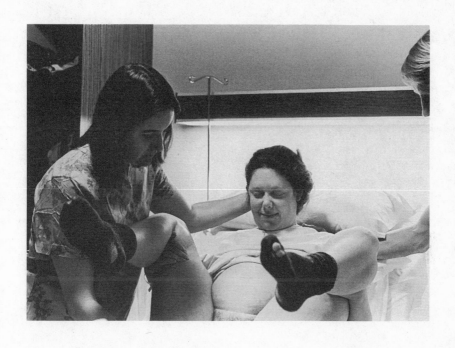

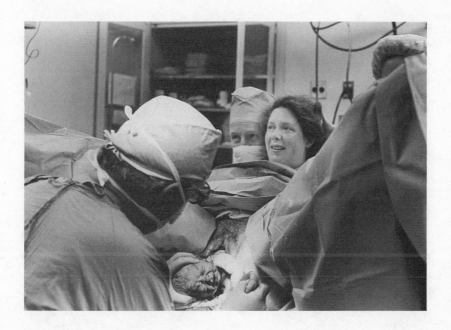

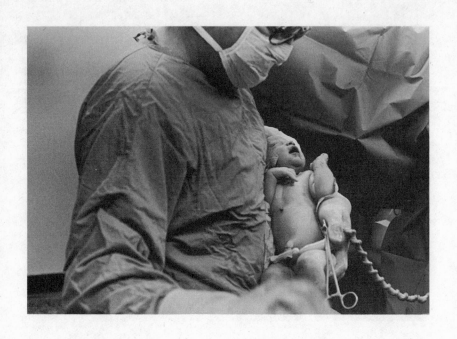

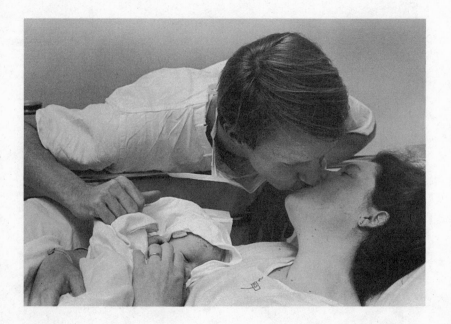

FRITZI KALLOP'S BIRTH BOOK

PART ONE

Pregnancy

You're pregnant! Don't those simple words bring a million pictures to mind? If it's hard to envision yourself ever sporting a very-pregnant belly or you and your husband holding your own little baby, Nature very generously provides a long, nine-month "taking-in phase" to help you prepare for the momentous event of having a baby.

Being pregnant for the first time is a unique condition to find yourself in, and it's easy to misinterpret the facts. If, for example, you've heard that hormonal changes at the onset of pregnancy cause women to be nauseated, you might naturally conclude that this is going to happen to you. It might—but it might not. Some women feel great from day one to the very end of the pregnancy. Others are able to avert their nausea with various measures described in the coming chapters.

To help give you the confidence you need to relax and enjoy your pregnant body and its precious contents, the first part of this book is a chronology of the normal experience of pregnancy—what goes on in your doctor's office, why you have certain tests and procedures, what's happening inside your body, how to cope with and alleviate possible discomforts, how to eat well and stay in shape. Hopefully, as you read about the predictable, normal

3

developments of pregnancy, you will gain a balanced view of how they may (or may not) affect your own condition.

What Is "Normal"?

Because having a baby is so new to you, it may be hard to determine what is considered the "normal" experience. The variations within the "normal range" are wide and they affect women to differing degrees. Although I always point this out in pregnancy and childbirth classes, after delivery someone will say, "I didn't have *any* nausea!" or "That first stage of labor that *you* said would be eight hours *wasn't*. It was only five!" That's perfectly normal. So as you read ahead, realize that the "normal" discussed is a range and undoubtedly you will have your own individual *special* variation. After all, no one is ever the exact "median of the bell curve." Neither will you be!

1

Confirming Your Suspicions

Some women are so highly attuned to their bodies that they say they actually feel the moment the egg implants into the wall of the uterus, about eight days after conception; others have no inkling of being pregnant until a month or two later, and even then can hardly believe their doctor's firm diagnosis. In either case, as the days stretch beyond the time you would normally expect a menstrual period and your suspicions of being pregnant grow stronger (perhaps noticing tenderness in your breasts or fluid retention in your body), you will naturally want to confirm them. You can buy an at-home pregnancy test at the corner

"Just prior to my pregnancy being confirmed, I experienced 'lead breasts'—my breasts became so heavy I had to hold them when I awoke and got out of bed. I also felt some minor cramping. I was very excited and a little nervous."

drugstore if you wish, but first call your doctor's office, say what's going on, and make an appointment for an office visit.

"When my home pregnancy test turned positive, I ran out and blew about a hundred bucks on competitive tests and spent the next morning peeing merrily and setting up a science lab in the kitchen."

YOUR FIRST OFFICE VISIT AND DOCTOR'S DIAGNOSIS

At your doctor's office a blood or urine sample will be taken to confirm or negate your suspicions. You'll get the results of the test either immediately or, if the sample has been sent out to a laboratory, in a few days.

Your doctor will do a physical exam to back up the findings of the lab test and get some clue to where you are in the pregnancy. First he'll measure the size of the uterus externally, from pubic bone to navel, using either calipers, which look like a pair of large ice tongs, or simply finger breadths. If it's the latter, you might not be aware you are being measured and he might say to the nurse (or he might just write it down on the chart himself), "three finger breadths below the umbilicus," or "one above" or whatever. There is no specific number he is looking for, so if you meet someone in the park that afternoon who is just as far along in her pregnancy but two finger breadths lower than you are, it's really not important. Measuring the uterus is merely one way your doctor can chart the pattern of fetal growth, and he will do this all through your pregnancy. He's not concerned about whether you are carrying a baby a little bigger or a little smaller than the next person's, only that the *pattern* of growth is consistent throughout your particular pregnancy.

Next, your doctor will probably do a vaginal exam to look for the physical signs of early pregnancy, checking the color of the mucous membrane of the vagina and the cervix, the neck of the uterus that juts down into the vagina. During pregnancy both of these areas change from a light pink to a purply color due to the increased blood supply.

He'll also examine the consistency of the cervix. If you were to put your finger into your vagina and touch the cervix, which is easy to reach when you are lying in the bath, you would find when you are not pregnant that it feels very firm, almost like the tip of your nose, with a noticeable little indentation or tiny hole in the center, leading up into the uterus. When you are pregnant, the increased blood supply to the area makes the cervix feel soft and fleshy, almost like the upper fatty part of your cheek when you smile. If you have never really explored your body, maybe now is the time to see just what's what.

Before finishing the vaginal exam, he will also measure the interior dimensions of your pelvic bones to determine whether your pelvis is "adequate for an average-sized infant." I've always loved the use of that all-encompassing medical term, so vague and unscientific, in describing how Nature manages to give each woman a baby the right size for her pelvis—at least in most cases. That's what's important anyway, not the exact measurement in pounds and ounces, and that term "average-sized infant" should really be "*appropriate*-sized infant."

The exam may be uncomfortable, but slow, deep breaths will help you relax and make it easier. There are two inside measure-

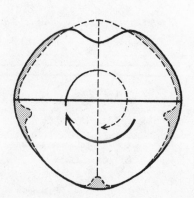

A woman's bony pelvis, with its widest diameter through the inlet being the transverse and its widest diameter through the outlet being from front to back. Arrow shows how the baby's head rotates through the bony pathway.

ments he's calculating: from side to side, two little bones that protrude into your pelvis; and from front to back, pubic bone to sacrum. Using only his fingers and hand may seem quite unscientific, but he knows what he's feeling in relationship to the size of his own hands. If he finds that your pelvis is particularly flat or narrow, for example, he might say something to you immediately about it or he might wait until later on in the pregnancy and say, "You know, the architecture of your pelvis is a little unusual. If you have a good-sized baby, we may have a problem getting the baby through, which would warrant a Caesarean birth."

The appearance of the hips can be deceiving. Most people assume that a woman with big hips can accommodate a baby the size of a horse. Actually, she might have prominent little spines,

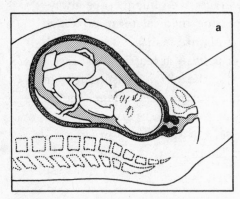 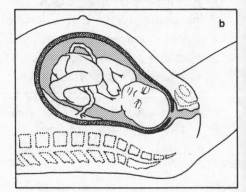

Pregnancy at term: before the onset of labor, head "dipping," cervix long, thick, and not effaced.

Early labor: cervix completely effaced and beginning to dilate.

Active labor: cervix 5–6 cm. dilated; vaginal exam being done prior to rupture of membranes.

Transition: cervix 8 cm. dilated; baby's head rotating.

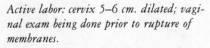

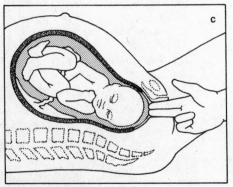 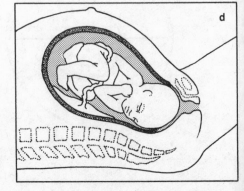

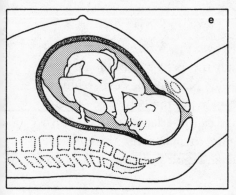

Cervix fully dilated to 10 cm.

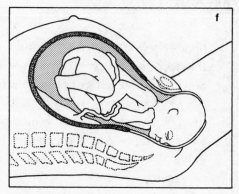

Baby's head visible at vaginal opening.

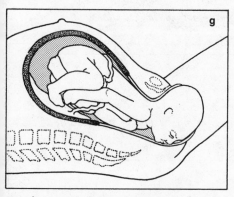

Head crowning just as episiotomy is about to be made.

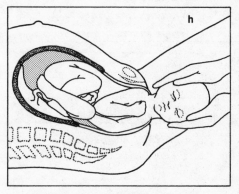

Assisted external rotation of baby's head just prior to the rest of the baby's body being delivered.

Separation of the placenta.

Immediately after placenta expulsion.

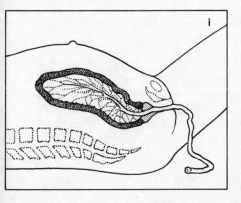

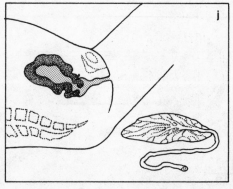

or a coccyx that bends in and narrows the inside dimension of the section of pelvis through which the baby's head must pass. Since it is a very tight passage anyway, Nature does everything it can to facilitate the birth process by having the baby's head, with its soft spaces and skull bones that can overlap if needed, turn and pivot up under the pubic bone to maneuver through the pelvis. The pelvic joints even "loosen" a bit near the end of the pregnancy.

> *"The whole conception process seemed a miracle. I wanted to learn more about how this had happened, and began to read every book I could find on children and childbearing. I also felt pressure to reevaluate our family budget, to see if we could get along on a single income." (Father)*

> *"Learning that I had conceived after a miscarriage and several months of trying was the most exciting part."*

Doctors are usually very open about their findings and will routinely tell you what is going on. You can consider that no news is good news, but if you hear nothing you might ask what he has found out about your own pelvic measurements.

When the examination has been completed, you will have a chance to sit down with your doctor to go over his findings, discuss your concerns, and get answers to any questions you might have.

> *"Our doctor asked us if we had planned this baby. 'Yes,' we said, 'we planned it for two years from now.'"*

Your Due Date and How It's Calculated

Faced with our irregular calendar of 28-, 30-, and 31-day months, there always seems to be a good deal of confusion about how many months pregnant one really is. When you confer with your doctor, he will ask you to tell him the first day of your last period. This is the date on which he will base his calculations. Now you might think to yourself he must be making some mistake because you certainly were not pregnant on the first day of your last period, and in fact you may suspect you conceived on, say, Monday, March 3, exactly fourteen days *after* the first day of your last period. In fact, there is a good reason why your last period figures into all this: the hormones that caused the lining of your uterus, the endometrium, to slough away and become your last period are the same ones that prepare the underlying tissue for implantation of a fertilized egg two weeks later. Both activities are part of the same cycle.

A birth wheel (a small cardboard wheel that spins on a calendar backing) makes it simple for your doctor to instantly calculate your due date by adding forty weeks to that first day of your last period. This gives you a specific date to focus on, but it is almost *never* going to be the exact date of birth. You could deliver two weeks before or two weeks after your calculated date, and it would still be considered perfectly normal. It's a myth that all first babies are born late, because in fact, 35 percent of them are born early, 60 percent are born late, and only 5 percent are born exactly on their due date.

Or the doctor may take a slightly different approach to making his calculations. Rather than count forward from your last period, he might apply Nagele's rule, taking the first day of your last period, subtracting three months and adding seven days. Either way, he'll arrive at the same date.

As for predictions that you are "definitely having a girl because you are carrying low and left" or you are "carrying a boy because it is high and hefty," you can dismiss them right away. Anyone

Jan Oct	Feb Nov	Mar Dec	Apr Jan	May Feb	June Mar	July Apr	Aug May	Sept June	Oct July	Nov Aug	Dec Sept
1 8	1 8	1 6	1 6	1 5	1 8	1 7	1 8	1 8	1 8	1 8	1 7
2 9	2 9	2 7	2 7	2 6	2 9	2 8	2 9	2 9	2 9	2 9	2 8
3 10	3 10	3 8	3 8	3 7	3 10	3 9	3 10	3 10	3 10	3 10	3 9
4 11	4 11	4 9	4 9	4 8	4 11	4 10	4 11	4 11	4 11	4 11	4 10
5 12	5 12	5 10	5 10	5 9	5 12	5 11	5 12	5 12	5 12	5 12	5 11
6 13	6 13	6 11	6 11	6 10	6 13	6 12	6 13	6 13	6 13	6 13	6 12
7 14	7 14	7 12	7 12	7 11	7 14	7 13	7 14	7 14	7 14	7 14	7 13
8 15	8 15	8 13	8 13	8 12	8 15	8 14	8 15	8 15	8 15	8 15	8 14
9 16	9 16	9 14	9 14	9 13	9 16	9 15	9 16	9 16	9 16	9 16	9 15
10 17	10 17	10 15	10 15	10 14	10 17	10 16	10 17	10 17	10 17	10 17	10 16
11 18	11 18	11 16	11 16	11 15	11 18	11 17	11 18	11 18	11 18	11 18	11 17
12 19	12 19	12 17	12 17	12 16	12 19	12 18	12 19	12 19	12 19	12 19	12 18
13 20	13 20	13 18	13 18	13 17	13 20	13 19	13 20	13 20	13 20	13 20	13 19
14 21	14 21	14 19	14 19	14 18	14 21	14 20	14 21	14 21	14 21	14 21	14 20
15 22	15 22	15 20	15 20	15 19	15 22	15 21	15 22	15 22	15 22	15 22	15 21
16 23	16 23	16 21	16 21	16 20	16 23	16 22	16 23	16 23	16 23	16 23	16 22
17 24	17 24	17 22	17 22	17 21	17 24	17 23	17 24	17 24	17 24	17 24	17 23
18 25	18 25	18 23	18 23	18 22	18 25	18 24	18 25	18 25	18 25	18 25	18 24
19 26	19 26	19 24	19 24	19 23	19 26	19 25	19 26	19 26	19 26	19 26	19 25
20 27	20 27	20 25	20 25	20 24	20 27	20 26	20 27	20 27	20 27	20 27	20 26
21 28	21 28	21 26	21 26	21 25	21 28	21 27	21 28	21 28	21 28	21 28	21 27
22 29	22 29	22 27	22 27	22 26	22 29	22 28	22 29	22 29	22 29	22 29	22 28
23 30	23 30	23 28	23 28	23 27	23 30	23 29	23 30	23 30	23 30	23 30	23 29
24 31	24 1	24 29	24 29	24 28	24 31	24 30	24 31	24 1	24 31	24 31	24 30
25 1	25 2	25 30	25 30	25 1	25 1	25 1	25 1	25 2	25 1	25 1	25 1
26 2	26 3	26 31	26 31	26 2	26 2	26 2	26 2	26 3	26 2	26 2	26 2
27 3	27 4	27 1	27 1	27 3	27 3	27 3	27 3	27 4	27 3	27 3	27 3
28 4	28 5	28 2	28 2	28 4	28 4	28 4	28 4	28 5	28 4	28 4	28 4
29 5		29 3	29 3	29 5	29 5	29 5	29 5	29 6	29 5	29 5	29 5
30 6		30 4	30 4	30 6	30 6	30 6	30 6	30 7	30 6	30 6	30 6
31 7		31 5		31 7		31 7	31 7		31 7		31 7
Jan Nov	Feb Dec	Mar Jan	Apr Feb	May Mar	June Apr	July May	Aug June	Sept July	Oct Aug	Nov Sept	Dec Oct

Check your baby's due date. Look down the columns of the chart at the figures set in bold type to find the first day of your last period; the date next to it is 280 days later, your due date (EDC).

who could accurately foretell the sex of a baby would probably not be walking around blithely making predictions but would undoubtedly be using his or her talent to make a fortune. You have a fifty-fifty chance of having a boy or a girl, plain and simple.

Incredible as it may seem, there are almost exactly the same number of girls as boys born in the world! When I worked in labor and delivery, we might have nine girls born in a row but, sure enough, two days later nine boys would bring it to a tie again, and at the end of the each year, when we averaged 3,400 deliveries, there would be 1,700 boys and 1,700 girls, give or take one or two. Statistically, there are more women alive today than men, but that is because many men die at a younger age, not because of birth quotas. Infant girls are usually a little sturdier than infant boys, which is why the nurses usually root for a girl when a mother is in premature labor with birth imminent.

In most people's eyes, your due date is never going to seem an accurate reflection of "where you are." When you tell people you are, say, five months pregnant, the reaction is invariably something like "Oh, but you are so small!" or "Oh, but you are so big!" It's never "Oh, you look just right!" As you stand there smiling patiently at these well-intentioned souls, you can rest assured it has nothing to do with your actual size, appearance, or anything else but the confusion that surrounds the due date and how people perceive the pregnant body in relation to it.

If you've always been a person who likes to plan things out exactly and has been on time for every appointment, you may find the uncertainty of your due date a little unsettling. All you can do is chalk it up as one of those curves Nature throws, adding to the suspense of one of life's great events.

YOU ARE PREGNANT!

If a blood or urine test is done prior to your first visit to your doctor, you will find the suspense builds steadily until that call finally comes from your doctor to report that your pregnancy test has come back positive. Much as you may have been prepared for the news, it's always a shock. One student of mine described the confusion she felt when her doctor told her the test was positive. Suddenly she forgot what that meant: was she positively pregnant, or positively *not* pregnant? For most couples, it truly is an overwhelming moment, and everyone reacts differently to it.

> *"I had no real expectations of pregnancy, but when the test came back positive, I found myself being scared of the unknown."* (Father)

There's a tendency to want all the world to know the news, to make it official, and yet many couples want to keep it a secret for a while, enjoying together the quiet fact that their tiny baby now exists. One newly pregnant woman called me excitedly to say, "I want to sign up for pregnancy class, please, to get things going! I have not been able to tell anyone, but I knew I could tell you!" As the impact of the news begins to sink in, ambivalent feelings may surface. Many women worry needlessly that they have no mothering instincts. Mothering is a skill that develops over a long period of time, and only after that baby arrives. And although he is not experiencing the physical changes, your husband too is undergoing his own psychological adjustments to this large event in your lives together. In a society like ours in which, despite evidence to the contrary, fathers are considered breadwinners and mothers are considered nurturers, your husband may understandably feel sudden pressure and anxiety about the financial responsibilities of raising a family.

There are also new concerns about your body. Is it, with a baby inside, too fragile to work, play, make love? I can assure you that it is not, but only time will help you and your partner adjust to its changing, resilient shape.

No matter what your age, for most couples the time to have a baby never seems to be perfect despite its being a time of great joy. Something in your career or family life may make the decision to start a family questionable. I know that for me, although I had wanted for years to become pregnant, when it happened, I felt delighted three days out of four—and miserable on the fourth. One woman told me that although she and her husband had talked about having a family later, she was numb when she heard the news. She'd just gotten a full scholarship for graduate school, and "later" was not now!

A professor of mine in nursing school described the prime childbearing years as between sixteen and nineteen years of age. Perhaps physiologically that's the optimum time, but psychologically, the right time for many women today seems to be when they are over thirty, or even thirty-five, when they've had a chance to establish their careers. And it's certainly common today to hear women say they wished they'd waited before having their children—they would have enjoyed mothering more had they first gotten a head start in a field they could pick up again later, and a chance to gain broader experience of the world.

Whatever feelings either you or your husband have about pregnancy, share them. Talk over your fears, hopes, and joys, recognizing that the ambivalence either of you might feel is perfectly normal. Opening up to and nurturing your feelings toward this new, growing baby will provide the foundation for parenthood. But take one step at a time, too. You may be filled with joy that you are pregnant, but it's perfectly normal not to feel anything much toward the baby, at least for a while.

> *"I feel a bond with all expectant mothers (including my own sisters) and with mothers in general. I feel connected with women, more so than I had ever felt before."*

Finally, remember to retain your sense of humor and keep your priorities in order. When doubts of being a good mother overwhelm you, remember the millions of children who have had parents far less concerned and loving than you and your husband. One father expressed it well: "We aren't sure if we'll be good parents, but even if we aren't, our baby won't know it—he can't compare!"

With your pregnancy confirmed, begin now to learn about the

changes in your body and what you can do to take care of your baby. Awareness of what goes on during the many routine visits to your doctor's office—with your body and that of the baby growing inside—will bestow confidence that all is well in this very special time in your life.

2

What Goes on in Your Doctor's Office and Other Medical Concerns

*M*onitoring pregnancy with medical tests and procedures allows a degree of positive control unheard of in the past, usually assuring a healthy, normal baby and a happy, thriving mother. Pregnancy itself *is* a healthy, normal occurrence—humans, unfortunately, are the only species with the ability to worry about it. If you happen to be the kind of person who worries about every little thing that can go wrong in your body, the medical procedures and tests during pregnancy are guaranteed to keep you busy with anxiety and concern. But things can go wrong even when you're *not* pregnant, and it would be foolish to single out your pregnancy for this kind of anxiety.

Just as each pregnancy is different, so too is each woman's attitude toward it. You may sail through with no need for medical attention, or you may be watched intensely by your doctor. In either case, to repeat, you'd be foolish to worry about what could happen. If you dwell on everything that can go wrong you will have a terrible time because of that worry, and your fantasies are far worse than the reality.

In this chapter, you will find basic information and a reasonable assessment of the tests and procedures that are typical during pregnancy. Focus on what you need to know as it comes up in your individual pregnancy, but do not dwell on areas that do not pertain to you. At least if you know what to expect when certain tests are done, you won't be as anxious about them as you would be if you knew nothing. As you read, do not assume that you'll undergo every procedure that's described!

THE ROUTINE OFFICE VISIT

Usually you will see your obstetrician once a month until the thirty-second week, then every two weeks until the last month, and then weekly. You are in your doctor's office so often during pregnancy—probably more than throughout a healthy lifetime—that it's a good time to become familiar with the terminology, and then feel free to discuss it.

ABBREVIATIONS AND NOTATIONS ON YOUR CHART

G	Gravida: the number of pregnancies you have had
P	Para: the number of births you have had
	(A first pregnancy, then, would be described as G 1, P 0)
Ab	Abortion: the number of induced or spontaneous abortions you have had
△	1st, 2nd, or 3rd Trimester: the gestational stages of your pregnancy, approximately 3 months each
LMP	Last menstrual period
EDC	Expected date of confinement: due date
Hgb	Hemoglobin: an oxygen-carrying substance present in your blood. If your Hgb is below 11% you are considered anemic and an iron supplement will be prescribed.
Fe	Iron: usually refers to an iron supplement prescription
BP	Blood pressure
FHR	Fetal heart rate: heard, not heard, or rate and location when it becomes easily audible
Edema	Swelling
Fundus	Top of the uterus
Vtx	Vertex: baby's head presenting (directed toward vaginal canal)
Br	Breech: baby's bottom presenting (directed toward vaginal canal)

DATE (MO., DY., YR.)	LOCATION	SERVICE		Susan Smith
1/18/88				

AGE	DOCTOR	
25	Dr. John Jones	IF NO NAME PLATE, PRINT NAME, SEX, AND HISTORY NO.

Date of Birth 2/27/61 Education AB Occupation Secretary Race W Marital Status M Religion ___

Patient's Address 400 East 63rd St. NY NY 10021 Tel. No. PL 8-2225

Name of Child's Father Bill Occupation Engineer Emergency Name ___ Message Tel. No. ___

Newborn's Physician Dr. David Smith Office Address 525 East 70th St. NYC Tel. No. ___

PREGNANCY HISTORY

No.	Date (Mo./Yr.)	Grav. Wks. Gest.	Term. Labor (Hrs.)	Prem. Spont.	Abort. Ind.	Live Type of Delivery	Interval between menses Alive/Dead	days Baby's Weight	PMP Months Nursed	LMP EDC Complications (Both Maternal and Neonatal)
1	8/86	spontaneous abortion at 12 weeks, D+C at hospital								
2	current pregnancy									
3										
4										
5										
6										

PRESENT PREGNANCY	GYNECOLOGICAL HISTORY	MEDICAL HISTORY	FAMILY HISTORY	Circle All Positive Findings. Detail Below
1. Bleeding	12. Menarche 14 yrs.	22. Rheumatic Fever	42. Hypertension	② at start and end of day
② Nausea, emesis	13. Interval 28	(32) Anemia Hct 11%	43. Kidney disease	④ due to iron supplement
3. Edema	14. Duration 5	33. Epilepsy	44. Diabetes	
④ Constipation	15. Pain	34. Syphillis	45. Malignancy	
5. Pain	16. Intermenstrual bleeding	35. Gonorrhea	46. Tuberculosis	
6. Urinary	17. Leukorrhea	36. Migraine	47. Psychiatric	
7. Headache	18. Contraception	37. Psychiatric	48. Multiple pregnancy	
8. Emotional	19. Infertility	38. Transfusions	49. Bleeding	
9. Smoking	20. Other	39. Endocrine	50. Genetic	
10. Alcohol	21. Abnormal Pap	40. Drug addiction	51. Other	
11. Drugs and Medications		(31) Operations 41. Other appendectomy age 8		☐ See additional progress notes

LABORATORY DATA

DATE	TEST	RESULT	DATE	RESULT	DATE	RESULT
6/6/86	Pap ✓	Normal	1/18	B.P. 110/64 P-78	—	FHR not audible yet
	Urine Culture			R-18 to 37	—	No varicosities
1/18/88	Gonorrhea Culture ✓	Neg	—	urine neg. for sugar and protein	—	No edema
	1 h. GTT				—	No skin rashes
1/18/87	Alpha Fetoprotein ✓	drawn + sent to lab	—	fundus - gravid, large per dates		
"	Rubella "		—			
1/18	Ultrasound	scheduled for 2/22, due to ? large infant vs. twins	—	Breasts - soft no masses		
			—	Pelvic Exam - nl Transverse diameter nl		
	Tine Test		VDRL	neg.	Sickle Cell	neg.
	Blood Type	O pos.	Antibodies		Antibodies	

PROBLEM LIST

DATE	NO	PROBLEM	PLAN
1/18		weight gain during first 8 weeks 10 lbs. Pt. counselled re: diet to control excessive weight gain and treat nausea. Pt. verbalizes understanding of information. ante	partum literature given and questions answered. Pregnancy danger signs explained and emergency telephone number given). Sonogram date set and procedure explained. F. Kallop, RN BS

Rev - 6-80
43310

THE NEW YORK HOSPITAL

OBSTETRICAL ANTEPARTUM RECORD

ANTE-PARTUM RECORD

A typical prenatal record with its abbreviations.

Routine Procedures

At each scheduled office visit you will have a **urine test** to check how your kidneys, which act as a kind of filter, are handling the pregnancy. Excretion of protein, for example, in conjunction with an elevated blood pressure may mean that an expectant woman should cut back on her activities.

Urine tests also gauge whether an excess amount of sugar is being excreted by your body. Because of the increase in blood volume and the metabolic changes that occur in pregnancy, some women acquire "gestational diabetes," which is evidenced by elevated blood and urine sugar. Gestational diabetes is usually controlled by dietary restrictions and disappears after delivery. If it develops, your doctor will monitor the condition; otherwise, you won't hear about the urine tests if the results are normal.

You will be weighed at each visit; the general consensus is that you should gain somewhere between twenty and thirty pounds when you are pregnant. Weight gain is normal if it is not laden with sugar and fat. You can tailor your diet perfectly during pregnancy so that you and your baby will thrive—without eating heaps more food than you are used to. For guidelines, turn to chapter 6, page 86.

Your doctor will check your **blood pressure** to keep tabs on the rate at which your blood volume is increasing. (The volume of blood in your circulatory system usually expands by about 30 percent during pregnancy, which is why you see all those blood vessels on the back on your hands and in your legs and feet.)

Existing **hypertension** (elevated blood pressure) may become aggravated in pregnancy and some women (5 to 10 percent) develop preeclampsia, a condition that includes a significant elevation in blood pressure, an increase of uric acid in the blood, and severe retention of fluid. The cause of preeclampsia is unknown and usually does not occur until after the twentieth week of pregnancy, if it occurs at all. Fortunately, because it develops slowly, with good prenatal care preeclampsia can be detected and treated early with dietary changes, stress reduction, rest, and in some cases sedatives.

Signs of preeclampsia include severe headaches, blurred vision, nausea, and persistent vomiting and abdominal pain. If you experience any of these, notify your doctor right away. The unknown is almost always more frightening than the reality and with his guidance you can usually manage your own condition.

A battery of **blood tests** are also done at the beginning of the pregnancy. Through them, various aspects of your general health and vulnerability to diseases that in the past went undetected can now be routinely checked.

One of these tests reveals whether or not you have had *toxoplasmosis,* "the cat disease." People love to warn you, "Do not get near cats when you are pregnant or you will risk causing neurological damage to the fetus." Should you be worried about it and don gloves, face mask, and protective vest when you change the kitty litter—or even put your beloved feline up for adoption? Probably not. Let me explain toxoplasmosis.

First of all, if you have had cats all your life (cats who have eaten mice or rats), you probably had toxoplasmosis when you were a child and didn't even know it, as it only makes you feel like you have a flu bug for twenty-four hours and then you are usually immune for life. The *only* way a cat gets toxoplasmosis is by eating a mouse or a rat, a necessary part of the cycle. That's why cats who live in the city and have less contact with mice often have never had it, while those who live in the country or suburbs almost always have.

The blood test for toxoplasmosis confirms whether you've had it, how long ago you had it, and whether you had a severe enough case to make you immune. If you have no protective antibodies, your doctor will probably advise you to stay away from cat feces, which transmits the disease, while you are pregnant. If you have no contact with your cat's feces, you are safe. (You can even have your cat tested if you like. If he has antibodies in his system, he's never going to get it again, so you are both completely safe.)

The other way to get toxoplasmosis is from raw meat (*not* raw fish), and if you have not had toxoplasmosis, you should make sure you eat only meat that is cooked. (It does not have to be cooked until it resembles shoe leather, but it should not be red in the middle.)

As for eating raw fish, remember that you are more susceptible to gastric upset when you are pregnant and therefore should be certain that *any* seafood you eat is absolutely fresh.

The blood count of a pregnant woman is quite different from that of a woman who isn't pregnant, so do not be alarmed to hear that your *red blood cell count* has dropped substantially. Because your "red count" system is based on a percentage of your whole circulation and your blood volume increases by 30 percent during pregnancy, your iron component appears to drop, but its absolute value may remain unchanged. In any case, your need for iron increases substantially in pregnancy and an iron supplement is usually recommended. (If it makes you constipated, see pages 51 and 90 for relief measures.)

Another blood test, done as soon as your pregnancy is confirmed, checks your vulnerability to *German measles.* Chances are you had German measles when you were young and are now immune to it. If not, fortunately you will know by the tests and thus can avoid exposure—a reasonable precaution, as German measles can cause neurological damage to an unborn baby, especially if it is contracted within the first three months of pregnancy.

Another early blood test gauges the level of a substance called AFP, or *alpha fetoprotein,* in the mother's blood. No news is good news on this one, but be glad such a sophisticated check on the blood can be done. If the AFP levels were abnormally high in early pregnancy, a neural tube defect such as spina bifida or hydrocephalus (water on the brain) would be suspected in the fetus and an amniocentesis (see page 31) would be recommended to confirm the initial findings.

Fetal development. In addition to gauging the baby's gestational age by measuring the size of your uterus, during routine examinations your doctor will be listening for the baby's heart rate, which can be heard as early as ten weeks. If he uses a Doptone, which amplifies the sound, he can usually pick it up around twelve weeks. With a stethoscope, he won't be able to hear it until sixteen

> *"When I heard the heartbeat for the first time there were tears in my eyes. That, to me, was the most exciting moment: to hear such a strong beat from such a little guy."*

weeks or maybe a little later. When the heartbeat becomes audible enough, you may hear your doctor call out to the nurse, "Fetal heart rate, lower left quadrant," or wherever he picks it up.

Someone will undoubtedly tell you that if the heart rate is fast, it is a boy, or if it is slow, it is a girl, or vice versa—but do not believe any of it. It is fast or slow because the baby is either doing the jig or taking a nap.

In any case, it is (to put it mildly) exciting when you finally hear the heartbeat, so ask your doctor when he has located it to let you listen too. One of my favorite descriptions of hearing the baby's heart for the first time came from a student who had been a horseback rider all her life and had had to give up her usual riding routine early in her pregnancy. She was thinking of this while the nurse tried to find the heartbeat, and then all of a sudden, "magic—the sound of hoofbeats of the most beautiful tiny fairy horse galloping, galloping," and she was "totally enchanted that the baby made its first introduction in such an unexpected, evocative way."

In your own excitement, you may want to mark off the location and share the momentous discovery with your husband, who can try to hear it when you get home. Gentlemen, don't be disappointed if you do not hear it with just your ear. Later on, when your wife is a full nine months pregnant, it will be easier to pick up. When I first worked in labor and delivery as a student nurse, my instructor would often hand me a fetoscope positioned exactly over the baby's heart and ask me to count the heart rate. Not only could I *not* count it, I could not even hear it and wondered if the instructor really could, either. Then one day, clear as a bell, there it was! After that it became a lot easier because I knew what the sound was like.

The baby's heart really does sound like galloping horses in the distance, albeit very faintly and going at about 140 beats a minute. If you hear louder, slower *ka-ploosh, ka-ploosh* sounds, gentlemen, this is the pulsating of one of your wife's large blood vessels that sends blood into the legs and you've got to move your ear over a little bit until you pick up the little *kerplunk, kerplunk* of the baby's beating heart.

> *"The most exciting moment came during my office visit eleven weeks after conception. I had no idea that I was going to hear the fetal heartbeat. I will never forget the eye contact with my doctor the moment he found the heartbeat. It sounded like a puppy dog rapidly panting. I was so excited, I started crying joyfully. After I left the office, I could not find a pay phone fast enough to tell my husband and imitate the puppy dog panting."*

As you get further along in your pregnancy, at any point in the last few months, you may notice a kind of rhythmical movement and think this is the heart beating. Then after a minute or so, it stops. Do not panic! The heartbeat is too faint for this kind of reverberation and what you are witnessing is *hiccoughs*! Babies in the uterus frequently get hiccoughs, which come and go of their own accord. Hiccoughs are a good indication of thoracic muscle development. They signal that your baby is actually "breathing" in your uterus. His oxygen is supplied through the placenta and umbilical cord, but in anticipation of the need to breathe on his own after delivery, Mother Nature has him inhaling and exhaling amniotic fluid to test out the system early. Remarkable films taken inside the uterus show babies inhaling, exhaling, swallowing, and sometimes even coughing—much more respiratory activity than we would imagine goes on in there!

While we often consider hiccoughs to be an annoyance, they don't seem to bother babies, and after delivery, you'll see many a newborn sleeping soundly in the hospital nursery with such a vigorous case of hiccoughs that he'll appear to be jumping in his sleep.

Swallowing and drinking are fetal activities you probably have not envisioned, either; but Nature of course wants to ensure an efficient, functioning digestive tract at birth, so gastrointestinal functioning begins in utero. A baby's first bowel movement is a thick, dark, sticky blob of meconium, which is really just bile concentrate, usually seen in the first day or two after birth. In the uterus all your baby is drinking is amniotic fluid, which he then pees back into. (Doesn't sound too tasty, does it? But fortunately amniotic fluid is completely refreshed as it is replaced with new fluid about every six hours.)

Dialogues with Your Doctor

Bring your husband with you to the exam, if he is inclined to come. Make a list of questions and concerns that may surface between visits, and have it ready to discuss with your doctor. The rapport you have with your obstetrician during your pregnancy is important and you should feel free to call him between visits— and of course contact him immediately if you notice these warning signs: vaginal bleeding, severe headache, blurred or double vision, acute abdominal pain, fever over 101 degrees Fahrenheit, sudden swelling of ankles, hands, and face, or persistent vomiting.

SPECIAL TESTS AND WHAT THEY MEAN

New tests using blood, urine, other body fluids, and tissues are constantly being perfected for the expectant mother. Again, be glad that yesterday's miracles of medicine are the routine procedures of today, readily available if they're needed.

Chorionic villi sampling is one such test, which is especially suited for women who have previously had a difficult second-trimester miscarriage of a genetically abnormal baby. It is done early, about eight weeks into the pregnancy, and involves taking a tiny sample of the villi, precursors of the placenta, transvaginally and testing the genetic content for abnormalities. The risks of this procedure are higher than those of amniocentesis (see below), as the procedure is more intrusive, but may be appropriate in some women. Results are available in twenty-four hours.

Researchers are now beginning to identify the small number of fetal cells that are released into the mother's bloodstream in early pregnancy. Once perfected, this easy blood test will surely be the genetic test of choice, replacing such intrusive procedures as amniocentesis and chorionic villi samplings completely.

Sonograms. If, in the beginning of your pregnancy, your doctor finds a discrepancy between your size and your dates, he may decide to have a sonogram done to help determine the *gestational age* of your baby. With sonography, a photographic image is taken of your fetus with ultrasound waves. The waves are transmitted through the uterine wall by way of a transducer. They bounce back off the baby to form a series of "soundwave" pictures (a sonogram) that show up on a monitor. Sonograms are useful in determining not only gestational age but fetal position, multiple pregnancies, and the position of the placenta. Who would have ever thought a technique similar to the sonar used by the navy in World War II to detect submarines and by oceanographers to study the migration of whales would eventually be used to survey a baby in utero!

Sonograms are *not* done routinely, or just because you'd like to have a polaroid picture of your unborn baby. While it seems to be about as safe a procedure as possible, it is still relatively new (with long-term effects, if any, as yet unknown) and is therefore used only when warranted.

Sonograms will not help hit the due date right on the nose, if that's what you are hoping, but instead will be two weeks one side or the other of it, and they are much more accurate in determining the gestational age of the fetus at the beginning of the pregnancy than they are at the end. This is because the baby's head size, which is the key measurement of the sonogram, changes much more rapidly in the beginning than it does toward the end of the pregnancy, when the change in head size is very slight.

"My brother has spina bifida and I was concerned about the chance of having a child with spina bifida. I thought that I would need to have amniocentesis. My doctor assured me that a blood test plus a sonogram would be able to detect birth defects with about 80 percent accuracy, and since my likelihood of having a child with spina bifida was about a half of a percent, I didn't need to risk miscarriage with the amnio. The percentages were reassuring."

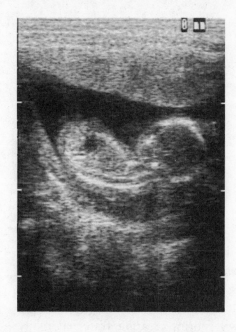

With an explanation from the technician, the sonogram becomes an exciting first picture of your little baby.

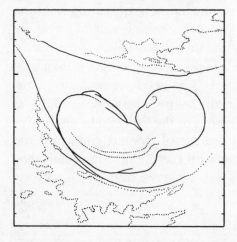

An ultrasonic scan usually takes about ten or fifteen minutes. Two hours prior to the procedure, you will be asked to drink extra fluids, usually four glasses of water, and avoid urinating, as a full bladder pushes the uterus up and ensures a better view of the fetus. Warm oil or cool gel is poured over the mother's belly and the transducer, which looks much like a microphone hooked up to a monitor, is slowly passed over the whole area. As it moves across the abdomen, the transducer conveys a variety of sonic images onto the monitor screen.

> "When I had amnio and the sonogram was being used to locate the baby, the sonographer pointed out the baby's various organs. Suddenly he said, 'There's the vagina.' I almost jumped off the table as I exclaimed, 'It's a girl!!' He proceeded to correct that impression: 'It's your vagina. That's what I mean.' "

As to whether you are carrying *twins,* sonograms will definitely confirm or negate your doctor's suspicions, which he may have had if he found your uterus to be consistently larger than your dates would indicate, if you have a family history of fraternal twins in you family, or if he heard what he thought were two fetal heartbeats. Normally, one egg is fertilized by one sperm. Seven out of ten pairs of twins result from a woman releasing two eggs that are then fertilized by two sperm, creating fraternal twins. Identical, or maternal, twins result from a fertilized egg splitting in two. If you are carrying twins, everything will be carefully monitored, with attention focused on the possibility of premature delivery—twins are usually born early as they outgrow their stay in the uterus earlier than singlets. With good prenatal care, however, two babies can thrive in the uterus just as successfully as one, with some sets even making it to the estimated due date.

Naturally, the earlier the existence of twins is confirmed the better for everyone, and today, with the use of ultrasound, they rarely go undetected. This was not always the case, and as recently

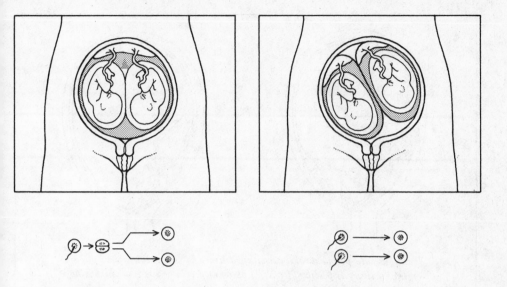

Identical twins form as a fertilized egg splits.

Fraternal twins occur when two eggs are fertilized by two sperm.

as fifteen years ago, one out of ten couples was in for a big surprise when that second baby burst on the scene, the parents having no inkling in advance. I remember once, after a beautiful five-pound baby girl had been delivered, diligently holding my hand over the mother's uterus, waiting for early signs of the placenta detaching from the uterine wall. The placenta seemed particularly large, and trying to be astute, I turned to the doctor and said, "Dr. Simmons, this is a very large placenta!" Dr. Simmons examined the mother and responded, "Miss Farber, here at New York Hospital we call those 'large placentas' the second twin!" And sure enough, out came a five-pound baby boy whom none of us, mother included, ever knew existed until that moment.

The ultrasound scan also shows the position of the placenta—a determination that for that one in a hundred mothers with *placenta previa* is very fortunate indeed for avoiding complications at birth. Usually, the placenta attaches high up in the fundus, or top of the uterus, well out of the way of the cervix. Sometimes, however, it will end up somewhere in the lower segment of the uterine wall (a situation that is referred to as placenta previa), where it might interfere with the baby's delivery. If the placenta

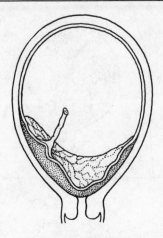 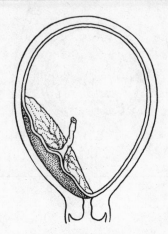

Total placenta previa would necessitate delivery by Caesarean, where often a vaginal delivery is possible if partial placenta previa occurs and there is no excessive bleeding in labor.

completely covers the cervix, a Caesarean birth would definitely be in order; but more often, if the placenta is at one side or the other of the cervix (partial or marginal placenta previa), and there is no excessive bleeding in labor, a vaginal delivery is possible. Painless, bright-red bleeding in the second trimester is usually a sign of placenta previa, and you should notify your doctor if any such bleeding occurs. A sonogram would then be ordered to locate the exact placental position.

If for whatever reason you do have a sonogram done, make sure that you take your husband. It is very exciting to see the images of the baby emerge on the screen, although of course it will not be a smiling little face and pudgy hand waving at you but rather blobs and shapes and lines that will probably require identification by the ultrasound technician. Do not be embarrassed to ask about what you see, and if you don't want to know the sex tell him and he'll say, "Drop your eyes, we're passing over the genital area." One couple in my Lamaze classes were sure they were having a boy—the penis had been picked up on the sonogram—and while awaiting the birth they had painted the baby's room blue and bought a whole wardrobe of infant clothes for boys. The night of our class reunion, in walked the Cavanaughs with a darling little baby girl (dressed in blue, of course).

Apparently, a little loop of cord had been positioned between the baby's legs as the ultrasound scanner passed over the genital area, and it was mistakenly identified as a penis. So you cannot always trust the sonogram for sex determination—although many parts of the baby's developing body, such as the skeleton and pulsing heart, are remarkably clear on the screen.

Amniocentesis is usually recommended for women over thirty-five and those with a history of genetic abnormalities in the family. For both of these groups, the chance of having a baby with a genetically transmitted defect, such as Down's syndrome or mental retardation, outweighs the risk of miscarriage inherent in the procedure. It might also be performed if your doctor has scheduled you to have a Caesarean birth and wants to check the baby's lung maturity at the end of the pregnancy.

Amniocentesis is done by withdrawing a small amount of fluid

"I'm only twenty-eight, so my doctor advised me that he wouldn't recommend amniocentesis, but I wanted to be tested just to make certain the baby was normal. After considerable thought, however, I decided not to be tested—I had come to grips emotionally with the realization that I would never have control over all the possible dangers that might affect my baby. I have to accept the constant risks, and while it seems my responsibility to minimize these risks as much as possible, I can't eliminate them. After much talking with my husband, I have confirmed trust that this child, however it turns out, will be right for us."

from the amniotic sac by syringe and evaluating the genetic content of the cells. It is usually performed between sixteen and eighteen weeks of pregnancy and the lab results relayed to your doctor within three weeks.

Amniocentesis not only picks up genetic diseases (some of which are pretty rare) but it also confirms the existence of neuralcord defects such as spina bifida or hydrocephalus. This occurs when the spinal cord is forming and a hole in the spinal-fluid cavity forms, eventually leaving the child paralyzed from the point of the lesion down. These defects are not genetic aberrations but rather flukes of nature, and if the defect is present, a little of the spinal fluid leaks into the amniotic fluid and can be detected with amniocentesis. Since neuralcord defects usually cause an elevated AFP level in the mother's blood, they would be picked up in an early pregnancy blood test, as described on page 22.

The reasons why more pregnant women are choosing to "have an amnio" are that more people having babies today are over thirty-five and also that the test has been perfected over the past twenty-five years and therefore is safely available to more women. In the 1940s and 1950s, the risk of miscarriage with amniocentesis was so high that the test was done only on women over forty, when the chances of having a baby with Down's syndrome, a genetic abnormality, is one out of sixty. Now, with ultrasound to define the position of the fetus and placenta, the procedure is much safer and more widely available.

> *"I had amnio because I wanted to know for sure that my child was healthy. Although I'm thirty years old and my doctor didn't feel the test was at all necessary, I'm glad I did it. I had peace of mind for nine months."*

I think eventually everyone will (and should) have amniocentesis, regardless of age, although now it is not warranted or even recommended for those under thirty-five. The number of technicians trained to administer the test is increasing, just as the risk of miscarriage is decreasing—now it's only one in six hundred tests, and even that statistic is improving. If you are particularly worried about your baby's genetic well-being and really want to have an amnio, say at age thirty-one, tell your doctor. In this case, you must be willing to accept the slight risk of miscarriage, which, if it were to happen, would usually be within forty-eight hours, caused by a rupture in the amniotic sac that is believed to occur if the sac membrane is abnormally fragile. But this is rare.

When I worked in the clinic at The New York Hospital, I would often hear pregnant women over forty who were adamantly against having amniocentesis. "If there is something wrong with the baby, I won't have an abortion," they would say. But when they were confronted with the reality of knowing in advance (from the AFP blood test, for example) that something was wrong, even couples who in the abstract didn't think that they would ever choose an abortion, did, in fact, make the choice. Should the baby be defective, amniocentesis at least allows you and your husband an opportunity to sort out your feelings and decide what course of action is right for you. Although statistics supposedly offer reassurance—that only one out of sixty-six mothers will have a baby with Down's syndrome when the mother-to-be is over forty—if you are the mother who has that baby, a small statistic becomes a lifetime commitment and perhaps a devastating one.

If you do have amniocentesis done, it will be scheduled between the sixteenth and eighteenth weeks of your pregnancy. You will have a sonogram to determine the exact position of the baby and a clear area of amniotic fluid nearby where the needle can go in. Then the area on your belly just above the pubic bone will be scrubbed, usually with a kind of sticky, brown iodine solution, Betadine, and your doctor will take a fine needle about three to four inches long and, with a little stab, insert it carefully into the

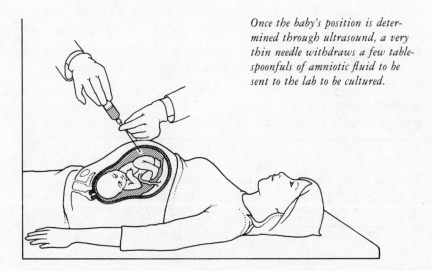

Once the baby's position is determined through ultrasound, a very thin needle withdraws a few table-spoonfuls of amniotic fluid to be sent to the lab to be cultured.

uterus. Some women feel a cramp when the needle goes into the uterine wall, others feel nothing; it probably depends on where the needle penetrates the muscle. About five tablespoons of straw-colored amniotic fluid are withdrawn, to be sent off to a laboratory for testing.

Bed rest is not required when the procedure is over, but you shouldn't go jogging back to work, either. Take it easy; go home and lounge around, or go to a movie. At the lab, the cells of the amniotic fluid are incubated, and the results are ready in two to four weeks. Sometimes cells do not grow—this would be evident within the first few days—and your doctor would be in touch with you to reschedule the test. If that happens, do not think, "Oh, no, there must be something wrong." Probably all it means is that some inefficient soul did not keep the amniotic fluid warm enough on the way to the laboratory.

As for the needle touching the baby, which is understandably a concern of many couples, it is extremely rare. The sonogram and "amnio" are done together, right then and there; sonogram equipment locates the baby and a wide area of amniotic fluid to one side of him, and the needle is inserted right away where there is definitely just fluid. When I had amnio with my first baby, the procedure was positively archaic. I had my sonogram done one day, and the next day I went for the amnio. My husband to this day believes the little mark that was visible at birth on our first son's shoulder was where the needle accidentally touched him.

By all means have your husband there for the sonogram, but let him choose whether to be present for the amniocentesis. One woman's husband was encouraged by her obstetrician to stand nearby during the procedure (most doctors today assuming this would be the husband's preference) and as soon as the needle was withdrawn from his wife's belly, he passed out right there on the floor.

While some tests are done early in pregnancy, there are others that might be warranted at the end of your pregnancy.

As the days past your due date increase, your doctor may want to evaluate the efficiency of the placenta. A placenta begins to deteriorate if it stays too long past its invited time in the uterus and, to be sure the baby is being well nourished, the following procedures may be done:

Blood or urine test for estriol. Estriol is excreted into your urine when you are pregnant, signifying a high level of estrogen and a well-functioning placenta. If the placenta is beginning to deteriorate, a low level of estriol is evident in your urine and blood. The urine test is usually done on a twenty-four-hour urine collection that you would bring to the hospital lab or your doctor's office. Proper collection is essential, so be sure you understand the procedure.

Nonstress test. Another way of checking placental functioning is the nonstress test. By attaching an external fetal monitor, your doctor can see the pattern of your baby's heart rate as you experience occasional Braxton Hicks contractions (page 68). If the pattern remains steady throughout these contractions, there is no need to induce labor; but if the baby exhibits distress in the form of a lowering heart rate during or right after these mild contractions, your doctor will want to get you delivered either by induction (page 166) or by Caesarean section (page 255).

Stress test. This test begins as a nonstress test (above) to determine a baseline for fetal heart rate and uterine activity. Then an oxytocin drug is administered by intravenous drip to slowly cause efficient, good-quality uterine contractions. The baby's reaction to these contractions is monitored and, again, if he shows any signs of distress or a declining heart rate, your doctor will want to get you delivered either vaginally or by Caesarean section very soon.

Once again, it's natural to be anxious about tests. But they should bring you some peace of mind, too: they provide a view into your pregnancy that could not have been imagined a generation ago, check the health of you and the baby, and, if needed, result in medical intervention that can ensure a healthy, properly developing child.

Your worries during pregnancy may surface in your dreams, which is a perfectly normal outlet for them. You may dream that your baby is abnormal, or that you cannot find him after you have delivered, or that you won't be able to handle the pain of labor. I had a recurring dream: my baby was so tiny that he was hidden in the folds of my sheets; I worried that I would roll over on him, and wouldn't let myself move all night. I was always so relieved to wake up, stiff from trying to stay still all night but delighted to see I was still pregnant. Another woman dreamed her husband gave birth to their baby—went through the labor and every-thing—and she was left pregnant!

Verbalize your dreams; write them down if it helps—and then forget about them.

After one mother delivered, she said she had never allowed herself to joyfully anticipate a healthy little baby; instead, all through her pregnancy, she let her mind run rampant to imagine the worst. Probably it was just from the fear of the unknown, but after delivery she was sorry that she had denied herself the plea-sure of envisioning her "scrumptious, perfect little baby, now the source of so much happiness."

Let the tests and routine procedures set your mind free to nurture that healthy, normal emotion that is love for one's own child. This deep feeling has just as much right to blossom and grow as the little baby inside you, so do not be afraid to open up to it.

LOSING A BABY—CONFRONTING
THE UNTHINKABLE

For the vast majority of women who worry about it, losing a baby proves to be an unfounded fear of a normal pregnancy. The relief and contentment that couples radiate as they return, baby in arms, for their Lamaze reunion is a blissful state that almost all couples can look forward to beyond the ordeal of pregnancy and birth.

It would be wonderful if this were always the case, but some women—not many, but still some—must confront the loss of a baby. There are no reliable statistics, but it has been estimated that about one in five conceptions actually end in miscarriage—some so early on that they go undetected.

Usually there is an initial period of time when bleeding indicates a problem but the actual outcome is still unpredictable.

If you've been bleeding and placenta previa has been ruled out by sonogram, a miscarriage, or spontaneous abortion as it is referred to in the medical profession, may be inevitable. If you experience any bleeding, keep in touch with your doctor and collect any passed clots or tissue in a clean container for your doctor to examine. Uterine contractions that result in painful cramps and cervical dilation usually lead to abortion. Bleeding that lessens when bed rest is prescribed and is not accompanied by uterine contractions often indicates a pregnancy that will continue uneventfully.

An ectopic pregnancy is one in which a fertilized egg begins to grow in the Fallopian tube between uterus and ovary. It usually will rupture through the walls of the tube at about six weeks, necessitating immediate surgery to remove the embryo and in some cases the tube as well. A positive pregnancy test with a uterus of normal, unpregnant size would alert your doctor to the problem. Ectopic pregnancies are rare, and an early visit to your doctor could avoid rupture. Severe lower abdominal pain usually accompanies the rupture as well.

A cervix that does not remain snugly closed in pregnancy can allow the fetus to slip through, resulting in a miscarriage, usually in the second trimester. A special purselike stitch, a Shirodkar, can be inserted into the cervix before or during the next pregnancy to prevent another miscarriage. This stitch remains in place until the end of the pregnancy, when it can be cut to allow for a normal delivery.

If a baby dies in the uterus after twenty-eight weeks of pregnancy, it is designated a stillbirth. Why it occurs is not always clear. Most physicians think that labor should be allowed to begin naturally, which is usually several days after the baby's death, but

" 'You're young, you'll have another baby,' they said. 'You can always adopt.' 'She's in a better place.' I grew furious as the suggestions became repetitive. Didn't they understand? I didn't want a new baby, I didn't think she was in a better place, I wanted my baby back.

"In the weeks of shock and grief that followed the loss of our baby, I needed answers and reassurance more than at any time in my life. I turned back to the books that had guided me through my pregnancy, but I felt greatly disappointed and deserted. There was a feeling of emptiness and total despair that seemed to erode me more each day, and gradually I realized I needed help. I called a counselor, a specialist in grieving, who had been recommended by the hospital. I felt safe talking to her. There was a tremendous sense of relief to share the pain with someone who was trained to help me cope. I met other parents who had lost a child; it helped to talk with them.

"I felt confused and alienated by my husband's behavior after the death of our baby. He didn't talk about it, didn't cry, but went back to work, laughing with friends and engaging in his usual sports and pastimes. One night, as I was trying to escape the memories so I could sleep without painful dreams, Bob reached out and took my hand. He pulled me close and held me tightly. Although we did not share any words, I knew the power of a touch would help to heal us so that we could talk.

"A year has passed. A year which taught us that time does heal. We wanted another child. Not a replacement, but the child we have always wanted. I needed to feel life inside me again, to reaffirm something deep within me that I cannot explain.

"Now, at twenty-one weeks, we look forward to the birth of our second child. We feel a great sense of joy and anticipation as we count down the weeks to delivery."

you and your doctor should discuss this. Seeing or touching your dead baby is a natural and appropriate part of the process, allowing you to pass through the stages of loss more easily.

Whatever the reasons, losing a baby is a devastating experience for any couple, usually aggravated for the mother by the effect of plummeting hormonal levels after the baby has died. You and your husband will both need to grieve—first with sadness and shock, then anger, then with a slow integration of the painful reality into your being. Usually talking with other parents who have lost a baby can help to understand your own reactions.

3

The Pregnant Body

*I*f you were to ask a roomful of pregnant women, "How do you like your pregnant body?" the response would be as varied as those answering. One would say, "It's great, I love looking in the mirror and seeing that glow of pregnancy!" while another would blurt out, "What glow? I've got blotches and spots coming out of the woodwork!" One poor soul would moan about being nauseated for three months straight, while the lady beside her would remark that she's never felt healthier in her life.

Although the word *pregnancy* means many different things to many different women, there are common "assets and liabilities" caused not only by the enlarging fetus as it affects the mother's internal organs, but also by an increase in hormones as they orchestrate major, though more subtle, changes inside and out. Comparative diagrams of female anatomy help to explain the changes in the body at various stages of pregnancy, although I was once surprised in class when one father-to-be, on looking at a very obvious cross section of a woman turned to the right, very politely asked for an explanation of what it was he was looking at. As I explained the position, I could not help wondering exactly how that man's wife had ever gotten pregnant!

In any case, when you look at a diagram of a woman who is not pregnant, you see a uterus that is smaller than your fist. When

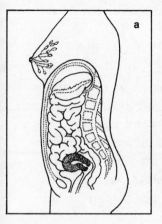

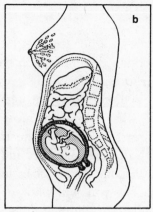

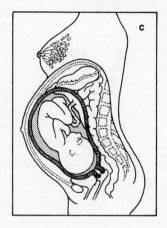

Basic anatomy prior to pregnancy.

Baby and placenta in the twentieth week of pregnancy.

At term, baby's head "floating."

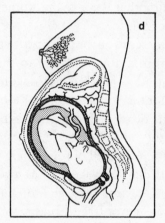

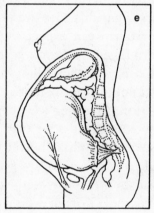

At term, baby's head "engaged," or deep into the pelvis.

At term, with uterine support system.

you deliver, that same uterus is the size of a large baby plus placenta and plenty of amniotic fluid. Over the course of nine months of pregnancy, the uterus progresses in size from an orange at three months to a cantaloupe at six months and a small watermelon toward the end of the third trimester. It is a pretty astounding sequence, particularly when you see a diagram of a woman three to four weeks before delivery with her stomach up to her eyeballs and her bladder pressed down to her knees. It's a wonder (gentlemen, take note) that she's able to function at all, much less breathe, walk, talk, and work!

More physical changes occur in a woman's body during pregnancy than in the whole of a healthy lifetime, changes that elicit a wide range of reactions depending on the individual. Some women revel in their pregnancy, delighted with it every day; others are plagued by discomforts throughout. But these are extremes and despite what you read, most women experience relatively few discomforts in light of the momentous transformation within. As with the medical tests and procedures, do not expect every possible discomfort to occur; instead, be aware that if they do, there are—as you will find in this chapter—many remedies that can alleviate or eliminate them.

Breast changes occur right from the onset of pregnancy, usually with a little tenderness and swelling that is for many women one of the first signs that they are pregnant.

Every woman can expect an increase in breast size over the course of pregnancy. If you go from a double A cup to the full-blown B cup in the first three months, which is not uncommon, you may think that in six more months you are going to look like Dolly Parton. This won't happen. Most of the change occurs in the early months and after that, the rate of increase slows down. For those of us who have been flat-chested all our lives, it is pretty spectacular to look down over all that cleavage. It was awesome to have my bony ribs covered by soft, firm flesh, and my husband was in heaven! Women who have extra-large breasts to begin with, however, find their increased breast size to be more of a challenge than an asset, and for them, extra support is essential.

> "At thirteen weeks I feel luscious when naked, with full breasts and belly, even if I feel just tubby in clothes."

> "What's all this talk about women not being particularly sexy during pregnancy? All I know is that my wife has become the most beautiful Botticelli bride imaginable."

Whatever your breast size, I recommend that you wear a bra during pregnancy. Regardless of whether she breast-feeds or not, every mother eventually loses some of her breast elasticity and firmness; you are going to lose a lot more of it if you walk around with full bosoms unsupported and swinging in the breeze, and a bra will help save as much of the elasticity as possible.

If you are used to an underwire bra, you can certainly continue to wear one during pregnancy until the baby becomes so big that it's uncomfortable.

If you have a full bosom and plan to breast-feed, I would suggest buying breast-feeding bras for your pregnancy; just be sure the straps are wide and comfortable so they will not cut into your shoulders. (Guidelines for choosing a nursing bra are given in chapter 23.)

You may notice a darkening of the nipple and areola, and several little bumps developing along the outer edge of the areola, the Montgomery glands that are getting ready to release a natural oil to help prevent your nipples from becoming chapped and sore during breast-feeding. (To help prepare the nipples for breast-feeding, see page 288.) When you take a shower, you might notice on the top of the nipple what looks like a little yellowish, dried-up, cakey stuff. It is colostrum—what the breast produces as the baby's first food before milk production begins—which has leaked out and dried there. It's perfectly normal. If you see nothing, it does not mean there *is* nothing—just that there's no leakage. The appearance of colostrum can occur early in the pregnancy, all the way through, or never, and if you decide to squeeze some out "just to see if there's anything in there," you'll have a hard time getting tangible proof.

You may see some stretch marks on the underside of your breasts, down around the pubic bone, or wherever; do not be duped into buying a vitamin-E-and-estrogen "miracle cream for the childbearing years" to take them away. If you like to use cream, fine; but stretch marks seem to have something to do with individual pigmentation or skin type and fade after pregnancy.

Fatigue is common during pregnancy. For most women, it seems to be worst in the beginning weeks, probably from the rapid hormonal changes, and at the very end of the pregnancy, probably due to the sheer bulk of the body and additional drain on maternal nutrients to support a bigger baby. In early pregnancy it's perfectly normal to want to sleep eleven hours or more and even then wake up exhausted. Huffing and puffing toward your due date, you find yourself tired once again, but this time with everybody saying, "Don't move! Stay where you are, let me do that chore for you." Since you're about to undergo the greatest physical endeavor of your life, giving birth, you'd be much better off getting ready for it with exercise than settling back into a club chair for the last month of your pregnancy. You will feel better, too—a basic exercise program not only improves circulation but also releases endorphins into the body that help you relax.

Of course rest is important in pregnancy; you don't want to overtire yourself. Long naps may not be possible, but even fifteen minutes of "time out" from your activities can regenerate your whole system. As you take your break, try this relaxation technique: resting in a comfortable position with your feet up, close your eyes and take long, deep breaths as you slowly exhale, concentrating all the while on relaxing different parts of your body, beginning at the top. With each exhalation, say to yourself, "relax neck and shoulders," or "relax arms and hands," and so on down the body. If you have trouble relaxing muscles, contract or tighten an area and then relax it, squeezing out the "tiredness chemicals" as you focus on each part—and don't forget your face.

If you find stressful thoughts creeping in, blocking your ability to relax, say to yourself, "I'll think about it when I am rested; in fifteen minutes, I'll work on that problem," and then put those anxious thoughts out of your mind until after you are rested and are better able to cope with them. Or have your husband give you a back rub. It may be exactly what you need to trigger the relaxation process.

Fatigue in the last months of pregnancy is heightened by the baby's activity after you settle down for the night. Many women are so exhausted that they fall sound asleep at nine o'clock, but then at midnight the baby starts moving around and they find themselves wide awake with a good case of insomnia. Most unborn babies seem to be like nocturnal animals. They are relatively

> *"I expected to be more tired than I was. I really only had two weeks of intense fatigue. The size of the stomach was difficult to imagine prepregnancy. Toward the end, I'd say I hadn't expected nine months to be so long."*

quiet and docile as they are gently rocked through your daytime routines, and then they are lively and active for a good part of the night, once the rhythm of your body has ceased. Actually it is this same pattern, which carries over after they are born, that makes the first few weeks with a baby so difficult, in many cases.

> *"My pregnancy was better than my expectations. I was thirty-four and expected to have some difficulties (nausea, et cetera) and had a very smooth time. Except for the first three-month fatigue and the last two weeks, I sometimes even forgot I was pregnant!"*

When you find yourself wide awake in the middle of the night, try to induce your body back to a restful state. Begin by doing some simple, not-too-strenuous exercises (page 75) for ten or fifteen minutes, then take a relaxing, moderately warm bath and drink a glass of warm milk (or a little wine or beer) as you languish in the tub. Return to bed with several pillows to position yourself as comfortably as you can. Chances are you will get a few more hours of sleep. If that does not work, try napping during the day when you can—maybe you can sneak in half an hour of sleep before the baby realizes you have stopped rocking him.

As for sleep positions, you can ignore what you read about *always* lying on your left side during pregnancy. You are going to have trouble enough sleeping, period. It is true that the vena cava and aorta, your two major blood vessels, lie underneath your baby and that lying on your left side relieves pressure on them. You won't, however, cut off any blood supply while you sleep. Furthermore, it is only at the very end of pregnancy, in labor,

"Morning sickness and fatigue were the pits!"

really, when there might be some concern about pressure on those major blood vessels if the baby exhibits signs of distress when the uterus is tightening—then you might be asked to lie on your left side as your doctor tries to further diagnose the problem.

Suggested positions for sleeping more comfortably:

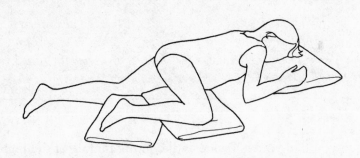

Lie on your side, upper leg well supported on pillows.

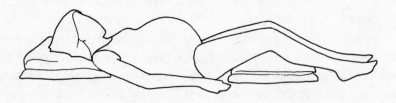

Lie on your back with extra pillows under head, shoulders, and knees.

Mood swings and emotions. Some women are on a perpetual high all through pregnancy and never experience radical mood shifts. Many women delight in the feelings of "ultimate femininity" or motherhood, and the whole idea that deep inside their body, a new little person that they and their husband have made together is growing makes them feel like smiling at any moment. At the same time, coping with the prospect of having a baby in their life may seem overwhelming: loving and caring for a baby whom they don't even know; managing a career, much less a marriage.

If you feel as if your emotions are on a swinging pendulum, it's because they are. Furthermore, you are not alone. Due to hormonal changes and fatigue, tearful or irritable bouts are common in early pregnancy. Many women who experience the moodiness of premenstrual syndrome (PMS) say that being pregnant is worse. As your body slowly adjusts to the physical changes it is experiencing and you begin to accept and become used to the idea of being pregnant, you will become less tearful. However, there is no denying the many conflicting emotions you will feel. Take one step at a time and many of your concerns will be resolved.

"Out of the blue I would start crying. Sometimes it was because of the changes I was going through, others because of the anticipation and fears, and sometimes for no reason at all."

Do some reading or share your concerns with other newly pregnant women in your exercise or pregnancy classes. Their concerns may not be the same as yours, but they know very well what you are going through because they are going through it too. More importantly, talk things over with your husband. He may not be the pregnant half of the couple, but he has certainly contributed an equal share to the state you are in. While he cannot do much about physical discomforts, he certainly can listen and give you support as you try to cope with anxiety and depression.

Grappling with his own conflicts about starting a family, he'll probably welcome an open dialogue! Communicating with each other during pregnancy can make this a special time of growth for your marriage. Do not feel guilty if you are ambivalent or depressed—these emotions are just as healthy as the joy and excitement you also feel about being pregnant and they confirm a normal, realistic outlook on the prospect of having a baby.

The digestive system reacts to the hormonal changes of pregnancy with an increased production of hydrochloric acid in your stomach and an overall slowing down of peristaltic activity in the intestines. The latter accounts for the excess acid just sitting there in your stomach—which is why over 50 percent of all pregnant women experience varying degrees of *nausea* for at least part of their pregnancy. Olfactory sense is heightened, too, and many women prone to nausea find that their sensitivity to odors exacerbates the stomach problem. Mild odors become intense. You may open the refrigerator and mistakenly think something has gone bad, or find that simple chores (feeding the cat, for example) become monumental tasks. For some women, all it takes is the smell of a garlicky pizza or the whiff of a cigar to retch immediately. Others feel nothing more than a slight queasiness at times, perhaps while riding in a car or bus.

> *"I did not immediately suspect I was pregnant, but the first change I noticed was a heightened sense of smell. The cooking smells (fried, spicy foods and tomato sauces) suddenly became very bothersome to me. I slept as much as I could, as I was very tired."*

In the first few months of my pregnancy, when nothing of it showed, I stood on many a crowded bus, my stomach heaving with every jolt. I often thought about wearing a sign saying "I am pregnant and nauseated. Please give me your seat now—I promise I won't take it when I am nine months along and big as a house!"

If nausea seems to be your biggest problem, the remedy is to

> *"The first three months were pretty bad. I felt nauseated at commuter hours, which made my subway rides to and from work living nightmares. Fortunately, I never actually got sick. The nausea and fatigue ended after fourteen weeks."*

> *"I feel slightly claustrophobic for the first time in my life being pregnant."*

make yourself eat every two hours during your wakeful state, awful as that sounds. Your natural inclination is to give that poor stomach a rest and *stop* eating, but since food helps absorb the excess hydrochloric acid and maintain blood sugar levels, you must try to eat something if you are ever going to improve the situation.

What you eat is important, too. A glazed doughnut might leave you feeling great for the next fifteen to twenty minutes because your blood sugar level rises quickly, but afterward, when it falls (and it does that just as quickly because there is so much sugar and so little protein in the doughnut), you feel even worse. You need a high-protein snack every two hours—peanut butter crackers, cheese and crackers, yogurt, a hard-boiled egg—anything high in protein that will bring your blood sugar up to a lower, but more stable, level than a doughnut will.

Herbal teas can be soothing when your stomach feels queasy, or even after a bout of vomiting. With such a pleasant variety of these caffeine-free drinks on the market today, you are bound to find at least one you can enjoy.

For some women, an increase of vitamin B may be helpful. The high hormone levels in pregnancy almost completely prohibit vitamin B absorption from the digestive tract—just when you most need its benefits as an antinauseant. You can increase your intake of green, leafy vegetables, but in order to get what you need to help combat nausea, you would be required to almost double the usual amounts of kale or collard greens, for example. If you cannot bear the thought (or aroma) of all those vegetables on your plate, talk to your doctor about a vitamin B supplement of up to 100 milligrams daily, by injection if your nausea leaves you incapacitated. When I got vitamin B injections, I felt better within a few hours and continued to feel fine for about four or five days; then I would again feel like throwing up on the spot.

If after trying every relief measure you are still miserable with constant nausea, try to keep busy so you cannot focus on it, and be sure to get plenty of rest. Increased salivation is often part of the syndrome and chewing gum or sucking a mint may bring relief. A piece of spearmint gum was often a lifesaver for me when I was pregnant, but to this day I cannot chew it for the memories of nausea that surface! Finally, take heart. The great majority of women report that their nausea disappears around twelve to fourteen weeks of pregnancy.

Heartburn and indigestion are also common in pregnancy, usually starting at about five months. These are due once again to the overabundance of hydrochloric acid in the digestive tract and the slowdown of the whole system in tandem with the baby pressing up under your stomach as he grows larger, causing some of the stomach acids to rise into your esophagus and give you that burning sensation.

If you know that soon after having the "ziti and broccoli laced with garlic" in your favorite restaurant you must counter it with Tums, Maalox, and Pepto-Bismol, it would probably be better if you just passed up this dish for the time being. Most antacids are high in sodium and encourage fluid retention, with hands and feet puffing up, particularly in the later months of pregnancy. If you are prone to this condition, watch your salt intake. A wonderful

> *"I had a one-week bout of unbelievably painful indigestion. I tried to be a martyr about it, not wanting to take any medication. When I finally called my doctor, he scolded me for not calling sooner and suggested Maalox Plus, which did the trick."*

Chinese lunch with lots of soy sauce could cause your legs, ankles, and feet to swell up by suppertime, looking as if they belonged to Babar the Elephant.

> *"Pregnancy was much easier than I thought it would be. There was very little that I couldn't do, especially during the second trimester. Fortunately, I didn't get any morning sickness, which I thought was a part of being pregnant."*

It has been said that three ounces of warm milk is just as effective for heartburn and indigestion as an antacid, and as unappealing as warm milk might sound, before you give up your favorite foods you might try it. Sometimes plain seltzer water helps, or you can look for antacids without sodium.

Try sleeping with large pillows under your neck and shoulders at night; sometimes this helps get rid of indigestion and that burning sensation, encouraging any gas that is forming in the digestive tract to come up and gastric juices to stay down.

Constipation. At the other end of the hormonally influenced digestive tract, many women find that when they are pregnant, they get constipated. The reason for this is the slowdown of the intestines, perhaps further aggravated by the iron supplement required during pregnancy.

If all the natural remedies—the high-grain cereals and breads, the green leafy vegetables, extra fluids, and walking—have simply not helped, I can recommend the "cure."

Maybe you've seen those not-too-appetizing dried fruits in the supermarket. Maybe you have even tried them and they have helped a little. Well, these fruits are also available *glazed*. High in iron, not only are they delicious (maybe a little *too* sweet), but also the glazing process does something to the pectin in the skin to make it very potent. Glazed fruits are a bit hard to find, but definitely worth looking for (see Resources, page 380). Although they are expensive, only a small box is necessary to cure you. Eat half a glazed peach, pear, apricot, or orange a night when you need it, pregnant or not, and you will never be constipated again.

> *"I felt it imperative to see a nutritionist mainly because doctors know very little about nutrition these days and I totally disagree that you can get all your vitamins from your food—unless you live on a farm and grow it yourself. Happily, the nutritionist cured my acute constipation immediately with linseed-oil capsules, one at breakfast, one at dinner, and I've had no problems since. This advice was worth everything!"*

Glycerine suppositories, which act merely as a lubricant, are fine for constipation if they solve the problem, but laxatives should be used with caution. Avoid using the systemic kind: they pull fluid into the bowel from other parts of the body. These fluids are needed elsewhere—in the circulatory system, for example, where they are ultimately put to use supporting the baby, and you should not interfere. Fiber laxatives such as Metamucil are usually fine—they just give you fiber. Certainly you should check with your doctor if this is the route you want to take, but first try the glazed fruits.

Hemorrhoids, those painful, itchy swellings formed by the dilation of veins at the anal opening, can develop at any time during pregnancy and are aggravated by constipation. They may not appear until the last trimester, the result of inner pelvic pressure on the rectum that builds in the later months and during delivery.

Keep those bowel movements soft and drink lots of water. For some women with hemorrhoids, cold witch-hazel compresses are soothing, while for others, a moderately warm bath feels great. Standing on your feet all day is likely to make the condition worse, so try to sit or, even better, lie down with a cold witch-hazel compress in place. To relieve the symptoms of pain and itchiness, ask your doctor for a soothing, numbing ointment that will enable you to gently tuck the hemorrhoids back into the rectum and encourage them to shrink. Fortunately, they usually disappear several weeks after delivery.

Bladder pressure. One of the earliest signs of pregnancy for many women is frequency of urination. "But how can that be?" they say. "How can a baby the size of a pinhead put pressure on my bladder?" Actually, it is not the baby at all; rather, hormone stimulation causes a change in the lining of the bladder so that it becomes ultrasensitive to pressure.

At the end of the pregnancy, of course, the urgency to urinate really is from the pressure of the baby and not the lining of the bladder. A diagram of your pregnant body from about six months on shows the baby sitting right on top of your bladder. At the very end of your pregnancy, you would have a hard time finding the bladder at all—on the diagram it is a thin black line under a towering uterus. (See *d*, page 41).

One word of warning about the urge to urinate frequently. You might think it occurs only because you are pregnant, but it could conceivably occur because you have cystitis, a urinary tract infection, and then you would look for other symptoms. If you felt a burning sensation, or if your urine were cloudy (urinate into a glass; it should be crystal clear), you may have a bladder infection that needs attention. Although not very often, urinary tract infections go completely undiagnosed in pregnant women because they think they are just experiencing the normal pressure from the baby when they have to go to the bathroom frequently. Don't wait until you have a fever. Cystitis can be easily treated, so just keep it in the back of your mind without being overconcerned.

As for the effect of the baby pressing on the bladder, what always used to leave me flustered was that I would be riding along on the bus, minding my own business, when all of a sudden the baby would wind up and give me such a strong kick in the bladder that I would involuntarily release a little urine and think, "My heavens, how do I get off this bus?" A kick like that does no permanent damage to the bladder—you are just not braced for the impact of those little feet pummeling it at that moment.

As you realize that your bladder capacity is getting less, it is tempting to cut back on drinking fluids. It is important, however, that you keep up your fluid intake all through pregnancy—and to compensate, persist in finding bathrooms. It always amused me how, when visiting those precious little shops along Madison Avenue in Manhattan, if you were not pregnant and asked for the bathroom, the shopkeepers would literally let you die on the floor before conceding they had a bathroom, whereas when you came sailing in with that pregnant belly, they would immediately point you in the direction of the bathroom (the same one that did not exist two years ago) to use "whenever you need it." Take advantage of this temporary gallantry!

Skin changes. If you take a look at your veins and other *blood vessels* during pregnancy, you will see that they appear to be much larger than usual. This is perfectly normal, although women who are prone to varicose veins, those protruding, purplish blood vessels close to the skin, should watch out for them—particularly if varicose veins are a family trait. Your doctor will not go over your body each visit with a fine-toothed comb, and you should call protruding veins to his attention when they appear. Look for them at the back of your knee, then on the back of your upper thighs. If you see them coming, it's far better to get into a pair of support stockings now to help try to maintain the elasticity of those blood vessels, then to have them lose it all and stay very large when your pregnancy is over. Just don't make the mistake of buying "maternity hose"—after you walk four blocks, the so-called maternity panel will be down at your knees. Instead, shop at the nearest bargain basement or chain outlet and buy several different brands of inexpensive support pantyhose one size larger than your usual size. When you hit on the pair that fits (cut the waistband if necessary) buy a few more of them. If you still need more support, your doctor may put you into some very heavy support stockings (available by prescription) for the duration of the pregnancy. Never mind what they look like. It's worth it if you want those veins to be able to shrink down to normal later on.

Some women experience vaginal varicosities, also due to increased blood volume, and a miniature ice pack, a clean cotton glove filled with crushed ice, can bring relief to the area at the end of a long day on your feet.

Others get *hemangiomas,* tiny red "spiders" on the hands, face, or other areas. These are actually dilated blood vessel ends and they are perfectly normal—due, again, to the increases in the circulatory system. Other than a little concealing makeup for the ones on your face, there is nothing to do about them. They'll shrink and fade away after pregnancy.

Some skin changes can be attributed to the changes in your circulatory system, but there are several others that are not so easily explained, particularly those having to do with skin *pigmentation.* Why the skin tends to get darker in some places remains a mystery of pregnancy. Some women get what is called "the mask of pregnancy," or chloasma, with what look like suntanned blotches on the face. You might think a little sun will even it all out, but it won't (the areas that are browner absorb more sun than the other areas). If you are tempted to eliminate the blotchy areas with "bleach cream for the childbearing years," that won't work, either. It is purely a bleach and probably not so great for your skin. Everything will fade after delivery (and breast-feeding) when your hormone levels return to normal.

Not only does the areola around the nipple get darker, but so does every mole and freckle on your body. These can also become enlarged and puffy, but it's perfectly normal and they will shrink after you deliver.

To me the most fascinating skin change during pregnancy is the *linea negra,* the little darkly pigmented line that gradually appears around the sixth month or so and runs from the pubic bone to the belly button and on up to the sternum. After you deliver and your skin shrinks down, it becomes very dark and as brown as an eyebrow-pencil mark. Then, all of a sudden one day in the shower about six weeks after you have delivered, it just washes away. During pregnancy you could scrub and scrub to try to get rid of it and it would do no good. Amazing!

Skin tags, or tabs, may develop during your pregnancy. These are tiny flaps of skin usually seen on the neck, breasts, and areola. Don't worry that they might interfere with breast-feeding, if that's how you plan to feed your baby. Most skin tags are quite tough and insensitive to the touch, and while you may not like the way they look, your baby will not be examining your breasts with a critical eye. If you really find them bothersome, however, you can have them removed by a dermatologist later, after you have weaned your baby from the breast, and your body has fully recovered from the childbirth process.

If your skin feels tender or itchy, there are remedies to try. One is to use a rich cream, such as Nivea or Keri lotion, which you might put into the bath or onto the skin after a bath, at night so you will not stain your daytime clothes. The other remedy, more for burning or soreness due to the skin stretching, is a colloidal oatmeal bath. This soothing treatment is available in packets at any pharmacy. Keep them in mind for future use when your child has a rash or chicken pox.

Hair. When you are pregnant, your hair will be thicker than it has ever been in your life. This is because all during pregnancy, the high hormone level keeps every hair on your head from falling out. When you are not pregnant, defoliation is a normal, ongoing process. Your hair is constantly growing in and falling out. If you look at your brush now, while pregnant, you won't see much hair in it at all.

In the weeks after delivery, however, many women worry that they are going bald; they seem to lose so much hair. But the only reason why you lose hair after pregnancy is that you do *not* lose it while you are pregnant! You can talk to your doctor about taking medication to slow the process, but really you should not be concerned. What you are losing is probably no more than what you would have lost over the nine-month period of your pregnancy.

Breast-feeding delays the return of the defoliating process, and so if you add that period to the nine months of pregnancy, you may well have over a year to enjoy an extra-thick head of hair. Some women say their hair changes texture when they are pregnant, but it's more likely that it's the additional amount of hair that they notice. Other women do not notice any difference in either thickness *or* texture.

Fluid retention. More than 50 percent of pregnant women notice some degree of fluid retention at the end of their pregnancy, causing hands, feet, and ankles to puff up. Sitting with legs crossed aggravates the situation, as it impedes return circulation; if you are at a desk for long stretches, make a conscious effort not to cross your legs. Toward the end of your pregnancy you will find you do not have much of a choice about how you sit—your legs will seem to want to stay apart, knees angled down, feet flat on the floor. Unattractive as it might be, that spread-legged position is the healthiest way to sit at the end of pregnancy, with the fewest bends in the legs to encourage free-flowing circulation.

Standing up for long periods can also result in swollen legs and ankles. When I was pregnant with my first child and working as a nurse in labor and delivery, I would come home after nine hours on my feet with ankles so swollen I could make little pit marks in them with my fingers. I began to think I would never see my toe or ankle bones again, but happily they did return. If you always see your doctor before going to work, when ankles are slenderest and bones prominent, tell him what they are like at the end of the day or schedule an appointment for then so he can see them.

One way to reduce swelling around the ankles is to lie down with your head at the bottom of the bed and your feet propped up straight against the headboard or wall for about ten minutes. With summer pregnancies, fluid retention is usually more severe: body fluids ooze into the tissues of your extremities in an effort to cool your overheated body. Try a cool bath with your feet raised.

Most women find that at the end of pregnancy their feet are about a half size larger than usual. Buy a roomier pair of shoes to wear for most of your pregnancy, rather than stretching all of your regular shoes. Of course if the weather is warm, sandals are a good, comfortable alternative.

One of my students noticed another, more generalized problem with her feet—they did not seem to want to go anywhere. Try as she might to get them out of bed and off to work in the morning, they just stayed put. Before I could help her on this one, one of the husbands in the group said, "Gee, I know the feeling well, and I'm not even pregnant."

If you are getting that kind of message from your tired, achy feet, how about giving them a warm bath? Or maybe a massage, by your husband, or foot circle exercises (page 84)? The pace and activity of your day may be too much for your pregnant body. If you are tired and uncomfortable and are still working in an office, consider moving up the date you begin your maternity leave. Cut back on your commitments. You owe it to yourself and that growing baby inside to take it easy!

Some women experience swelling in the tissues of the wrists, also known as *carpal tunnel syndrome.* Hands may be numb or tingly in the morning as the swollen tissues exert pressure on ligaments and nerves. To help alleviate this discomfort, stretch your arms high above your head and hold the position while you clench and extend the fingers. If the condition worsens and becomes painful, talk to your doctor about it; sometimes hand splints worn at night can help tilt the wrists outward in a position that relieves pressure.

Increased blood volume can cause the fingers to swell, particularly in hot weather, so be sure to remove your rings while you can still get them off.

Occasional **dizzy spells** and **hot flashes** are perfectly normal, and again these are due to increased circulation. Hot flashes occur when lots of blood rushes to your head, making you feel flushed and hot all over. Dress in light, loose-fitting clothes. If you're pregnant in winter, consider yourself fortunate that you have not only your own built-in body warmer, but also "the glow of pregnancy" to bring color to your face.

Dizzy spells can occur when you stand up quickly—the blood drops right out of your head and you feel faint. You'll be fine if you get your head down. Pregnant with my first baby, I could discreetly lean down and pretend I was tying my nurse's shoes. With my third baby I was not working, so I would lean over and pretend to look for my keys. Whatever your ploy, be calm and lean way down. If you stand up and pretend nothing is happening, hoping the dizzy feeling will pass, you may pass *out.* To avoid feeling dizzy in the first place, move slowly when you change from one position to another. Because of the increased cardiac load, some people get a little palpitation—and then it's gone. This, too, is normal.

Some women have more **headaches** during pregnancy, which in part may be due to your increased circulation but also may be from fatigue and stress. Again, take it easy. Try to get more rest and modify your life-style to decrease anxiety—but do not take medication without discussing it with your doctor first. The good news is that women who have a history of migraine headaches usually find themselves completely free of them during pregnancy and breast-feeding.

Cramping. Leg and foot cramps when you are pregnant are caused by a metabolic imbalance between calcium and phosphorus, due to increased hormone levels. You can increase the amount of calcium in your diet; but since the problem is metabolic, this does not help most people. If you feel cramping begin in the middle of the night, straighten your leg, flex your foot up, and in a sitting position, lean forward and press down on your knee. This will help to stretch the muscles in your leg and take away the cramp.

Do *stretch out leg and flex foot muscles to relieve the cramps.*

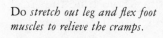

Don't *draw up your knees and point your toes—those cramps will only get worse.*

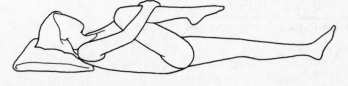

Eye-pressure changes occur in some women, and it is not your imagination if your hard contact lenses feel uncomfortable. If this happens, use your prescription glasses for the duration of your pregnancy.

It is very common for **gums** to become a little more sensitive when you brush your teeth or when you go to the dentist and he works in your mouth with that little hook. Tender, puffy gums that are apt to bleed more easily than usual are again caused by the increased circulation and hormonal stimulation. Your inclination might be to forget about the Water Pik or dental floss, or not brush so diligently, but that would be a big mistake—you have got to keep up all your good dental habits during pregnancy. You are more prone than ever to tooth decay and gum disease. The old wives' tale that "with every pregnancy you lose a tooth" is rubbish, but undoubtedly many expectant mothers did not take care of their teeth because their *gums* were tender. If your toothbrush is too hard, use a softer one; but keep brushing, flossing, and seeing your dentist regularly.

At each visit, remind your dentist that you are pregnant, particularly if it doesn't show, so that he can accurately evaluate the need for X rays, dental work, or local anesthesia.

Rhinitis of pregnancy. Some women notice that they have what is called "rhinitis of pregnancy," which makes them feel they have a kind of low-grade cold or stuffy nose the whole time they are pregnant. If this happens, buy a vaporizer (you'll need one for the baby eventually) and use it in your room at night—the extra moisture can help to soothe a stuffy nose. Put a little Vaseline or A&D ointment around your nose to keep it from getting chapped.

Both the heightened olfactory sense, described earlier, and rhinitis of pregnancy are due to hormonal stimulation and increased circulation to the mucous membranes. The same hormones that are preparing the mucous lining of the vagina to be able to expand and deliver a baby, are, in a wonderful, nondiscriminatory way, also preparing the mucous-membrane lining of your nose and mouth—just in case you have to deliver orally or nasally!

> *"My ears clogged up as if I had a bad head cold; I could hear myself speak inside my head."*

Women who suffer from rhinitis all through pregnancy report that it miraculously seems to disappear at the onset of labor.

If you get a full-blown cold during pregnancy, discuss how to treat the symptoms with your doctor before taking any medications, including those you may have routinely used in the past. If you blow your nose too hard you might have a little nosebleed—again nothing to worry about.

Vaginal discharge. As pregnancy progresses, your increased hormonal levels will probably cause an increase in vaginal discharge, which is normal. Because the vagina is self-cleansing, daily bathing is sufficient. Douching is not recommended in pregnancy. You can use a light panty liner, but underpants that have a cotton crotch panel are usually sufficient for absorbing any discharge.

Changes in pH make you more susceptible to yeast infections, and if you experience vaginal itching, burning, or redness, consult your doctor. Treatment is easy, effective, and safe for the baby, so do not let the condition go for more than three days.

Sexual intercourse. You may have noticed changes in how you feel about having sex. When the discomforts of the early months have passed, most women find that their pregnant bodies are more sexually sensitive than ever before—due in part to the increased circulation to the vaginal area, and perhaps also to the freedom from using contraception. On the other hand, some

> *"I particularly enjoyed talking to my husband about the baby; discussing names, preparing his room, trying to imagine what he'd be like. There was a special closeness that evolved during that time that keeps growing now."*

women are not interested in sex at all when they're pregnant—also perfectly normal.

If you have been told that having sex will endanger the baby, it's just not true, unless your doctor tells you to refrain for a specific medical condition. The cautions of the past about intercourse in pregnancy have gone by the boards, as have the admonitions against taking a bath or going swimming. We think that between the mucus plug, the amniotic sac, and the uterus itself, the baby is well protected. I remember one doctor saying, "I tell my mothers to stop having intercourse when labor begins," which may be a little too liberal for you but certainly rings true when the baby's safety is the case in point.

If the cervix were to begin to open or dilate early, your doctor would want you to be extra careful, and would probably suggest special precautions to take. Otherwise, you can do everything you normally do, confident that the amniotic sac amply protects the baby in a cushioned, perfectly regulated environment all through the pregnancy.

In fact, even if you ran into a cement wall the baby would still be cushioned and safe. One father came to a Lamaze class with a mayonnaise jar and an egg, determined to show everyone just how well-protected the baby really was inside the mother. First, he filled the jar to the top with water and got rid of all the bubbles. Then he cracked the egg, dropped the yolk into the water, and closed the lid tightly. Holding up a crisp, new hundred-dollar bill, he proposed to the class that anyone who could break the yolk without breaking the jar would win the money. Everyone took turns vigorously shaking and tapping the jar—and all the while that little yolk just floated around in a leisurely fashion, without even touching the surface of the glass, let alone breaking. That is kind of what the baby is like, nicely cushioned in the amniotic sac, oblivious to the turmoil of life in the outside world.

Like most women, you will probably have very few discomforts during pregnancy that require special attention. Your main focus will be on the baby developing inside, and the excitement this will bring far outshadows any minor, temporary ailments you may experience.

4

The Developing Baby

*T*he baby's growth in the uterus may not be as obvious as the changes a mother experiences in her body, but it is no less extraordinary.

The most exciting proof that the baby exists is early *fetal movement.* In Nilsson's *A Child Is Born* or Flanagan's *The First Nine Months of Life,* two books I highly recommend, you can follow your pregnancy along with photographs of the developing fetus, seeing each tiny detail of the baby's body miraculously come into existence—eyebrows and eyelashes, and fingernails. When you feel one "kick" in three different places and wonder, "Hmm, how can *that* be?" the photographs show with reassuring clarity how those limbs can move all at once. Phenomenal visual sequences show a wide variety of movement and positions: for example, some babies sit, almost tailor-fashion, sucking their toes, and then appear at birth with a blister where they sucked!

For many women, feeling their baby move for the first time happens just when they wonder if they will *ever* feel anything at

"Feeling the baby move? It was totally unexpected and absolutely enthralling."

63

all. Of course, you cannot *see* your own little baby yet, but the tangible sign that he or she exists inside is truly exhilarating. That first kick, swipe, or turn seems to make the pregnancy real—the "embryo/fetus" of the first few months becomes a "real live baby."

> *"Sometimes when the baby kicks hard it really tickles and I laugh out loud."*

Later, when fetal activity becomes more pronounced, your husband will be just as excited as you to put his hand on your belly and feel that baby move.

> *"The most touching moment was when I woke up one morning and my husband told me he hadn't been able to sleep. I asked him what he did and he said that he had put his hand on my stomach and felt the baby. I had never felt him doing this. But it overwhelmed me, since it made me feel we were really together on this. It was a very loving moment."*

Initial fetal movement has been described as "the flutter of angel wings," but with my baby it felt more like a gas bubble, scurrying from one side of my intestines to the other. Not uncomfortable, but nothing ethereal, either. If at first you doubt that what you feel is the baby, soon the "gas bubble" seems to have its own definite rhythm, more like a quick little bunny foot than angel wings fluttering, and a very definite sensation—the baby's muscles have become well enough developed to make their exercise sessions known.

Some women experience fetal activity as early as sixteen weeks, but don't panic if you are five months pregnant and have not really noticed it. If you are tuned in to the possibility, you may find that yes, there is a little something there.

One couple approached me after their first Lamaze class for a "private consultation." They were worried because they had not felt the baby move. The classroom had emptied, so I asked the woman to lie down on one of the sofas and I gently laid my hand on her thirty-two-week-pregnant abdomen. Her husband hovered over us anxiously. All was quiet, so I gave the baby a little jab with my fingers to see if I could get a response. Still nothing. Now both parents were looking pale. "Hmmm," I groped for words of reassurance—just as a big, pointy lump began to protrude at the left side of that large pregnant belly, gradually moved across it, and then disappeared at the other side. Immediately the husband exclaimed with relief, "Alice, that's not a gas bubble, you dummy!"—and we all had a laugh.

In the last trimester, the baby makes his presence known to all, mother, father, and siblings, if any, and as the photographs show, there is plenty of fetal movement from those beginning stages, when the fetus is minuscule, until the time he begins to outgrow his peaceful, cozy environment in the uterus. The umbilical cord, which tethers the baby to the placenta, is about two feet long and gives the baby ample freedom to move about, with somersaults, twists, and turns. The cord consists of a stretchy, fibrous substance called Wharton's jelly; it functions beautifully to supply the baby with nutrients and oxygen during pregnancy and birth. I even remember seeing two "true knots" in babies' cords in the delivery room that never caused a problem!

> *"The fun part was feeling the little one move around inside me, which occurred on occasion when I was in exercise class. When it did, everyone in class including the instructor would want to feel the movement. Sometimes it lasted long enough for them to experience (vicariously) this new life."*

Toward the very end of the pregnancy, some babies exhibit certain traits that will be evident after their birth. Some of them rub their cheeks over and over again with tiny fists, or hunch their shoulders up and down, or suck their toes. In those first days after delivery, as you marvel over your beautiful little baby, you may suddenly catch yourself exclaiming, "So *that's* what it was, that funny little movement!" At least you can *see* what just a day ago you could only feel.

> *"In the last trimester, I was able to touch what I think was a foot and the baby would pull her foot back. It was like a game."*

If you notice you are lopsided, that one side of your belly sticks up higher than the other side, it's because of the baby's position. The side that sticks up highest is where the baby's bottom is located. If you experience an excruciating pain on your left, under the ribs, where your baby has imbedded his right kneecap, pat or poke him there firmly, and he will probably move into another position. He's been kicking and pushing you all day; you can certainly push him back a little to rearrange him! If he is pressing on the sciatic nerve, push him again and he will move over. If this does not seem to work, you can increase your efforts by adding music and baths to the pokes.

> *"The best part for both of us was the fourth through the ninth month. Until I started to show, I didn't really feel like I was pregnant. I wasn't convinced there wasn't some big mistake until the baby kicked."*

We know that babies react to music, especially when base tones predominate. There was an obstetrician doing research at The New York Hospital who would visit Philharmonic Hall twice weekly and ask pregnant women coming to the concert if he could monitor their babies with a lightweight, ultrasonic belt to keep track of fetal activity. He found that all babies literally started to "dance" to the music, and when it stopped, they became very still.

One couple who found themselves at a loud rock concert in Madison Square Garden were so nervous about the effect of all the noise on their baby that they piled coats on the pregnant mother's belly. They need not have worried. What babies hear through the amniotic fluid is very different from what we hear through air conduction. It would be as if you were at the bottom of the swimming pool and a band was playing music on the lawn; you would hear the sounds as muffled, vibrating noises. On the other hand, women have had to leave concerts because their unborns kicked up such a fuss that Mom couldn't endure it.

In addition to music and little pokes, babies also respond to baths—something about their mother lounging peacefully in warm water seems to encourage them to move about.

Get in the tub, turn on the loud music, and gently poke him if you feel uncomfortable about his position. One mother found that a loud, firm tap of her wedding ring against the side of the porcelain tub would "startle" the baby into repositioning himself. If this sounds a bit insensitive, you can be assured you are not scaring him: his movement is only a reflex action; he does not yet know the emotion of fear.

The baby's position affects your own body in other ways, too, particularly toward the end of the pregnancy. You are probably used to seeing a cross-section diagram of the uterus, with the baby growing inside. What you are probably not used to seeing is that the whole uterus, when viewed as a solid mass, is really a big muscle bag. Attached to it there is a broad ligament that goes back toward the spinal column. As the weight of the baby pulls it, you might get a backache at the end of the day. There are two additional ligaments, one on either side of the uterus, that come out of the groin to help stabilize things, much the way long ropes steady those huge Mickey Mouse and Popeye balloons in the Macy's Thanksgiving Day Parade (see figure *e*, page 41). Although these ligaments stretch with the expanding uterus, it is

> *"A long-term client was making very little eye contact with me as I presented a piece I had written for his magazine. I finally asked him if something was wrong. He said in a very awkward fashion—as if doubting his sanity—'It seems like your dress is moving.'"*

not uncommon to feel an occasional ache in the groin. You might also experience a more intense sensation, a sharp, stabbing pain in the same groin area, which almost all women describe in their third trimester. It's sharp enough for you to think, "Oh, help, a ruptured appendix at eight months pregnant!" and then in five seconds, it is gone. As you walked one way and turned to the right, the baby moved in exactly the opposite direction and turned left, giving a good, hard yank on that ligament. It hurts, but if you wait for a moment the pain will be gone, with no subsequent damage.

Toward the end of your pregnancy, you may notice **Braxton Hicks contractions.** When they first occur, you might confuse them with fetal movement, thinking the baby has assumed a position in which his bottom is prominent. If you poke around, you will find it is not a bottom at all but rather the whole uterus that you feel, as hard as your forehead. After a minute or so, the odd sensation passes, and then only the part where the baby's bottom is actually located is hard.

What you have experienced is a Braxton Hicks contraction, also referred to as a toning-up contraction, as the uterus prepares itself for labor. With first babies, Braxton Hicks contractions are not painful and do not even compare with real labor contractions. They seem to come on without any forewarning and at odd times of the day, when suddenly you'll feel a large wave of pressure as if, in the words of many women, the whole uterus has been transformed into a bowling ball!

Women having second and subsequent babies experience Braxton Hicks contractions earlier and with greater frequency than women having first babies. Then they really can be uncomfortable, but again, not nearly so bad as real contractions.

As the final stretch of pregnancy comes into focus and the due date approaches, Nature bestows the last round of physical endowments to the little baby soon to be born. Babies who keep to their birth schedule put on an insulating layer of fat in the eighth month; this will also provide extra nourishment after the trauma of birth. Antibodies and gamma globulin from the mother's blood, placenta, and amniotic fluid bring the baby's immunity to infection and disease up to the level of his mother. Fetal growth slows substantially about a week or two before birth. The aging placenta triggers certain hormonal changes in the mother's body, which in turn signal the onset of labor. The pregnancy is over, but the climactic event of birth is just beginning.

The mother-to-be whose pregnancy might have seemed endless can pause for a moment to contemplate the phenomenal events that have taken place inside her body, in what is really a very short period of time. The development of her baby is so dramatic that it seems to defy comprehension. In nine months' time, two

> *"Sometimes I resent the invasion of this little creature in my body which I have controlled and disciplined for so long. It's been taken over by a growing parasite . . . but that's only what I feel when I feel overwhelmed."*

tiny cells have multiplied into two hundred million cells—a totally formed, full-term baby who is approximately six billion times heavier than the almost weightless egg that was fertilized at conception!

Today, we know that a mother can have a great influence over her pregnancy and the health of her baby. Good prenatal care makes a world of difference, not only from the medical standpoint where tests and keen observation assure the safest outcome possible, but also from the standpoint of becoming a responsible, loving parent. Having a baby in your life requires a long, slow adjustment, but you can get a head start with the nurturing pro-

> *"One day I walked by two men carrying a piano into a piano store. One of the men looked at me, didn't miss a beat, and pointing one hand at my belly called out, 'It's a boy!' I have yet to determine if he's correct but it made me smile, realizing that even unborn babies bring people closer together."*

cess if you take good care of yourself during pregnancy, when that little baby is forming and growing inside.

In the next two chapters, you will find guidelines for taking care of yourself and your baby during your pregnancy. Exercise will not only feel good and keep you in shape, it will also strengthen your body for labor and delivery. Healthy, nutritious foods and a sensible outlook toward what you put into your body will help to make a healthy baby.

5

Pregnant and Thriving

I remember one mother whose appearance was so healthy and attractive at the end of her third trimester that she stood out distinctly from the Lamaze group that I was teaching. When someone asked what she did for herself, she replied that she swam in a pool every day and planned to do so right up to her due date. Swimming freed her from the confines of her ungainly pregnant body, she explained, much as it does for a walrus when it hits the water. Many people feel that way about exercising in a pool when they are pregnant—but what was interesting about this student's explanation concerned her own mother and the shifting attitudes toward pregnancy. In the late 1940s, her pregnant mother had shocked a whole summer community by doing long laps in a Maine lake, and her husband (who happened to be a doctor) further amazed the group by digging a nicely rounded hole for his wife's pregnant belly. When she came out of the water she positioned her belly over the hole, plopped down on the beach, and lay flat on her stomach—sheer bliss at eight months pregnant!

If there is any merit to the slogan "You've come a long way, baby," it certainly holds for those nine months of pregnancy. So many of the cautions of the past—no sex, no exercise, no baths, and so forth—have been proved unnecessary that today women

"Being pregnant was much easier than I thought it would be. I continued to exercise until the day I gave birth, so I felt pretty good about my body, even in its new shape. The pregnancy did not change our lives very much. We continued to entertain and to go on day hikes and the movies. In fact, not until about the eighth month did it seem that we were really going to have a baby."

can enjoy their pregnancy with very few limitations on their healthy, active prepregnant life-style.

Fortunately, we know much more about prenatal care than we ever did in the past. You will be doing good things for your body and feeling a whole lot better about pregnancy if, along with making routine visits to your doctor to monitor the course of the pregnancy and following a diet that consists of healthy, nourishing food (see page 86), you carry yourself proud and tall, keep yourself *moving,* with regular exercises geared for your growing body, and generally ignore what anyone other than your doctor says to you about caring for your body. Your intuition, knowledge of yourself and occasionally, the advice of others—in combination—should prevail.

"I think that advice on activity, both from doctor and books, was confusing. Initially, I was scared to push myself too much in stretching and exercising. But I think that I could have been more active. Also, the eating/food question was confusing. The way some books stated it, the amounts of food I should eat were staggering. I ate about half as much as they said, which was still a good deal more than my nonpregnant consumption amount, and still gained forty pounds!"

"I did love being pregnant. I felt wonderful. The nine months plus passed very quickly."

Good posture, or correct body alignment, is the first order of business for maintaining a healthy, comfortable pregnant shape.

Have you been brave enough to look in the mirror sideways lately? Undoubtedly the view is not quite the way you remembered it! Are you standing up straight? If you were to walk behind a pregnant woman on the street, you could probably guess she was pregnant solely by the way she walks—or waddles. She does that for a very good reason. When a woman is not pregnant, her center of gravity is in the middle of her pelvis, giving her a sense of security and balance. As pregnancy progresses, her center of gravity is gradually displaced forward and she feels not quite as well balanced. To compensate, she broadens her base, spreading out those legs and feet; later on, as the baby gets a little larger, she is likely to let him hang down in front, with her head poking forward as a counterweight—the final touch to complete the image of a duck.

You can't always keep "chin up, shoulders back, chest forward." However, if you imagine that a string is attached to the top of your head and you pull on that string so that everything falls in line below, it will tilt your pelvis forward and up in such a way that it will become more like an upright basket that can carry the weight of the baby than an angled one, which allows the weight of the baby to pull on your back and presses on your bladder. This string-pulling posture will help you feel much better than if you just let your body sink with the weight of the baby. By tucking your bottom under and keeping your body in alignment, you should have many added weeks of feeling secure—at least until the final weeks of your pregnancy.

> *"Changes in my body (like gaining weight) were very difficult to deal with. I had a very strong sense of my physical appearance which I felt changed drastically, very quickly."*

Most backaches in pregnancy are caused by poor posture; you may find that they disappear entirely when you pay attention to how you carry yourself. If you still experience them, however, it

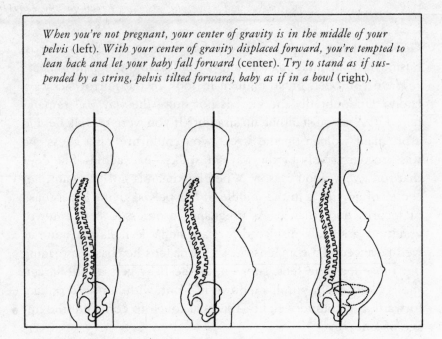

When you're not pregnant, your center of gravity is in the middle of your pelvis (left). With your center of gravity displaced forward, you're tempted to lean back and let your baby fall forward (center). Try to stand as if suspended by a string, pelvis tilted forward, baby as if in a bowl (right).

may be from overstretching the ligament that runs from the uterus to your spinal column. A warm bath or heating pad may help, as many women report heat to be a soothing remedy. Believe it or not, a small can of frozen juice concentrate wrapped in a linen towel and pressed against the aching areas can relieve backaches. Some women report that a good massage is the best cure, and it might be worth a session or two under professional hands, or enlisting your husband to massage a little lotion into the spot. A maternity girdle (don't be misled—it will neither squash your baby nor make you look like you're not pregnant) may provide to your lower back the support that's needed to rid you of persistent low-back pain.

Your **maternity clothes** should be comfortable; keep ahead of your changing size. Some women can continue to wear their old clothes for a while if they are loose-fitting, but there is nothing worse for morale or more tiring for your body than wearing that favorite skirt or pants until the buttons pop off. Your wardrobe doesn't always have to be "maternity," either. Dresses made from cool, Indian cottons feel and look great in summer—loose-fitting, light, and just right for enhancing the shape of your pregnant body. The "layered" look seems to suit many pregnant women, but be sure not to overdress, even in winter. Remember, you have your own built-in little body warmer and will hardly need even a sweater to combat a chilly winter if you live in the north.

If friends offer to loan you their maternity clothes, take them up on it. In a sense, your pregnancy is a special time for them and sharing not only brings you closer but also adds variety to your maternity wardrobe.

Low heels are best. With your center of gravity thrown forward, high heels not only aggravate matters but become a liability as well. The last thing you need is a broken arm from an accidental fall two weeks before your due date!

PELVIC-FLOOR EXERCISES

Along with good posture, I always recommend *Kegel pelvic-floor exercises*. Make a habit of doing them all through pregnancy to build strength, resilience, and tone. And to promote healing, do these exercises after delivery; they increase circulation to the pelvic floor as it recovers from the birth.

The pelvic-floor muscles consist of all of the muscles between your pubic bone and coccyx that encircle the urethra, vagina, and anus. They control elimination, intercourse, and pushing out a baby; and yet, if you are like the rest of the world, you probably did not even know they exist, much less support all of your pelvic organs and, during pregnancy, that growing uterus.

Strengthening the pelvic-floor muscles is easy. All you do is tighten the muscles encircling the urinary passage and rectum as if you were trying to hold back urinating or having a bowel movement. Hold for a few seconds, and release.

I had always directed the pelvic-floor exercises toward women in the Lamaze groups—until two urologists taking my class recommended them for the men, too. Apparently, it is not uncommon for men in their sixties and seventies to develop benign prostatic hypertrophy, a condition in which the prostate gland begins to enlarge and can even obstruct the urinary passage. So, gentlemen, you too should do these Kegel exercises to increase circulation to the area and ward off hypertrophy, if you are prone to it. Both you and your wife should do them twenty-five times a day every day for the rest of your life.

> *"Patty's extreme good health and mobility made us forget at times that there were really any limitations to being pregnant. In the final overview of the whole experience, I think it was much more than I expected . . . much richer, more joy-filled, more of a bonding between husband and wife." (Father)*

If your immediate reaction is "Sorry, I'm too busy," think of all those minutes you spend waiting—stuck in a traffic jam, on a street corner, in the supermarket, at the sink. Once my husband and I were standing in a long line for a movie when one of my Lamaze couples (also on line) called out, "Fritzi, we're doing our exercises!" Everyone else stared quizzically at the couple, who were standing perfectly still. You can do 150 repetitions a day without a soul catching on!

To vary the pelvic-floor exercises, do them as if you were patterning them on an elevator ride: Up you go, stopping at the third floor and holding the muscles only partially contracted, then on to the fifth floor, tightening a little more, and on to the tenth floor, tightening as much as possible. Now go down on the elevator, releasing the muscles in the same gradual way as you tightened them.

Gentlemen, you can help your wives by saying when you have intercourse, "First floor, third floor," and so on, and see how many levels they can master. At first it may only be one or two, but after some practice, they should be able to get to six to eight levels.

> *"Pregnancy was even better than expected. Outside of some minor discomforts, it was one of the happiest periods in mine and my husband's lives. I never felt better and the joy of the experience brought even more closeness and sharing into our lives."*

EXERCISE AND ENJOY AN ACTIVE LIFE

If it's your first pregnancy, it may be a little difficult to feel confident that you can enjoy an active life-style with a baby in your uterus. You may picture the whole situation as much more fragile and precarious than it really is—perhaps because those pictures of the developing fetus reveal something that *looks* so fragile and new. As described in chapter 3, the baby really is protected in the uterus, but if you still have doubts about it, I recommend that you join an exercise class for pregnant women. Working side by side with other pregnant women can give you the confidence you need, as well as a chance to meet new friends. The level of camaraderie is usually pretty high, and most pregnant women feel better after they begin to attend exercise classes once or twice a week and look forward to them.

Obviously, in choosing how you exercise, some common sense is in order. Because of your displaced center of gravity, you are certainly not going to ski down a mountainside or jump a horse or swim in rough ocean water when you are very pregnant and could risk injury.

> *"I expected to retain water but did not experience any swelling at all. I thought I would be able to swim through pregnancy but swollen nasal passages meant kickboard only, no crawl!"*

If you are a jogger, it is better not to jog once your uterus has grown out over your pubic bone because it is a very delicate bone and with each jog the uterus and baby bang down on it and put it under a good deal of stress.

Snorkeling is fine, but scuba diving, where there is a significant change in water pressure, should be postponed until after the baby arrives.

Air travel during pregnancy is safe because the air pressure in large passenger planes is regulated. What you need to avoid is flying very high in small planes in which unpressurized cabins with diminished oxygen could create a problem. Check with your doctor about travel at the end of your pregnancy.

> *"My greatest fear about pregnancy was that I would gain enormous amounts of weight and have a tough time getting back into shape. In reality I was able to continue strenuous exercise through the seventh month and moderate exercise thereafter."*

Exercises to Benefit Everyone

The exercises that follow are grouped to cover certain key areas of the body in hopes that you can keep them limber, strong, and free from discomfort. Some exercises are for early pregnancy, others are for later, and they are divided up accordingly.

Generally, exercise of any kind is fine except for straight-leg lifts, sit-ups, or any exercises that require good abdominal muscle tone. As your pregnancy progresses, your abdominal muscles split up the middle to let the uterus grow. When that happens, the exercises that usually work the abdomen and strengthen it only put strain on your back. If you want to do sit-ups, keep your legs bent. I am giving you the simple basics, but certainly there are many exercises to investigate further if you like; I recommend Noble's *Essential Exercises for the Childbearing Year.* (See Suggested Reading, page 375.)

EXERCISES FOR THE EARLY MONTHS

These exercises should be completed twice daily for about fifteen minutes each session. Adjust the program to fit your needs. If you feel that your back needs more strengthening, do more exercises for the back. Do the same with other parts of the body. Start slowly and breathe slowly as you do them.

For Torso and Body

Stand with legs apart, arms stretched over-head. Bend slowly forward (to waist level), then straighten up and stretch back. Repeat ten times.

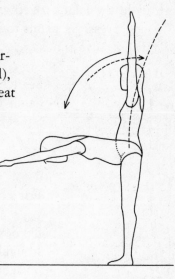

Stand with legs apart, arms straight out in front. Twist the body from right to left and back. Repeat twenty times.

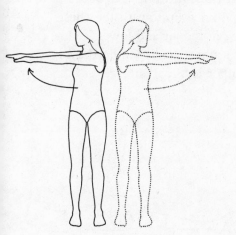

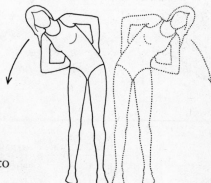

Stand with legs apart and hands on hips. Bend torso slowly from side to side. Repeat twenty times.

For the Breasts

Fold the hands together in front of breasts, and press the palms together. Repeat twenty-five times.

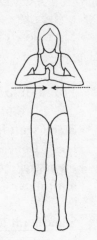

Stretch the arms out in front, hands holding a small pillow. Squeeze and release twenty-five times.

For the Legs

Lie down on your back with the legs out straight. Bend one knee up toward the chest, straighten that leg in the air and lower it slowly. Repeat ten times, and then do the exercise with the other leg.

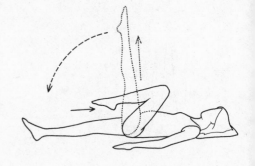

Lie down with the legs straight and the arms apart. Bring one knee up toward the opposite arm, then slowly lower it. Repeat the exercise ten times with each leg.

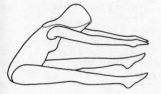

Sit with legs straight out in front, knees about a foot apart. Reach hands down toward toes as far as possible, and release up again. Repeat twenty times.

Lie down and rest your legs on a chair and pillow to support feet for five minutes, three times a day. Rather than strengthening, this position relaxes the pregnant body and encourages good circulation from feet and legs back to your heart.

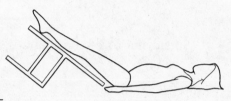

For the Back

Lie on the floor with knees slightly bent, feet together. Reach with hands toward the knees, rolling your head and shoulders up. Slowly unroll down. Do this ten times.

Get on all fours and reach forward with one hand as far as possible. Repeat twenty times. Change hands and do the exercise again.

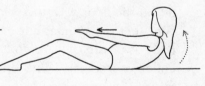

Sit on your heels and bend forward as far as possible with the arms out straight. Repeat ten times.

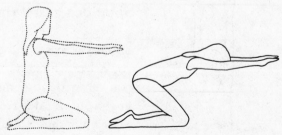

SECOND- AND THIRD-TRIMESTER STRENGTHENING EXERCISES FOR LABOR AND DELIVERY

Spend ten to fifteen minutes twice daily going through the following:

Tailor Sit

Sit cross-legged with the back slightly rounded and lean forward slightly to relieve back pressure. Do this for short periods of time several times a day.

Tailor Press

Sit on the floor with the soles of your feet together, as close to your body as possible. Place your hands under your knees, palms up. Lean forward, gently pressing your knees down against your hands (toward the floor). Hold this stretch for ten to twenty seconds and release. Do this several times at each exercise session.

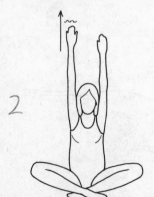

Shoulder-and-Arm Stretch

Sit cross-legged and extend arms straight up above your head. Gradually reach as high as you can with your right arm, wiggling your fingers as you do. Keeping both arms up, relax your right shoulder and let it come

2

down, stretch as high as you can with your left arm, wiggling your fingers as you do, then relax the shoulder.

Rib-Cage Stretch

3

Sit cross-legged on the floor and place your right arm across your tummy. Stretch your left arm over your head and to the right, stretching and reaching as far as you can. Don't let your head fall forward. Now reverse and again reach and stretch.

Shoulder Roll with Elbow Circles

4

Sit cross-legged on the floor and place your fingers on your shoulders. Slowly raise your elbows forward and as high over your head as possible and then gradually down as far behind you as you can, making two large circles in the air with your elbows and smaller ones with your shoulders.

Breast and Chest Muscle Support

5

Sit cross-legged on the floor and place your palms together in front, at breast level. Press them together gently three or four times, open them (keeping the arms at breast level), and press your elbows back as far as possible, as if trying to touch them behind you. Repeat.

Leg-Limbering Lifts

Lie flat on the floor with the right leg stretched out straight, the left leg bent with foot close to your bottom. Inhale slowly through the nose as you raise your right leg as high as possible. Flex the foot, still keeping the knee straight, and exhale through the lips as you gradually lower the right leg. Reverse leg positions and repeat with the left leg.

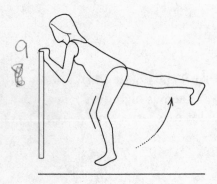

Thigh Stretch

Stand on the right leg, right foot turned out and the knee slightly bent. Raise the left leg behind you, with foot turned out. Lower your body down as low and as far forward as possible, extending your arms to the side (or resting one hand on a chair) for balance. Repeat with the left leg.

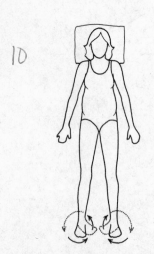

Ankle and Foot Stretch

When lying or sitting, position your feet at rest with heels about a foot apart. Point your toes inward and slowly rotate your ankles up and out, then slowly down and in, wiggling your toes as you circle.

Pelvic Tilt

Lie on your back with knees bent, feet close to your bottom about a foot apart on the floor. Breathe in through the nose as you relax completely, exhale through your lips as you press your back down toward the floor, tilting your pelvis and pulling down on your shoulders.

Back Roll

Lie on your back with knees up and feet close to your bottom, about a foot apart on the floor. Lift your bottom as high as possible as you inhale through your nose, then slowly exhale through your lips as you lower your back to the floor, one vertebra at a time, as if they were a string of pearls you were slowly setting down.

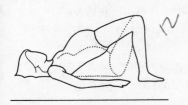

Back Press

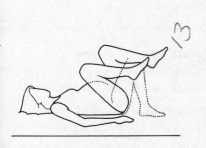

Lie flat on your back, legs bent and feet together close to your bottom. Inhale. Now exhale as you slowly lift your feet, allowing your knees to fall apart to make space for your belly. Bring your knees toward your shoulders while you press the small of your back toward the floor. Inhale as you return to your original position.

6

Making a Healthy Baby

*I*t has always been interesting to me that perfectly formed babies are made in exactly the same sequence of development, no matter what the mother's type or temperament. Environmental influences do have an effect, as seen in areas of famine or in mothers who are heavy drinkers or addicted to drugs; but these are extremes, and the consoling fact remains that in spite of not having the perfect diet or the perfect uterine environment, the vast majority of babies who arrive in the world are still healthy. Even so, a nutritious, healthy diet during pregnancy makes good sense: give your baby the best you can for his development.

WEIGHT GAIN—FACTS AND FALLACIES

I am amused when I read the recommendations for weight gain during pregnancy: No pounds for the first twelve weeks, seven pounds from twelve to twenty weeks, fourteen pounds from twenty to thirty weeks, seven pounds from thirty to thirty-six weeks, and no pounds the last four weeks. This projection is supposedly based on a bell-curve weight gain, tabbed at between twenty and thirty pounds depending on your build and metabolism. In fact, some women gain eighteen pounds and others forty pounds without a problem. It all depends on the individual.

If you are wondering how can you possibly come up with twenty to thirty extra pounds when the end result is only an eight-pound baby, here's how and where it is distributed:

- Baby, 7 to 8 lbs

- Placenta, 2 lbs

- Amniotic fluid, 2 lbs

- Increase in uterine size, 2 lbs

- Breast tissue, 3 lbs

- Increase in circulatory system, 4 lbs

- Retained fluid and stored body fat, 5 to 9 lbs

Don't be put off by the term "stored body fat." This is Nature's way of giving you and the baby a few extra pounds in case labor and delivery are so exhausting that you both need to lie back for a day or two, living off your fat reserves as you recover. This is not usually the case, of course, and these fat reserves are eliminated with the other twenty pounds in the first few weeks after birth, as are the retained fluids, which are perspired away and flushed out when you urinate. (Do not be surprised when you awaken during the night to find your hair and nightgown soaked with perspiration—think of it as excess weight falling away.)

Many women are tempted, as they see their waistline disappear

> *"I thought I would gain more weight—not that I ate a lot, but I anticipated that my calcium intake, particularly of milk, would bring me up to thirty to thirty-five pounds. The pregnancy did surprisingly cause me to eat sweets more than normal and to have cravings—not for pickles and ice cream, but dried apples, chocolate milk shakes, chocolate-chip cookies, and apricots."*

three to four months into the pregnancy, to decide that since no one will notice, they may as well go ahead and indulge in large fudge sundaes after lunch and dinner. The excess fat that they put on is not easily eliminated after delivery, and it will probably settle into your thighs and derriere. One way to check whether you are putting on too much fat from the foods you eat is to measure your upper thigh; it should remain the same size throughout your pregnancy.

> *"My appetite was if anything less demanding than normal—probably because I suffered greatly from heartburn and thus gained no extraneous weight, and six weeks after giving birth I weighed less than before pregnancy. I resumed exercise as soon as possible and after ten weeks muscle tone had been regained."*

While excess fats should be avoided, you can safely eat the following to your heart's content: meats; poultry; fish; skim-milk products; vegetables and fruits. (Daily recommendations are given on page 92.) Sweets and empty carbohydrates do nothing for you or the baby.

Many women have a tendency to think they should double what they eat to make a healthy baby—"eating for two" is the rationale. This is not a valid assumption if you look at what is required during pregnancy in terms of calories.

> *"I've reverted very instinctively to the 'comfort foods' of childhood and away from all grown-up, exotic flavors and textures."*

Normally, when you are not pregnant, you need about 1,500 to 2,000 calories a day. In the beginning of your pregnancy, you need only an additional 200 calories a day, and at the end of pregnancy, you need approximately 350 calories more than usual. That is not very many extra calories, when you realize that an eight-ounce cup of fruited yogurt contains about 200 calories. In any case, although you may be "eating for two," the baby is *tiny* and certainly does not need the same amount of meat and potatoes as you do.

So if you think of adding on those additional 200 to 350 calories with foods that are nutritious and high in protein, you will be just fine.

GENERAL NUTRITION REQUIREMENTS

Protein provides the building blocks for your body to create a healthy baby and placenta; when you are pregnant, your protein needs increase by 50 percent. To ensure that you meet this additional requirement each day, you could have a pint of skim milk or a quarter pound of hard cheese (cheddar, for example, has more protein than cream cheese) or a good helping of meat, poultry, or fish in addition to your normal intake. Good sources of protein include lean meat, fish, poultry, eggs, milk, cheese, dried beans, and nuts.

Carbohydrates are broken down and absorbed slowly and thus supply you and your baby with long-burning energy, and you will get them with your increase of varied foods. Good sources of carbohydrates are whole-grain breads, cereals, pasta, rice, fruits, and vegetables. Only a slight increase is necessary—say, an extra slice of toast.

> *"My diet improved dramatically during pregnancy. I gave up liquor, coffee, diet soda (I did continue to eat plenty of chocolate, though!) and I increased my intake of fruits and vegetables."*

Fats are already included in a balanced diet—you need not think about adding them on. In other words, if your weight is in the normal range, your consumption of fats remains as it has in the past. If you were overweight before you became pregnant, trim excess fats off meats and use less butter on your foods.

Vitamins. By incorporating varied foods into your daily diet, you usually take in the necessary vitamins. Many of the foods individual women crave during pregnancy seem to contain certain elements they lack in their current diet, but since you can't count on this, many doctors prescribe a vitamin supplement to be sure the increased vitamin needs are met.

Some brands of vitamins seem to aggravate the nausea that women experience and are therefore not recommended, but in general, the consensus still seems to be that a multivitamin designed for pregnancy will ensure essential vitamins for mother and baby should they be neglected in the average diet. Ask your doctor to recommend vitamins for your pregnancy. Don't be tempted to take the large-dose megavitamins that you see in health-food stores—they are unsuitable for pregnancy and could even be dangerous to you and the baby.

Minerals are trace elements found in many foods and are essential to a well-balanced diet. Iron and calcium are the two minerals to focus on in pregnancy; they are crucial for a developing fetus and healthy mother.

Iron is necessary for the formation of red blood cells, and your need nearly doubles in pregnancy. Many doctors prescribe an iron supplement which is most efficient if taken with vitamin C, so take it with orange juice. Avoid taking iron with milk products, and note also that iron absorption is compromised if it is taken with antacids.

If supplemental iron tends to make you constipated or increases nausea, try taking it in a different form. Usually, slow-release spansules cause the least amount of gastric distress and constipation.

If you notice that your bowel movements are black while you are taking an iron supplement, this is normal and means that your needs (and your baby's) have been met and now your body is getting rid of the excess.

Good sources of iron are liver, egg yolk, whole grains, dark-green leafy vegetables, brewer's yeast, and nuts.

Calcium is necessary for the formation of strong bones and teeth, and it enables blood to clot and muscles to function. Your need for this mineral almost doubles in pregnancy. Oxalic acid in spinach and cocoa reduces the absorption of calcium, so do not depend on chocolate milk or creamed spinach as your main calcium source. If you must flavor the milk, use something else to make it palatable, and eat the spinach separately from the cream. Good sources of calcium are dairy products, leafy vegetables, beans, and nuts.

Some people get muscle cramps in pregnancy and if you've been told that increasing your calcium will take them away, you can try that under your doctor's supervision; but for most people it does not work. As for dealing with a muscle cramp when it occurs, see page 59. If you do decide to try adding extra calcium, two Tums (calcium carbonate) with no sodium a day will do exactly what the expensive prescription supplements do and are much more pleasant to take. As for other calcium supplements, be sure they do not contain bone meal or dolomite, both of which are very high in lead.

Folic acid is essential for supplying the nucleic acids needed for the cell division of the embryo. You could meet your quota with a huge increase of leafy vegetables and liver, but again, a vitamin supplement is a much simpler alternative.

Watch your sodium intake in the last trimester. You should avoid salty foods, but in general there is no need to eliminate all salt from your diet if you are used to reasonably low amounts and you have no problems with fluid retention during your pregnancy.

A Nutritious Daily Diet

A good diet in pregnancy is essential, but do not be misled by what you might read. Much of the published literature seems to be written for robust women who toil in the fields from sunup to sunset, with food requirements quite different from your own. I don't mean to imply that you lead a sedentary life, only that the diets suggested might lead you to believe that you should triple everything you eat normally and then go on to eat kale and liver as your healthy between-meal snacks. If you stare in awe at those illustrated charts of "foods for pregnant ladies"—cornucopias with four fish springing out and three loaves of bread and potatoes rolling across the table next to six eggs and a pound of butter— do not despair. If you make sure "the basics" are included in your diet, you'll be fine. They are:

- *Milk Group* (3 to 4 servings)

    skim or low-fat milk (8 oz = 1 serving)
    cheeses (3 oz = 1 serving; the harder the cheese,
       the more nutritious)
    yogurt (8 oz = 1 serving)

- *Meat Group* (6 ounces or 2 or 3 servings of any
       of the following)

    beef, veal, pork, lamb, poultry, fish, liver
       (cut back on meats with additives, especially nitrates
       and nitrites—ham, bacon, and so on)

- *Vegetable and Fruit Group* (6 servings: 1/2 C fruit
       juice = 1 serving; 2 oz vegetable = 1 serving)

    all fruits or juices (at least 1 serving daily rich in
       vitamin C, such as orange juice)
    all vegetables or juices (at least 1 serving rich in vitamin A,
       such as dark green or yellow vegetables)

- *Bread and Cereal Group* (4 servings)

    rice (1/2 C cooked rice = 1 serving)
    pasta (1/2 C cooked pasta = 1 serving)
    enriched bread (1 slice = 1 serving)
    enriched cereal (3/4 C = 1 serving)

- *Other Foods*

  butter, margarine, or oil, for cooking and taste
  nuts and seeds as snacks
  iodized salt, to taste
  water or other liquids (at least 6 glasses daily)

- *Vitamin supplements*

  as per your doctor's recommendations

EXAMPLE OF A WELL-BALANCED DAILY MENU

Breakfast
  1 6-ounce glass orange juice (1 fruit-group serving and
    vitamin C source)
  1 egg and 2 sausages (1 milk-group serving; 1 meat-group serving)
  1 slice toast (1 bread-group serving)
  1 8-ounce glass milk (1 milk-group serving)
  1 vitamin supplement

Lunch
  1 cup cream soup (1 milk-group serving)
  1 tuna salad sandwich with lettuce and celery (1 meat-group
    serving; 2 bread-group servings; 1 vegetable-group serving)
  1 8-ounce glass skim milk (1 milk-group serving)
  1 apple (1 fruit-group serving)

Dinner
  1 broiled chicken breast (2 meat-group servings)
  1 4-ounce serving rice (1 bread-group serving)
  1 4-ounce serving beans (1 vegetable-group serving)
  1 small salad (1 vegetable-group serving)
  2 cookies (1 bread-group serving)

Totals:
  Milk Group, 4 servings
  Meat Group, 4 servings
  Vegetable and Fruit Group, 5 servings
  Bread and Cereal Group, 4 servings
  Daily vitamin supplement

Many nutritionists recommend a "cocktail" for pregnant women which, if taken daily, not only fulfills additional nutritional requirements but also gives you energy. Some women carry a thermos of this special drink around with them and sip it when they are feeling tired.

Pregnant Cocktail

Combine the following ingredients in a blender for ten seconds or so and chill the mixture before drinking.

---

2 C milk
1/3 C powdered skim milk
1 T brewer's yeast
1/2 t vanilla
1 raw egg
1/2 egg shell
1 T pasteurized honey
1/2 C fresh fruit

If you are plagued by nausea, see how a little of this drink goes down. If it makes you feel worse, wait until the stage at which your nausea is a thing of the past before trying it again.

A SENSIBLE APPROACH TO MEDICATIONS AND DRUGS

Information about **drugs** in pregnancy is relatively scant; there's no safe way to test the mother-baby unit and, obviously, there are no ready volunteers.

Once your pregnancy is confirmed, discuss *all* medications and drugs with your doctor before taking them. This includes any prescription drugs as well as simple over-the-counter remedies for colds, flu, or headaches. The one safe general rule during pregnancy is to *avoid* drugs and medications—with the exception of what your doctor may prescribe. Needless to say, *all* illegal drugs, including marijuana and cocaine, are out. We know LSD can cause chromosomal damage; the others are suspect.

X rays are hazardous to the fetus, especially when the organs are forming, and they should be routinely avoided during pregnancy. If it's crucial that you have an X ray, tell the doctor or dentist in advance that you are pregnant and be sure that you are well covered with an abdominal shield.

Caffeine is a stimulant and although it may be beneficial to get the blood flowing through you and in turn through the baby, too much of it can make both of you hyperirritable, overactive, and sleepless. It's better to avoid it altogether during pregnancy, but if you must have a cup of regular coffee to open your eyes in the morning, perhaps you could cut back on the amount of caffeine by using instant coffee instead of brewed or, even better, switch to decaffeinated. The best choice is water-processed decaffeinated instant coffee: it has the least caffeine and contains no harmful chemicals.

Tea also contains caffeine, but decaffeinated and herbal teas are now available in such a wide assortment of appealing flavors—almond, orange, peppermint, and so on—that switching over to them is an easy, safe alternative to drinking regular tea.

Many soft drinks contain caffeine, not to mention empty calories, artificial sweeteners, and preservatives. Check the labels. None of the artificial sweeteners have been available long enough to be classified as 100 percent safe. A little sugar during pregnancy is probably safer than saccharine or Nutrasweet, regardless of the extra calories. If soft drinks are a habit, your pregnancy may provide the impetus to break it. Switch to unadulterated fruit juices to quench your thirst—or fresh, cold water.

The alcohol controversy. Studies have concluded that babies born to chronic alcoholic mothers show signs of fetal alcohol syndrome, including mental retardation and other neurological disabilities. Chronic alcoholic mothers are classified as mothers who consume four ounces of 86 proof alcohol daily. The general reaction to this news was total abstinence from *all* alcoholic beverages by women who were pregnant, for fear of adverse affects on the fetus. Of course drinking should be limited or omitted during pregnancy, especially in the early months when the laying down of organ systems in your baby is under way. However, there is *no* documentation that an *occasional* glass of wine or beer is harmful, and for many women, especially at the very end of pregnancy, that is exactly what helps them relax and get some much-needed sleep after a long, tense day of work—or when they are evaluating whether what they feel is real or false labor (see page 105).

Fortunately, drinking hard liquor at business lunches or cocktail parties is rapidly becoming a thing of the past, as is the social standard of drinking liquor at parties. Today there are many nonalcoholic drinks (lemon- or lime-flavored Perrier and seltzers, Moussy beer, for example) available for these occasions.

Smoking should be curtailed during pregnancy, as studies prove it endangers the fetus.

There's a film documentary that shows the effect of smoking on the unborn baby's circulatory system. First, we see a thermographic view of a baby's delicate little fingers in the uterus, clearly outlined because the blood reaches every cell, and then we see that same tiny hand after the mother has taken her first few puffs of just one cigarette. The hand has almost faded away as all those little blood vessels have lost their blood supply and constricted. It makes you wonder, If this is what happens to a baby's hand, what is happening to his brain? Rarely is there an expectant mother who does not choose to totally give up smoking after seeing the film.

If your objective is to provide the very best for your developing baby, you'll approach food and nutrition with good sense and a heightened awareness of making your diet healthier than ever during, and also, for yourself, beyond your pregnancy.

PART TWO

Preparing for Labor and Delivery

In the final weeks of pregnancy, watch for the little signs, mere hints, really, that your body is shifting gears, readying itself for labor. Be ready, not overanxious. "Impending labor" is not real labor at all, but rather the preparatory stage when labor, in a most general way, is on the horizon.

I urge that you take childbirth classes. Most are given weekly, beginning six weeks before your due date, and you should sign up for them *in your fourth month* to be sure of reserving a place for you and your husband. Whatever "school" of childbirth education you choose (some are described in chapter 8), you should learn, review, or at least consider the Lamaze techniques presented here. *Skim the pages in chapter 9 now,* and then, six weeks before your due date (ideally, in tandem with your childbirth classes) begin practicing the techniques with your partner. Lamaze has helped thousands of couples to cope with the process of labor and delivery.

7

Signs of Impending Labor

*T*oward the end of your pregnancy, most likely during one of the routine visits to your doctor's office, you might hear the phrase "the baby has dropped." This sounds as if all of a sudden the baby has gone *kerplunk!* and fallen down into your pelvis. Nothing quite so abrupt has happened. What this really means is that the baby has gradually settled down into the pelvis, assuming the position he will be in when labor begins. When he is not there yet, he is "floating"; when he has "dropped" and is actually wedged into the pelvis, he is "engaged"; and when he is in between the two, he is "dipping." The medical terms, even though they may not sound very medical, will often be used as your doctor examines you around your due date.

THE BABY'S PRESENTATION

In women having first babies, the baby drops or engages anywhere between two and six weeks before labor starts. So if your doctor informs you that the baby is engaged, do not rush home, pack your suitcase, call your husband, and head for the hospital. You

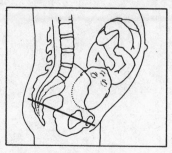

Baby floating, −4 cm.

Baby engaged, 0 station.

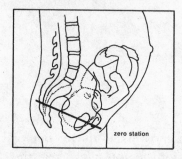

zero station

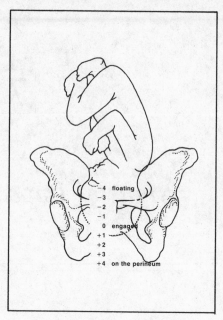

−4 floating
−3
−2
−1
0 engaged
+1
+2
+3
+4 on the perineum

Stations −4 through +4 delivery.

could be waiting another six weeks. With second babies, however, labor usually begins before the head is engaged, in other words, when it's not as deep into the pelvis as for a prima para (a woman having her first baby).

When a baby is engaged, most likely it is with his head down, in a "vertex presentation": 96 percent of all babies engage as a

At left, *a baby presenting as a vertex—96 percent of all babies.* Center, *a baby presenting as a breech—approximately 4 percent of all babies.* Right, *transverse presentation—less than ¹/₂ percent of all babies and usually necessitating a Caesarean.*

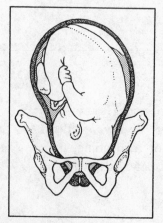
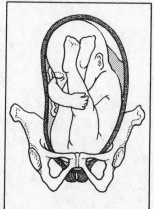
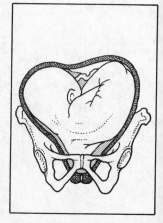

vertex; about 4 percent engage as a breech, with bottom down; and about ½ percent assume a transverse position, in which case they must either be maneuvered from the outside in hopes of being repositioned as a vertex or breech or delivered by Caesarean section.

If it is a vertex, the position of the head can influence what kind of labor you will have. Usually the baby is curled up, head flexed with chin on chest, and facing the mother's right side. Almost *all* babies face the mother's right side but why, no one knows. If he faces front, he is in what is referred to as the posterior position. This often causes a longer, less efficient labor that is felt in the back and is commonly referred to as back labor (see page 178). Although one out of four babies maneuver into a modified posterior position for part of labor, only one out of ten will deliver in a true posterior, or "sunny-side up," position. Some babies who get into this posterior position in labor have trouble passing through the pelvis and may warrant a forceps delivery, which is described later, to gently turn the head into the normal position.

At the end of your pregnancy, your doctor will check whether the baby has engaged and whether the presenting part is a vertex or breech by externally placing his thumb and forefinger on either side of the baby's head, just above your pubic bone, and sort of jiggling it. He can do this while you are on the examining table or while you are standing. Once the head (or whatever the presenting part) is engaged, it is too deep in the pelvis to be wobbled at all.

When you are actually in labor, your doctor will continue to check the baby's position with a vaginal exam every few hours, feeling the edge of the cervix on each side and measuring how wide open it is. At about four centimeters dilation, he could actually feel the baby's head or bottom and confirm once and for all that it is a vertex or a breech. It's not all guesswork until then, of course, as he can usually identify the presenting part just by feeling your abdomen at the end of your pregnancy. But he is not 100 percent sure until he actually feels what is there. Some years ago, as the assisting nurse, I stood by as the chief resident examined a laboring mother and quickly called out of the delivery room to the attending physician, "It's a vertex, her third baby, and you'd better hurry or you will miss the delivery!" Dr. Sweeney rushed in, took one look at the baby as it appeared, and yelled back to the resident, "If that's a vertex, it's the first one I ever saw having a little bowel movement on its way out!"

Breech Babies for First-Time Mothers

If, at the end of your pregnancy, your doctor feels sure your baby is a vertex, everyone is delighted. On the other hand, since Mother Nature, the "fabulous master planner" in obstetrics, cleverly brings most babies down into the pelvis head first, she almost seems to be saying *"Beware!"* when a baby comes down as a breech, particularly with first-time mothers. This is because the head of a baby in the breech position does not have an opportunity during the hours of labor to "mold" or elongate, which facilitates its passage through the mother's bony pelvis. A breech baby's slender, resilient body could slip right through the bony convolutions of the pelvis, and then the head could get caught— not in the cervix (that's tissue and can be stretched or even cut if need be) but in the bony pelvic ring.

Fortunately, to help compensate for the baby's size and position, the pelvis has a little give in labor—Nature's way of preparing for a *slight* expansion, if needed, for the baby to pass through. At the end of pregnancy, some women are actually aware of a loose or "greased" pelvis at the joint in the front at the pubic bone and in back at the sacrum, a (sure) sign of impending labor. But this is nothing to count on for a breech; thus, to avoid unnecessary risk, most women whose first babies are breeches are delivered by Caesarean. (For women who have delivered one or more seven- or eight-pound babies in the vertex position, a breech does not pose the same degree of risk as with first-time mothers because unless the second baby is substantially bigger, the internal bony pelvic ring has shown itself to be adequate, or "proven," for a good-sized head to pass through.)

There are always exceptions, of course, and sometimes first babies are born vaginally in a breech position without a problem.

I know one woman who went into labor three weeks prematurely with the baby in the breech position; nothing would slow down her labor and there she was with a breech birth. In another instance, a woman who had made it to her full term arrived at the hospital fully dilated with the baby in the breech position and birth imminent. Fortunately, both babies were in the five-pound range, with heads small enough to pass through the mother's pelvis, and everything went smoothly.

The presenting part of a breech is not always bottom first, deep in the pelvis with legs neatly folded up, as is shown on page 100. Instead, it could be one foot, two feet, a pair of knees, or any combination. When I first worked in labor and delivery, there was a mother who was rushed upstairs in a wheelchair. On arrival in the labor room, she announced in a very blasé tone, "I am about to have the baby." Wondering if this could be true, judging from her extreme composure, I asked, "How do you know for sure?" To which she replied, "Follow me, my dear," got out of the wheelchair, climbed onto the bed, took her panties down, lay back, and dropped her knees apart—and there in plain view were two little wiggling feet! When the resident came in and examined her, the baby pulled his feet back in! Indeed she was about to deliver her baby, and sure enough she did so about five minutes later.

But these births are exceptions and, repeating once again, to avoid risk the greater majority of women who are having first babies as breeches are delivered by Caesarean.

Breech or vertex, you can well understand why your doctor concentrates his full attention on determining the baby's position: he wants to know as much as possible beforehand about what to expect when labor begins. And so should you. When he checks for your baby's position at the end of your pregnancy, feeling your belly and trying to jiggle your baby's head, you can say to him, "Hmmm, Dr. Saary, is it a vertex, engaged? Or is it a breech?" He would *love* to discuss it with you if you would ask! Imagine how boring it must be to see fifty women every day and say to them nothing but "Everything's fine."

One way you yourself will know that the baby has dropped is that all of a sudden your indigestion and shortness of breath will seem to improve—you can actually *feel* space that has been gained above. This is a short-lived triumph, however, since in fact you have merely traded one battle for another, and all the space you gain above is now lost below. If you thought the bladder problem was bad before this, well, you will have to think again. An anatomical drawing (see *c* and *d*, page 41) shows a tiny black line to indicate what *used* to be the bladder and, what with the baby's head pressing down, the bladder at the end of pregnancy has a maximum capacity of only about half a cup whereas ordinarily it's several cups.

If you have a baby that engages as a vertex, you will deliver a vertex. He will no longer do flips. However, even with the head engaged deep in the pelvis, there will be fetal movement; those little arms and legs will still have a good thrust. If your baby engages as a breech, he will not turn to become a vertex. Usually at the end of the pregnancy the baby does not do much somersaulting anyway, but if he is *not* engaged, it is possible that he could turn, probably right up to the onset of labor.

THE NESTING URGE

Many women experience a spurt of energy for a day or two prior to the onset of labor—a sudden compulsion to clean out all the closets and wash the windows. While it is fine to take cues from your body and psyche, do not allow yourself to get overtired—it

> *"My brain went on vacation in my ninth month; all rational thinking seemed to click off. A week before my due date, as the baby's room was being wallpapered, I stood in the doorway watching the lovely repeat pattern my husband and I had carefully chosen go up on the walls, and only when the whole room was finished and the men were cleaning up did I realize the paper had been hung upside down!"*

could happen that you go into labor just after you finish cleaning for six hours and are thoroughly exhausted. One mother I knew who bred horses did just that. At the end of her pregnancy she spent one whole day with a stable hand cleaning out stalls. As soon as she finished and put her feet up, a fourteen-hour labor began.

> *"The couple of weeks off from work before the due date were very special not just from the point of accomplishing errands but the peaceful aspect of waiting. I'd encourage women to take time off to 'be alone with themselves.'"*

FALSE LABOR FOR SOME

About 15 percent of women having first babies (and about 25 percent having second babies) will experience what are known as false labor contractions during the days prior to the onset of real labor. They can occur in series that last a couple of hours at a time and, although the contractions are stronger and more uncomfortable (even painful) than Braxton Hicks contractions (see page 68), they do not *progress*. This means that while they may be quite regular, lasting forty seconds each and occurring every five minutes for two hours, *if they do not get stronger, last longer, and come more frequently,* you can be fairly certain that what you feel are false labor contractions.

If this is your first baby and your first bout with labor contractions, you are irresistibly going to leap to the conclusion that true labor has begun. Fortunately, there is a way to determine whether what you feel is real or false labor, so rather than get yourself all worked up about it, you can put those contractions to what I call the "dip and sip" test.

Take a relaxing, twenty-minute bath in comfortably hot water and, as you lounge in the tub, sip an ounce or two of wine or beer. The very low alcohol content will have little effect on your full-term infant, while the combination of warm dip and cool sips will relax the uterus and false labor will peter out—if that's what it is. When their patients call with contractions, some doctors even say, "Have a little brandy and see what happens."

What is happening in your body when false labor occurs is that your pituitary gland, for some unknown reason, spurts out a little splash of oxytocin, the chemical that stimulates uterine contractions. Alcohol gently quiets the pituitary, false labor subsides, and you can get some much-needed rest to be ready to handle true labor when it starts.

If the contractions really *are* the beginning of labor, your bath and sips of wine will have no influence on them and their progression will become evident soon enough.

Early bouts with false labor (especially in women having second or third babies) can result in some changes in the cervix or neck of the uterus. It may begin to efface or even dilate (see page 154) up to two or three centimeters. Some women are elated to hear of this change when their doctor examines them vaginally, believing they will have an easier labor with this head start and delighted that they barely noticed the contractions that caused this cervical change. Don't count on gaining any advantages. Although early cervical changes may seem like a little bonus before you begin, there are no guarantees of a fast or easy labor.

Occasionally, a woman's cervix will dilate "significantly" several weeks before her due date. In that case, a specific medical regimen such as bed rest, no tub baths, and so on may be necessary. Your doctor will explain this to you if it happens.

Remember that many women do not experience any of the above before real labor begins and may, instead, face another situation—that of being overdue.

> "I really want to get this pregnancy over with. I want my figure back, my work, my husband/lover—but I know it'll never be the same. Everything will be richer, deeper, and all the days of my life I will have added a dimension to everything I do."

BEING OVERDUE

Since only four out of ten babies are delivered on or before the due date, there is a good chance that yours may be late. Menstrual cycles vary, and being overdue may reflect a cycle slightly longer than the usual twenty-eight-day period that is used in calculating the due date. In any case, you might find yourself feeling a little despondent when the Big Day has come and gone and everyone you know says, "What! You still haven't delivered?" Get plenty of rest and keep your spirits up by planning some special, relaxing activities for these days, which may add up to a week or two.

"I was ten days overdue and each day dragged by, I felt so heavy and exhausted. Finally I decided to get up and play tennis with a friend. That did it—two sets from three to five and labor started at eight!"

As the days past your due date increase, your doctor may want to do some tests to evaluate the efficiency of the placenta (see page 34).

The last few visits to your doctor before the baby is born are quite different from the routine visits in the earlier months. Time hangs heavy and most likely you are more than ready for your pregnancy to be over. The suspense seems to mount each time you climb onto the examining table and your doctor proceeds with the all-too-familiar rounds of checking the baby's position, vital signs, and the progress of your pregnancy. Chances are, you are just plain tired, too, and find your emotions tied in with these visits, including some apprehension about what is determined from them. This is only natural.

While your doctor is as hopeful as you are that labor will begin spontaneously, he or she is also determined that you and your baby progress through the ordeal of birth as safely as possible. As you and your doctor assess your situation at the end of pregnancy, keep an open mind and stand ready to accept the decisions that might be made. Having options at this point is one of the rewards of present-day medicine and all its technology, providing many routes that can be taken to safeguard the welfare of mother and baby.

Hold fast to the relationship of trust and openness that you and your doctor have enjoyed for close to a year. Ask questions, share your feelings, listen carefully—and be glad you are having a baby today, when so many of the past risks in childbirth are no longer a consideration.

8

Childbirth Education, and Some Thoughts on What to Anticipate

When I begin a new series of Lamaze classes, I ask each couple to explain to the rest of the group why they are taking the course. One couple will usually describe "wanting to learn all we can about childbirth"; another, "to get a crash course in biology"; and still another, "because we have nothing to lose." Sometimes a father or two will elicit a few smiles and chuckles with, "Because she's pregnant and I'm responsible," or, "I was there at the beginning, so I thought I'd see it through to the end."

So it goes around the room, until invariably one husband describes "being coerced" into coming, while his wife admits that her prime motivation for attending is "fear of death." Now the cat is really out of the bag, and the response of relief and nervous laughter confirms the shared feelings of the rest of the class. *Everyone* is scared about the prospect of giving birth, even if he would love to say otherwise.

For whatever reasons, the couples who attend these classes have chosen to be involved, as husband and wife, in the birth of their child. Their spirit of camaraderie, of wanting to experience the event together, may seem to be a very natural part of the process, but in fact it is very different from how most of our parents bore us, with husbands "in the general vicinity," as one

> *"I only went to Lamaze classes because my doctor insisted, and thank God he did! Lamaze doesn't give you a painless birth, but at least I knew what was going on and the breathing helped, and most important it helped my husband learn how to help me."*

father put it, but definitely not in the delivery room, and *definitely* not right in there coaching their wives through labor.

The presence of fathers during labor and delivery is a vast improvement to the situation. It leaves you no room, gentlemen, to imagine that your wife is dying as the long hours of labor mount and you pace the halls. And it gives you a chance to participate during labor—staying beside your wife, with a significant opportunity to help. If you are nervous about how you might react to what will happen, I assure you that however gruesome the task might seem now as you try to envision it, when you are actively needed to support your wife, you will not *think* of the task at all. You simply focus on helping in the best way you can, holding her head if she throws up in transition, applying more pressure (although your hands are exhausted) to her aching back if she has back labor. When she tearfully whispers, "I want to go home now, I don't want to do this any more," being there to say "You *can* do it, breathe with me, he-he-he-blow" (or whatever childbirth technique you use) can do wonders to help get her back on the track. She needs the support of someone she loves.

Labor *is* going to be tough, and that's the best reason of all to be together through it. No matter how nice the nurse is, her presence is not the same as having someone right there who knows you and loves you, someone who can see what *you* need at that moment: a pat on the leg, a reminder to keep breathing, or whatever it may be.

Working together in labor and delivery creates a very special bond between a husband and wife. One father who was "coerced" into attending his first Lamaze class stayed for them all. His wife delivered the day before the last class. He made a special trip to attend that final meeting, to tell the group about the delivery, and he did so in memorable terms: "When *we* went into labor *we* had to begin our first breathing, and when *we* got into the cab *we* had to get into our panting, and when *we* got to the hospital, *we pushed!*" Everyone laughed, and then he said, "I know you don't believe it, but she couldn't have had it without me."

As for the birth itself, seeing that baby arrive is unlike any other event you will witness in life. With advance permission, most hospitals today will even allow photographs to be taken in the delivery room. One father, a professional photographer, came in prepared to take a million pictures of his baby's birth, with several cameras and light meters around his neck, and film for every possible situation in his pockets. As the baby appeared, I noticed that this father just stood there, cameras still around his neck but arms hanging limp at his side. Very gently I reminded him, "Mr. Friedman, what about your pictures?" Rooted to the floor, the tears streaming down over his mask, he replied, "I don't have to take any pictures, I'll never forget this moment."

This is the way many people feel about the birth of their baby, and if you can share it, together as a couple, it's all the more awesome—an experience neither of you will ever forget.

Even with husbands and wives participating, what kind of labor you will actually have is still a big toss-up. You can work perfectly together as a husband-and-wife team, practicing your childbirth techniques every evening, but that will not guarantee that labor and delivery will be any faster or easier than it was for women a generation ago. Certainly it is safer today, but I think it's very important to be open-minded and flexible about what you antic- ipate. If, on the one hand, you are convinced that you are "going to learn that Lamaze breathing inside out, pass up any medication, and breeze right through labor"—forget it. On the other hand, if you are depending on an epidural (the medication that numbs you from the waist down) to see you through and eliminate all the pain, you may not have that option. One person will be lucky enough to have a three- or four-hour labor and pop a baby out, and another will go through twenty-four hours of labor and have a Caesarean birth at the end. You simply do not know what will happen until you are there.

Don't believe a word of it when someone says to you, "Well,

dear, you have such a low pain threshold, don't bother with those classes." Baloney! To repeat—you either luck out and get an easy labor and delivery, or you don't. Having been with so many couples in labor and delivery, I can tell you it's that simple.

Do not be enticed into another popular line of thinking: "But my mother had an easy labor, and my sister had one too. . . ." While there may be some relevance to this because you have similar genes, don't forget that you have a different husband and a different baby in there and it will never be *just* the same. You may have heard the old adage, "It's just as easy to fall in love with a rich man as a poor man." Well, in obstetrics we always would kid about its being "just as easy to fall in love with a small man as a large man"—and maybe if you'd been smart you would have considered that before throwing away your contraceptives! Although size is not the only factor in determining how easy or difficult your childbirth will be, it certainly has some influence.

No one grades your performance in labor and delivery. No one gets an A-plus, and no one fails the course. Your behavior is irrelevant to the outcome. Whether you have some pain-relieving medication or not really doesn't matter, either. Labor is not a contest to see who can "go the distance with the least assistance." Of course, the more you know how to help yourself, the less medication, if any, you will require; but there's no award or benefit for needless suffering—just see how it goes.

As for any innate abilities we may have possessed to cope with childbirth, we seem to have lost them somewhere along the evolutionary ladder. In general, we approach labor with the burden of having sublimated our instincts, so that the term "natural" childbirth (which for many people is a scary phrase to begin with) really no longer applies. The fact is, when left to our own devices, most of us humans respond very poorly in labor, whereas the lower animals seem to manage very well on their instincts. If you've ever seen a cat or other animal give birth, there is very little distress or pain apparent and Nature works things out easily—the mother appears to know exactly what to do. Most humans, unfortunately, do just the opposite. When feeling pain in the abdomen (an inevitable fact of labor), we curl up in a ball, clutch the belly, hold the breath, tighten every muscle in the body, and cry "Aaarrrggghhh"—a response that only makes labor that much more uncomfortable. You have to put aside this reaction and recondition your body to cope with the situation. This is where childbirth techniques come into play.

Childbirth preparation, or education, can teach you what you probably wouldn't do naturally. The basic education is quite enlightening. Even if you took a college-level biology course, the chances are it never went further than a study of the lower order of animals. You spent all year looking at chicken-embryo eggs and working over frogs, but human biology was always beyond the scope of the course. With Lamaze or other childbirth techniques, at least you will *know* what is going on, why it is happening, and how long it is likely to last—all of which helps give the experience some perspective and make it a lot easier to handle.

I remember one student who came to her Lamaze class reunion, baby in her arms and husband at her side, candidly admitting that after it was all over, she found herself angry that her labor had hurt so much. She felt that people had lied about it—until she realized that she hadn't really listened or taken the preparatory exercises seriously enough. Now, again, you may be the very rare and lucky one whose labor isn't too painful—*very rare*—but I assure you it is important to practice your childbirth techniques as if your life depended on them.

Of all the different approaches to coping with pain in labor and delivery, I believe Lamaze techniques are best. However, there are other techniques to consider. In the late 1950s the English doctor Grantly Dick-Read popularized his **Read Method.** Since childbirth was a normal, physiological process, Read believed that it should not be painful. He theorized that the reason women had pain in labor was because their fear and ignorance of the process produced tension and the tension in turn caused pain. He referred to this cause-and-effect relationship as the pain-tension-fear cycle. With education and relaxation, Read demonstrated that when the cycle was broken women did not experience the degree of pain they anticipated. To be candid, Dr. Dick-Read worked very closely with his mothers. He stayed with them all through labor and in mesmerizing tones would tell them that the wave of the contraction was coming, that they should imagine lying on the beach, the waves of the ocean ebbing and flowing over them—in other words, he did his best to lull the laboring mother into a relaxed, hypnotic state. Many who observed Dr. Dick-Read with his patients claimed that his techniques were more disciplined than the term "relaxation techniques" one might lead to believe, that he in fact did partially hypnotize his patients as he led them through labor minute-by-minute. Most women, I think, no matter how well educated or how beautifully relaxed they are, will feel pain. Helpful as the relaxation techniques may be, the Read Method as it is written seems to fall short in the area of using distraction to cope with pain.

> "I always wanted to participate in the birth of our child, and when I read Marjorie Karmel's book Thank you, Dr. Lamaze, it presented a method that would give me the tools I would need to accomplish what I wanted—so I found a Lamaze teacher and we devoured everything we learned."

The **Bradley Method** also embraces education and relaxation, but then encourages the mother to "flow with" the tide of labor. That is, rather than focus away from the sensations she is experiencing, she should turn her thoughts inward. This may be the perfect approach for some women, but in thirteen years of observation as a nurse in labor and delivery, I have seen that most women need to focus away from the pain or it becomes overwhelming.

The Lamaze Psychoprophylactic Method is based on the philosophy of Dr. Ferdinand Lamaze, an obstetrician who studied in Russia and France. Lamaze felt that no matter how well relaxed they were, most women were still going to experience some degree of pain and would have to learn how to cope with it. At the time he began to explore this idea, Pavlov's studies of stimulus-response conditioning in dogs were just coming to light. Lamaze saw the value of the conditioned response and its potential for helping women to cope with labor. He believed that if a woman were trained to relax and to focus her attention away from painful contractions (using complicated breathing techniques as active diversion), the pain would become peripheral.

I am sure that everyone has had the experience of waking up one morning and feeling horrible, but knowing that the commitments of the day took precedence over staying in bed. You do what you have to do, and when it is all over, you finally can say, "I feel awful and now I am going to go home and go to bed." During the time you were fulfilling your obligations, you really didn't think about how horrible you felt because your commitments distracted you from your physical discomfort. That is basically what the Lamaze techniques are meant to do.

> *"My husband and I attended all the Lamaze classes and practiced our lessons religiously every evening. We felt we were ready for anything—except the Caesarean that was performed before contractions ever started! Knowing the breathing techniques was still useful; I depended on them in recovery."*

The Lamaze Method seems to help most people regardless of their degree of discomfort. We can gauge blood pressure, pulse rate, respiratory rate, contraction strength during labor, but it is impossible to establish just how much pain a person feels. This is why it is reassuring to have a variety of Lamaze tools to choose from, to help you cope with varying degrees of pain and intensifying contractions.

So the three goals of Lamaze are, *first*, to gain a basic knowledge of what happens in labor; *second*, to master the art of muscular relaxation to keep the body from tensing with each contraction; and, *third*, to consciously impose rhythmic, patterned breathing over the wavelike pattern of the contraction, as distraction from the pain.

Strengthening exercises that begin on page 78 are also an important part of your preparation for labor, but since they do not require your husband's participation, you can do them alone every day before beginning your Lamaze practice sessions together.

9

Lamaze Childbirth Techniques

*T*his chapter is your Lamaze primer. It contains explanations, guidance, and practical hints for learning the concentration-relaxation exercises, Lamaze breathing, and pushing techniques, as well as suggestions for packing a "Lamaze bag" of practical items to help you cope with pain when you are in the hospital labor room.

Although you will not be using your Lamaze techniques until after true labor begins, you and your husband should start practicing them together daily about six weeks before your due date. Regardless of what school of childbirth education you embrace, I can assure you it will be to your advantage to have the Lamaze Method ready to use as a viable option.

Author's Note: Because Lamaze involves a two-partner team, the laboring mother and her coach, some of the practical information in this chapter is directed specifically to the mother or to the coach, depending on which partner will need it during labor.

The role of the coach can be filled by whomever the mother chooses. In this book, however, it is assumed that the partners will be husband and wife; thus the masculine gender will consistently be used to address the coach. Obviously, the two-partner team that practices together should be the team that works together in labor.

Tip for the Coach: You need to learn the Lamaze techniques better than your wife does. When that first really strong contraction hits, she may forget everything she's learned and will depend on your cues to see her through labor.

THE CONCENTRATION-RELAXATION EXERCISES

Recognizing that relaxation is one of the greatest weapons to use against pain, Dr. Ferdinand Lamaze developed a series of "neuromuscular control exercises" to use when labor contractions become so strong that they can no longer be ignored. You will know you have reached this point in labor when you find yourself involuntarily tensing as each contraction builds. That's when you should start putting your Lamaze techniques to use.

One of your goals in labor is to keep all of the muscles in your body relaxed, absolutely limp—not only to conserve energy and decrease pain, but also to allow the uterus to work freely, unhampered by tension. It may sound easy; it's not. Staying relaxed when you're in pain takes practice. It's a skill you must develop with your coach beforehand so that in real labor you can instantly call it up from memory. As you practice, you might wonder why you would want to pay attention to parts of the body that seem to have nothing to do with labor. The pain that is felt as the uterine neck dilates with contractions will probably be low, down in front, and deep in your body, but the reaction to that pain is going to be the tensing of other parts of the body. The coach will never say, "Contract your right arm" in the labor room!

If you are good at the relaxation exercises, practice twice a week, for ten minutes in the evening. If you're not, take more time to practice, maybe even with a beer or warm bath beforehand to help you relax.

Practice Session

Lie on your back with pillows under your head, neck, shoulders, and knees so you feel comfortable.

With your coach at your side, take a "cleansing breath" (just a deep sigh) and relax from head to toe.

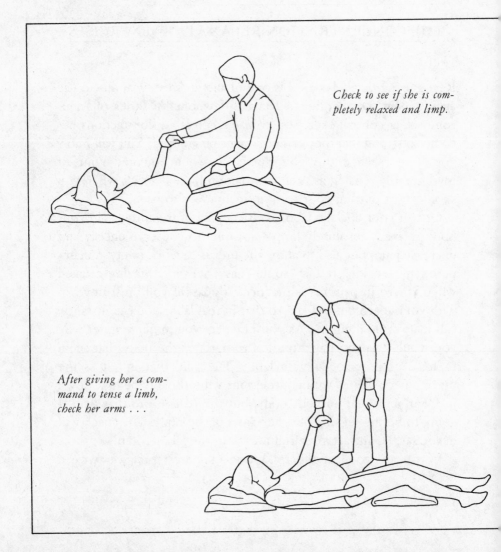

Check to see if she is completely relaxed and limp.

After giving her a command to tense a limb, check her arms . . .

Gentlemen, check to see that she is totally relaxed. Pick up her arm, and when you feel you have the weight of it, swing it lightly, then let it flop gently to the floor. Check her legs. If she holds them neatly together, with the feet parallel and the toes pointing up, she is not relaxed. To be completely relaxed, the outstretched legs must be loose enough to flop apart. Slide your hands under one of her knees, lift it gently about two or three inches off the floor, and rotate it from side to side. It should feel heavy and loose. With this gentle motion you will know if the hip and knee joints are relaxed. (There's no need to lift her whole leg to the ceiling!)

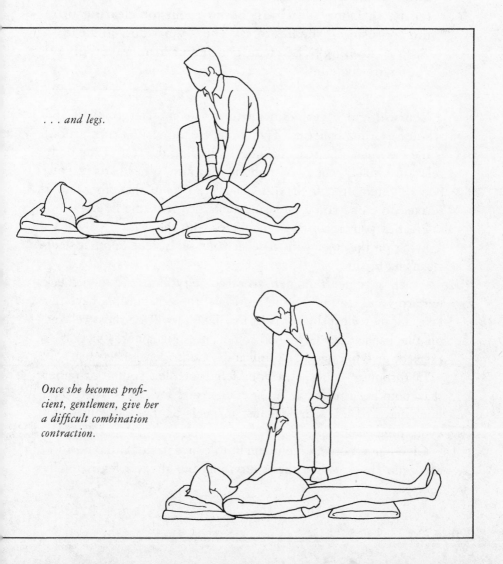

. . . and legs.

Once she becomes proficient, gentlemen, give her a difficult combination contraction.

Now give her a command: "Contract your right arm."

In response, ladies, make a fist, lock your elbow, and hold your right arm about six inches off the floor, simultaneously trying to keep the rest of your body totally relaxed.

Check to see that she's doing this, gentlemen, and then tell her to "Release" (or "Relax") the arm. Then, ladies, let everything go limp again.

Tip for the Coach: When you are cueing your wife to relax, it is important to use a specific word—*relax, release,* whatever—for the command, and to use it consistently. In labor, there will be no room for clearing up the confusion if she has to ask you, "What do you mean, 'Stop tightening'?" Be clear, gentle but firm, as you give your wife the cues.

You will find it very difficult to isolate muscle groups if you are not a prima ballerina. Tightening (to simulate a contraction) is the easy part; the real challenge is leaving the rest of the body relaxed. Usually when you tighten your arm, other parts of your body tighten up. Or, if you manage to keep the other limbs relaxed, the one you are tensing sinks slowly to the floor.

Practice your relaxation techniques with the legs.

Lying on the floor with arms at your sides, take another deep cleansing breath.

Coach, give her a moment to relax everything, and then check her arms and legs as you did before. If there is tension, have her take another cleansing breath; usually she will be most relaxed on the exhalation. Give her some encouragement. Once she's relaxed, give her another command: "Contract your left leg."

In response, ladies, flex your left foot (flex your foot rather than pointing it to avoid a leg cramp) and lock your knee. You don't have to lift your leg, just make it tight. Hold, and keep everything else relaxed.

Give her a moment, gentlemen, to concentrate on the position and then check to see that everything but the left leg is totally relaxed.

If this seems impossible, which it is with about 50 percent of the women who are new to Lamaze, have your husband get down on the floor and you, ladies, assume the role of the coach for a few minutes. With your husband on the floor, pick up his arms and feel how heavy and loose they are, almost dead weight—exactly the feeling you are after. Too bad he can't be the pregnant one! Switch roles again and see if it might be a little easier.

Take your cleansing breath and relax completely.

> *"Although Jane is always eager to give me a lot of credit for making the delivery easier for her, I can't help but feel that the part I played was relatively small. I did enjoy the whole thing a great deal, however, and can't imagine doing it any other way. In fact, I find myself feeling sorry for the fathers of years past who never had a chance to be so actively involved, from beginning to end, as I was."*

Gentlemen, check for relaxation and when she is ready, ask her to tense one limb and keep the others relaxed. Vary the limbs. Once she has the hang of it, ask her to contract two limbs at once. Here's where more concentration is required, especially when the two limbs are diagonally opposite.

Tip for the Coach: Watch your wife closely in real labor and you will know right away what areas of her body you can help her to relax. If she suddenly starts to grip your wrist or roll her toes under or bite her lip as the contraction comes, you must immediately tell her to relax the area; and because of your practice sessions with this conditioning, she will (you hope) relax.

Some couples develop a system of "touch relaxation": instead of giving a verbal command to relax a tensed area, the coach places his hand gently on it and the laboring mother responds to this warm, gentle touch by releasing the tension under it. This touch system in labor can also be comforting, which further helps you to relax—provided, of course, that your husband uses a gentle hand. I remember watching aghast as one expectant father literally hit his poor wife's stiff shoulder, shouting at her, "Here, dear, relax it here!" The effect was that she became more and more tense with each hit—surely not the kind of teamwork Dr. Lamaze had in mind.

Gentlemen, during labor your encouragement will be crucial to your wife's performance and you should give it to her all through your practice sessions. Build up her confidence by telling her she is doing well; in labor, it may be exactly what she needs to relax.

Ladies, when you finish your practice session with the concentration-relaxation exercises, you will probably feel like a turtle on its back as you struggle to get up—your abdominal muscles are practically useless at this point in your pregnancy. Draw your knees up toward your chest, roll over onto your side, and push yourself up with your arms and hands. From there it's easy to stand, and you'll have done it without the need of assistance. (Remember this at the end of your pregnancy as you struggle to get out of bed!)

To rise, draw up your
knees, roll to your side. . .

. . . and push yourself up
with your arms.

Review

The concentration-relaxation exercises prepare you to relax in labor, when the pain makes you want to tense your muscles. Remember, tension makes the pain worse. With your coach's verbal cue or gentle touch, you can condition the tense areas of your body to relax on cue.

Once you master this technique, you will have it at your command, with or without a partner present, to use throughout life, whenever you need to relax. For example, when you have only an hour to catch forty winks while your baby naps, being able to release all the tension and let every muscle go limp lets you drift off to sleep in seconds. You'll see.

> *"Labor hurt more than I ever imagined! Fortunately it did not last too long, however."*

THE LAMAZE BREATHING TECHNIQUES

Just as the relaxation techniques help you conserve energy, release tension, and allow your body to flow with the uterine waves, the Lamaze breathing techniques help divert your attention from the labor contractions, giving you something active to do when they come. The breathing techniques will not make the pain go away, but they will not let you helplessly dwell on it, either.

Lamaze breathing for all parts of labor should be light, shallow, and rhythmic.

Think of each uterine contraction not as a "labor pain" but as a wave with a gradual increase in intensity, a peak of five to twenty seconds, and a gradual decrease. The pattern will always be wave-like, but the contractions will intensify as labor progresses. Therefore, you will need to adjust your breathing to what you feel, choosing from three different Lamaze breathing techniques—given here with their most typical time of use:

Slow-Paced Breathing, Technique #1 for *Phase One, Early Labor*
Cervix effacing to 100% and dilating to about 3 centimeters
Duration: 6 to 8 hours

Modified-Paced Breathing, Technique #2 for *Phase Two, Active Labor*
Cervix dilating from 3 to 8 centimeters
Duration: 3 to 4 hours

Pattern-Paced Breathing, Technique #3 for *Phase Three, Transition*
Cervix dilating from 8 to 10 centimeters
Duration: 1 hour

Remember, in labor, you should try to hold off with your Lamaze breathing as long as you can. Don't even start doing it until you can no longer "walk, talk, or joke" through the contractions, probably four to six hours after real labor begins.

Feel free to use the breathing technique that helps you most—trust your body to give you its cues. I remember one woman who was frantically performing her "transition breathing" as she was being admitted to the hospital; this breathing is usually reserved for the very end of the first stage of labor, when contractions are at their absolute worst. I quickly got one of the residents to examine her, fearing she might be just about ready to deliver, but she was only three centimeters dilated. When I tried to encourage her to go back to one of the earlier breathing patterns (not only to conserve her energy, but also to save this more complicated technique for later when contractions are strongest), she vehemently insisted, "But I have to do this breathing, I'm sorry, I just *have* to!" With that, another very strong, untypical "early-labor" contraction hit—and in only one hour, she was nine centimeters dilated! She was right, she had listened to her body experiencing an unusually strong and fast labor, and responded perfectly.

> *"Labor and delivery were nothing like what we expected. I expected twelve hours of labor with stages of breathing and pain. That is, I expected an orderly progression. It wasn't anything like that. We delivered in the hospital, but only by the skin of our teeth."*

For most women, of course, labor progresses more slowly and the tendency is to speed up the breathing, probably in the hope that it will speed up labor or because the contractions turn out to be tougher to handle than expected. Do listen closely to what the nurses or your doctor suggest to make you comfortable, and try to stretch out the effectiveness of the simpler breathing patterns. You'll know what's right by how you feel.

> *"I went into labor not knowing what to expect. It was like opening a door and not knowing what was behind it. I was scared and nervous, to say the least."*

Slow-Paced Breathing—Technique #1

When to use it: When you feel you can no longer ignore your contractions. This will probably be several hours into early labor, toward the end of phase one, when you become too uncomfortable to continue other distractions—walking, watching a movie, and so on. Contractions at this point will probably be several minutes apart, lasting about forty-five seconds and feeling like a strong, aching pain.

The Procedure Summarized

Focus your eyes on one spot—your "focal point" (see below).
  As the contraction begins, take a "cleansing breath" (see below).
  Breathe comfortably and rhythmically, six to nine breaths per

minute, inhaling through your nose and exhaling through your mouth.

"Effleurage" (see below) or gently massage your belly throughout.

As the contraction ends, take another deep cleansing breath and relax completely.

A full practice session for Technique #1 will follow but first, a brief explanation of some of the basic elements used in Lamaze.

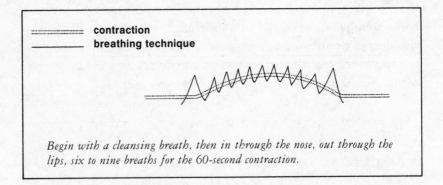

············ **contraction**

——————— **breathing technique**

Begin with a cleansing breath, then in through the nose, out through the lips, six to nine breaths for the 60-second contraction.

The "focal point." When they use Lamaze breathing to cope with contractions, most women find that it is effective to focus their eyes on an object, a comfortable distance away, to further distract them from their discomfort. Perhaps you think you would feel more relaxed with your eyes closed. This may be true as you practice for labor, but once labor begins and contractions become strong, you might find yourself overwhelmed when your eyes are shut. You will be more "on top of things" with your eyes open and focused on an object, so at least practice this way.

For labor in the hospital, you will bring a "focal point" with you: perhaps a little picture the nurse can tape to the wall for you. One woman brought in a great picture of a roast beef sandwich on rye bread, with Russian dressing oozing out the side—it's enough to make me salivate as I describe it. Now, most people do not feel very much like eating in labor and should not do so once labor is progressing, in case of the need for an emergency Caesarean delivery (you are offered ice chips, but *nothing* else), so I thought it rather funny that she had chosen a picture of a sandwich and was mesmerized by it during seven hours of labor. When we went to the delivery room, the picture was hurriedly stuffed into her husband's pocket, and she delivered so quickly that it was forgotten. We placed her baby girl in her arms and after she and her husband had had a chance to enjoy her for a bit, the proud new mother suddenly turned to her husband and said, "Now, darling, do you remember my picture of the roast beef sandwich? I want *two* just like it!" *Chacun à son gout*—to each his own if it helps you get through labor, but a picture that is devoid of responsibility or incapable of eliciting emotion is best, while one of your "firstborn" dog may make you worry about him at home. (I used flower stick-on decals, starting out in early labor with a tiny one and having my husband substitute bigger and bigger ones as labor got stronger—nice to have a change. But now, of course, I can't look at them as they always remind me of being in labor!)

The cleansing breath is taken at the very beginning and the very end of each contraction. This slow, deep breath not only helps you to relax, but also gives you and the baby a good supply of oxygen. It also lets the coach know when a contraction is beginning, so he can begin timing it and coaching you through it.

Timing contractions. During practice sessions, gentlemen, you will time "contractions" for your wife by using a watch or stopwatch and saying, "Contraction begins," at the start of a minute. On this cue, ladies, take your cleansing breath and begin your Lamaze breathing pattern. In labor, gentlemen, you will take your cue from your wife: as you hear her take a cleansing breath, you know a contraction is starting and will begin timing from that point. Divide every contraction into fifteen-second segments, saying, "Fifteen seconds. Thirty seconds," and so on. Chopping up a long, painful minute makes it seem much shorter. When you hear your husband say "Forty-five seconds," ladies, you know it's almost over!

Effleurage is soothing. Many women have difficulty relaxing completely during the contractions; a gentle stroking massage, or effleurage, of your own large belly not only feels lovely but also ensures that your hands are not clenching. Place your fingertips just above your pubic bone and gently stroke up the center of your belly and down the sides, making two large ovals. Or, if you would rather, go the opposite way, down the center and up the sides. Try it. Feels nice, doesn't it?

If in labor you find the effleurage more distracting then helpful, put your hands in your lap, palms up and fingers slightly bent so they appear relaxed, and ask your coach to do the effleurage.

Tip for the Coach: Gentlemen, you should frequently check to be sure her hands are relaxed, wherever she decides to put them, and if they do tense, make her do her own effleurage to keep them busy. If and when you do the effleurage, gentlemen, make one large circle with your palm, staying away from her belly button, which is usually hypersensitive because it puffs out at the end of pregnancy.

It might be nice to use a little talcum powder, or cornstarch if you prefer it, to make the stroke smoother; the powder feels great no matter who is doing the effleurage. As one husband said, "It makes her belly look like a loaf of homemade bread!"

I remember one husband, in a zealous effort, "scrubbing" his wife's belly with almost the same short, deliberate strokes you might use to scrub a frying pan. She loved it, but for most women I think a slower, gentler pace is more appreciated.

You will use this effleurage all through labor, keeping it slow and soothing even when your breathing becomes more rapid as labor progresses.

Recognizing and coping with hyperventilation. As you breathe out forcefully you exhale more carbon dioxide than usual, which can cause dizziness or, for some people, a tingling around the lips and fingers and toes, even to such an extent that the fingers and toes may feel cramping. It can happen at any point in labor, and you should be prepared to deal with it.

The remedy for hyperventilation is simply to build up your level of carbon dioxide quickly, by either slowing down your exhalations or inhaling the air you exhaled. You can cup your hands over your nose and mouth as you breathe or, even better, hold a small paper bag over them. The bag should be a very little one. Once when a laboring mother was feeling light-headed in labor I suggested to her husband that he use the brown bag he'd brought with their Lamaze supplies, and at that point I was suddenly called out of the labor room for a time. When I returned, I found him trying to hold a large brown supermarket bag over her face! Don't make this mistake. Not only is a large bag bulky and unmanageable, it doesn't help at all. Use one of those little brown sandwich bags instead.

What to do when your mouth is dry. Use a little purse-sized mouthwash spray or plant sprayer filled with water when your mouth becomes dry. You won't really feel thirsty in labor, just dry. If you decide to use mouthwash spray, be sure to test it at home first, especially if you don't ordinarily use the stuff. Something mild or even plain water is better than something so strong you want to rub it off your tongue after each squirt. Don't make the mistake of one woman who went right out to the fanciest pharmacy in town and loaded up on an array of esoteric supplies to bring with her into the labor room, only to find that when she

> *"I was present during the whole labor and delivery except when my wife was getting an epidural. I feel I was of great use during labor as a source of support for my wife. From my standpoint, I must admit that the labor was more painful to my wife than I had expected. It was also difficult for me to watch her going through such intense pain. All in all, I strongly recommend husbands being present to provide their wives with emotional support."*

needed some moisture, the imported "pure rosewater" mouth-wash not only made her feel nauseated but it also clung vengefully to her tastebuds.

Moisture for those lips, too. Lip gloss or balm is also useful in labor. With all the breathing, licking, spraying, and swallowing, your lips can feel "labor chapped" the next day, so protect them as they start to feel dry.

If you start your active-labor breathing at home and use any of these items, remember to pack them up to take to the hospital so you can use them again after you've been admitted and settled into your labor room.

Practice Session

Lie down in a comfortable position on your back, with pillows behind your shoulders, neck, and head, or perhaps on your side.

Take a cleansing breath.

Gentlemen, begin timing the contraction.

Ladies, find your focal point and start your chest breathing: *six to nine breaths* per minute, each one going slowly in through your nose and out through your mouth. (During your first practice contraction, count how many breaths you take in a minute. If six to nine come naturally, stay with it. Fourteen breaths per minute is far too shallow, while four is too deep. Practice to be comfortable with six to nine.)

Effleurage as you do the breathing and, when a minute is up, end with a cleansing breath which, in labor, gives a finality to each contraction and signals the beginning of three or more glorious, pain-free minutes!

Now you have the first Lamaze breathing technique down pat. You will want to practice it together again after you do your concentration-relaxation exercises (page 117) once a day at the end of your pregnancy, probably for the last six weeks. Remember that the practice sessions need not take more than about fifteen minutes—but conditioning is important.

Modified-Paced Breathing—Technique #2

The second Lamaze breathing technique seems an appropriate distraction for the new, stronger contractions of active labor—but, as has been said before, you decide when it's time to use it, doing whatever technique helps you best. Perhaps, instead of going into the second breathing technique right away, you could slightly increase the pace of the slow-paced breathing (Technique #1) as an interim breathing pattern. Do, say, ten to fifteen breaths per minute instead of six to nine. On the other hand, you may decide that all of this breathing is tiresome and you'll just breathe normally with the next contraction, or maybe you'd prefer to hold your breath and tap your foot. If it works for you, fine. I predict, however, that it will be the first and last contraction you experiment with.

When to use it: When contractions become sharper and more intense; in other words, when the slow-paced breathing is no longer effective and no longer fits the character of the contractions. (For most women this will be in active labor with 45-to-60-second contractions coming two to three minutes apart and pain becoming sharp.)

The Procedure Summarized

Concentrate your eyes on your focal point.

As the contraction begins, take a cleansing breath and sigh it out.

Position your mouth partially open in a slight smile as if you were saying the word *he.*

Breathe shallowly and rhythmically to a count of 4/4—that is, accenting the first (or the last) *he,* as in "He-he-he-he; He-he-he-

he"—for sixty seconds, speeding up the pace as the contraction becomes stronger and slowing down the pace as it lessens at the end. Always keep the 4/4 rhythm, even when you are increasing or decreasing your pace.

Effleurage throughout.

End the contraction with a deep cleansing breath.

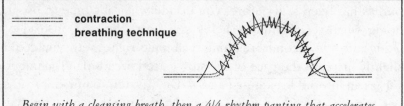

.... contraction
———— breathing technique

Begin with a cleansing breath, then a 4/4 rhythm panting that accelerates and decelerates with the intensity of the contraction.

Practice Session

Take a cleansing breath and sigh it out.

Now shape your mouth as if saying (and exaggerating) the word *he,* putting the side edges of your tongue against your teeth to help circulate the moisture a little bit. The pattern of the breathing is very light, all in the chest, breathing *in and out* and whispering a staccato *he* on the exhalation.

Do the breathing very softly. It should barely be audible; you'll just tire yourself if you do it more loudly than that. Accent the first of the four *he*s, making the next three (in-out) breaths softer. The 4/4 rhythm is important: it helps to keep you in control of the more painful contractions. With no rhythm, there's the tendency to panic as the contraction peaks; then the breathing can be haywire. Obviously, you don't want that to happen.

If you find that establishing a 4/4 rhythm is difficult for you at first, start the breathing by opening your mouth wide and panting like a dog in the summer, which will help to establish a steady in-out pace. When you have it, close your teeth to shape the word *he* in a slight smile, and now accent every fourth *he*. If need be, hum a little tune to yourself to keep that 4/4 rhythm.

One woman accented the last beat and whispered, "he-he-he-*shit*" to keep the 4/4 panting. That seemed to do the trick for her, although she felt the need to apologize for her language. (There's no need for apologies—anything goes in labor!)

As you breathe, do not bob your head. Keep it still, neck relaxed, resting against the pillows.

Accent the exhalation rather than the inhalation. You will almost automatically take back in what you've breathed out, which not only makes it a lot less tiring but also helps prevent hyperventilation (described on page 128).

When you first try Technique #2, the top of your tongue is going to feel as if you have been licking ashtrays, and there will probably be a pool of saliva collecting below. It gets better with practice. As you breathe, try swallowing or licking your lips as your first beat, or whatever works well for you, to distribute the moisture in your mouth. Use mouthwash or spray in real labor.

Once you have the 4/4 pattern down pat—*both* of you, with the coach as versed in it as you are—try a variation of the breathing which is actually more the way you will be using it in labor.

Because these strong active-labor contractions start out slowly, gradually increase in intensity, peak for, say, twenty seconds, and then gradually decrease, you will want to adjust your *he-he*-pattern breathing to what you will be feeling. If you find it odd to practice the breathing at a quick pace, in active labor you will know right away why this is done—those contractions come on much stronger than in early labor and you need the quicker pace to keep on top of them. Even so, you do not suddenly start breathing at a breakneck speed, but rather adjust the pace to the wavelike pattern of the contraction, starting slowly, progressing with the contraction to a faster pace, and then slowing down again.

Try this practice technique to simulate the pain of a labor contraction:

First, gentlemen, hold her upper thigh (not down by the knee or you will hit that ticklish spot) and squeeze it while your wife does her breathing. Start the squeeze as you say, "Contraction begins," build up the intensity for twenty seconds; squeeze harder for twenty seconds at the peak—as tightly as you can, making it hurt enough that she has to cope with the pain—and then gradually, over twenty more seconds, release the squeeze.

This leg squeeze, with its varying degrees of intensity, is only a practice technique to simulate the typical wave pattern of a contraction. Although the pain feels nothing like a labor contraction, it does make you experience a wavelike pattern, and it is hoped that if it hurts at the peak, you will need to focus on your breathing to cope with that pain. (Your coach will *not* be squeezing your leg in labor!)

Ladies, start your 4/4 breathing slowly, increase the pace as your husband squeezes tighter, level it off for the peak period, and then gradually slow down the breathing pace as the squeeze diminishes. As you breathe, effleurage gently or place your hands palms up and relaxed in your lap, and keep your eyes on a focal spot.

Tip for the Coach: Gentlemen, throughout the practice contraction, give your wife the time intervals and watch to see that her eyes are on her focal point and her body is relaxed as she breathes. Don't let her go too fast through the practice sessions, which often happens as she becomes more proficient. In labor, she'll automatically speed up, so it's important to develop control now.

When it's over, squeeze her leg again, gentlemen, this time when she's not doing her Lamaze breathing. Isn't it remarkable, ladies, how much stronger that squeeze felt when you weren't breathing with it? Reverse roles so that your husband can feel the difference!

Once she gets the hang of adjusting the breathing to the intensity of the squeeze, gentlemen, you should then vary the squeeze, maybe starting out quickly, or holding the peak for thirty seconds, whatever. *Real* labor contractions will probably not be beautifully divided into twenty seconds up, twenty seconds at the peak, and twenty seconds down!

Keep eyes on your focal point and your effleurage at a steady pace—in other words, don't speed it up when you speed up your breathing. The concentration required to maintain two differing paces adds another element of distraction from pain.

> *"Childbirth was exactly as we had learned in the Lamaze class. Each stage was noticeably different from the other."*

If all of a sudden you feel as if you don't have enough air, you could just take a deep breath, breaking the pattern, and start again. Or if you suddenly feel you have too much air, you could blow out *(whoosh)* and start again. After you practice a bit you will be much more comfortable with the pattern, and in labor you will probably be too busy coping to notice if this happens.

If you find the breathing very tiring, that's because it *is* tiring. But what are your options in labor? To be in pain, or to be tired. Besides, in labor you won't have time to think about fatigue or whether you are getting too much or too little air—you will be so busy keeping abreast of your contractions that you will not feel the need to fine tune your Lamaze techniques. But if, as you practice with your coach, you want to experiment with little variations to make you more comfortable, go ahead. One woman in my class insisted on putting the tip of her tongue against the roof of her mouth as she breathed. She thought it was great. I couldn't stand doing it that way, with my tongue edges dry and tingly and flapping in the breeze, but you'll have to decide what's best for you.

You, ladies, should build up your stamina so that you can do just the peak 4/4-pattern breathing for a full sixty seconds. Then, when you practice with your coach, he should get ahold of your leg and give you some variations: squeezing to simulate a contraction that has *two* painful peaks, for example, since that could actually happen.

Finally, gentlemen, keep in mind that you are the one watching and coaching. Very often in the practice sessions the mother-to-be will perch way up on the edge of a chair, almost hovering over her husband as she tries to do the breathing properly, while he lounges comfortably in his chair, casually watching the second hand of his watch tick by. Remember, you are the coach and *she* should be the one lounging back and taking it easy. Help her to be relaxed—*you* perch forward if need be!

Pattern-Paced Breathing—Technique #3

When to use it: Whenever the modified-paced breathing (Technique #2) is no longer effective. The pattern-paced breathing is more rhythmical and slightly faster than the modified-paced breathing, and, while the pattern can be varied (as described in the practice session below), its rate is constant. Breathing Technique #3 is appropriate for transition (see page 213), the most intense phase of labor, when contractions typically last 60 to 90 seconds and come 60 to 90 seconds apart. Pain is sharp and severe.

The Procedure Summarized

Focus on your coach's eyes rather than your focal point.
Take a quick cleansing breath.
Position the mouth partially open, as in shallow breathing, as if saying the word *he*.
Pant four to six times lightly and then blow out in a short, forceful little whistle on the next count. Keep up this pant-blow pattern for ninety seconds, as that's how long transition contractions can last.
Do not effleurage. Tuck hands down into groin or apply constant low-back counterpressure.
End the contraction with one or two cleansing breaths.

Practice Session

Since transition is the most painful and most difficult part of labor, you and your coach must both know this technique perfectly.

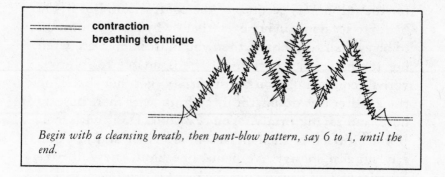

contraction
breathing technique

Begin with a cleansing breath, then pant-blow pattern, say 6 to 1, until the end.

In labor, you will need to be ready to vary the breathing pattern when more concentration is required to help regain control over very intense contractions. It could be six pants to one blow, or five pants to two blows, but always with more pants than blows or your whistling mouth will experience muscle spasms. One woman in labor used "pant-blow; pant-pant-blow; pant-pant-pant-blow . . ." till she reached six pants to one blow, and then worked down again. That certainly takes plenty of concentration—if you want to try it.

Keep your eyes riveted to each other's throughout the contraction.

Gentlemen, let her choose her own patterned pace for the first sixty seconds of the practice contraction, then for the last thirty seconds call out variations for her, say, six to one, four to two, et cetera; and ladies, you do them. Remember, there should always be more pants than blows.

Let's try it now. Ladies, you tell your coach what breathing pattern you prefer; gentlemen, you say, "Contraction begins."

After a quick cleansing breath, ladies, focus on your husband's eyes and begin the breathing.

Tuck your hands deep in your groin or under your coccyx.

Gentlemen, call out a variation at sixty seconds.

Finish with a cleansing breath or two.

Tip for the Coach: Gentlemen, if she's coping beautifully in labor, let her continue with the pattern she's chosen for the full ninety seconds of the contraction. But if you begin to see panic in her eyes (that's why it's so important to be eyeball to eyeball), then you must immediately tell her to change her pattern. If she is unable to follow a verbal command, you must firmly get her back on track—literally doing the breathing with her, nose to nose, and saying firmly, "You *can* do it! Do it with me!" If you sit back in the labor-room armchair and just quietly suggest she try five pants, one blow, she will have found a way of leaping out the nearest window. The key is catching that early twinge of panic in her eyes, and then putting your all into helping her get back on track.

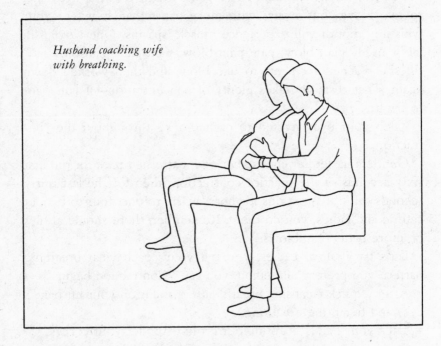

Husband coaching wife with breathing.

Once you've gotten Breathing Technique #3 down, practice it again, this time with the technique used to cope with the "early urge to push."

The early urge to push. Toward the end of transition, most women experience an overwhelming urge to push, or bear down (see page 217). This is because a firstborn's pointy head misleads her into thinking it is time to push. To avoid tearing the cervix, you must suppress that urge until you are fully dilated, counteracting it by breathing in and blowing out forcefully for about five to ten seconds when it occurs during the contraction, and then returning to the pant-blow pattern until the contraction ends.

In your practice session, at sixty seconds the coach will say "Early urge to push" and, ladies, you should begin doing a forceful blowing. Take in a deep breath, puff out your cheeks, and blow it all out, and quickly repeat. Purse your lips in a whistling position so that the air doesn't come out too quickly; otherwise you'll hyperventilate (see page 128 for remedies).

This blowing is very forceful, much more so than the little accent blow or whistle that you do as a punctuation for your pattern-paced breathing. It has to be. If you give only delicate little puffs, you'll undoubtedly give way to the urge at the end of each little blow and bear down involuntarily.

In labor, tell your nurse immediately when you feel you want to bear down so she can get your doctor to examine you, in the hope that he'll say, "Yes, fully dilated—start to push!" But until you have that confirmation (and usually the urge to bear down comes ten to fifteen minutes before it's really time), you must blow.

Try to practice now.

Gentlemen, you say, "Contraction begins."

After a quick cleansing breath, ladies, you begin your patterned-paced breathing.

At sixty seconds, gentlemen, you say, "Early urge to push," and let her blow forcefully for five to ten seconds. Then give her different variations until the ninety-second practice contraction is over.

Expulsion Technique

When to use it: When the cervix is ten centimeters dilated and you have been told by your doctor to begin pushing. Contractions come every two to three minutes. They last forty-five to sixty seconds and are much less painful than the contractions during transition.

Positions. *During practice sessions:* lying semi-inclined against your coach's legs as he sits in a chair (see page 138).

In the labor room: legs apart with hands under knees, or holding ankles, feet apart and flat on bed.

In the delivery room: legs up in stirrups with hands holding hand grips.

In birthing bed or chair: legs bent, knees up, feet resting in supports or on bed.

The Procedure Summarized

As the contraction begins, inhale deeply, exhale; inhale deeply, exhale; inhale deeply a third time and *hold your breath,* bearing down, while relaxing your pelvic floor.

Bring shoulders and head forward, with elbows bent, knees wide apart.

When more air is needed, quickly exhale through your mouth, take a quick breath, and resume pushing. This will probably be necessary three times during a contraction.

As the contraction ends, exhale, lie back, and take several deep cleansing breaths and rest.

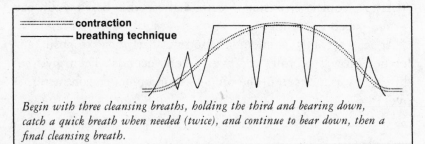

Begin with three cleansing breaths, holding the third and bearing down, catch a quick breath when needed (twice), and continue to bear down, then a final cleansing breath.

Practice Session

Although most women find pushing to be the easiest and least painful part of labor (some even say it's exhilarating), practicing the pushing is very difficult. This is because as you push, your baby is not yet in position for birth and all the pressure is under your rib cage. In addition, it's particularly hard to relate to pushing without that overwhelming urge to bear down.

Practicing the pushing will not hurt you or the baby; you are basically using the same muscles you use when you have a bowel movement. To help focus on those muscles while you practice, vary the pelvic-floor exercises, given in chapter 5, as follows:

Uncross your legs and slowly begin to tighten the pelvic-floor muscles as if you're rising in that elevator. Now you're at the top and you begin to come back down, slowly, from the tenth floor to the first floor. Relax those pelvic-floor muscles. Back at the first floor, when all is relaxed, take a deep breath, hold it, and bear down. Can you pretend that the elevator has just gone down into the basement? Feel the vagina bulge? In any case, when you do it you should feel as if you're about to urinate; that way you know that the pelvic-floor area is relaxed.

To practice the pushing, have your husband sit in a chair with his legs bent at about a 45-degree angle to the floor, knees and feet together. Put a pillow against his shins, sit on the floor in front of him, and lean back on his legs. In the practice position, one quizzical father once asked me, "Are we sitting on the headboard of the labor bed?" The answer, gentlemen, is no, you are just acting as her backrest. During labor, you'll be standing at her bedside, a far more effective position from which to coach the pushing.

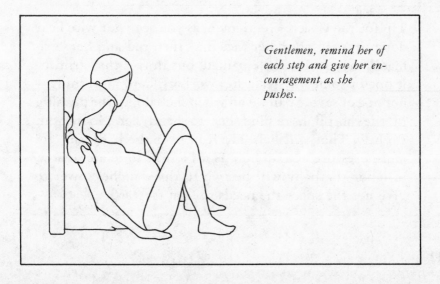

Gentlemen, remind her of each step and give her encouragement as she pushes.

(In labor your angle of sitting will be important. If you are too far forward, you push the baby's head into your coccyx and into the bed. The pelvis should be angled about 30 degrees from the bed to give the baby space to move out. If he is not coming very easily, the nurse will suggest that you change position a bit—one leg over there, the other over here, trying something different to get that angle right. So just be flexible about it. If you are tall, you will probably find that holding on to both ankles is a good position; if you are short, you will probably find it easier to hold on behind your knees or thereabouts.)

Now, gentlemen, say, "Contraction begins," and, ladies, take a cleansing breath. Take a second breath as the contraction is building up, and then on the third breath, take a deep breath and hold it. Bend your elbows a little, lean your head forward, and *push!* Blow out, catch a quick breath, hold it, *push!* Blow out, catch a third breath and *push!,* then release.

Take a cleansing breath at the end.

In labor, as you push you will be holding your breath as long as you possibly can so you won't lose ground. Every time you stop pushing, even for a few seconds to catch your breath, the baby slips back a little. A long steady push is much more effective than a series of short ones in which each time you catch your breath he slips back as far as you've pushed him. That's in real labor; as you practice, you need to hold the pushing breaths only

---

Tip for the Coach: Gentlemen, as you see your wife bear down in real labor, her face may turn red and her "grimace" may look a little pained, but in fact that grimace is one of someone straining, working hard at pushing— not one of severe pain. And when she's doing the pushing in the hospital, remind her to bend her elbows out slightly. That will help her lean over the baby and get more pressure behind him. Hard as it is to relate to now, in labor the baby will be two to three inches lower to give her the space she needs to lean forward.

for a few seconds, just to get the technique. No sense in getting hemorrhoids and a headache trying to sustain a long push now!

Remember, ladies, to practice with your knees wide apart—no one has ever delivered a baby with her legs politely crossed! And don't puff out your cheeks when you hold your breath. You can hold it with your cheeks in and your face relaxed. Try it.

> *"I had always thought my labor and delivery would be normal, long and natural, but was I in for a surprise. It was irregular, very long, and Caesarean."*

> *"When people asked me if I was going to have 'natural childbirth' I would say, 'I'm going to have childbirth, but I don't know yet what kind.'"*

THE LAMAZE "GOODY" BAG

About three weeks before your due date, pack a Lamaze "goody bag" containing all the items you think you'll want during labor and delivery. Keep it separate from your hospital suitcase which will, when you are admitted, be taken to your hospital room.

The Lamaze Bag Checklist:

- a small picture to focus on
- a small brown paper bag (4" × 6" or thereabouts)
- talcum powder
- a can of tennis balls
- an ice pack

- washcloth

- mouthwash spray

- stopwatch or watch with second hand

- lip balm

- book, needlework, or deck of cards

- split of champagne

- small change for telephone calls

- socks (optional)

- this book

Briefly, here is what each of these items is for:

A small picture to focus on will serve as your focal point or visual aid to help you concentrate on appropriate Lamaze techniques in labor. Choose one or two small (unframed) pictures, photos, or decals that can easily be taped to the wall in your labor room.

A small paper bag will help prevent or quickly diminish hyperventilation, if it occurs (see page 128).

A small can of talcum powder or cornstarch will not only feel soothing when you effleurage (see page 127) but may also be refreshing when you experience the "flush" of working hard in labor.

A can of tennis balls for back labor (page 178), if it occurs, to allow your husband a break from exerting counterpressure with his fists or massaging vigorously. One expectant mother in my labor room used a plastic rolling pin full of ice cubes—effective for both counterpressure and numbing combined.

An ice pack in a plastic container (not metal, as the edges are too sharp), also for back labor (page 178), the best size being that of a paperback book. If you have trouble finding one at the local hardware store (it's usually stocked for summer picnics), try a camping-supply shop. Keep it in the freezer until you leave for the hospital.

A split of champagne to celebrate the birth. A magnum is not only unwieldy but will also be warm after the long hours of labor, so a split is a better size. Keep it refrigerated until you are ready to leave for the hospital; then, to keep it chilled, tape the champagne and ice pack together.

A well-worn washcloth to mop your brow.

Mouthwash spray (purse size) or an atomizer like the ones used to water small plants, filled with water, to keep your mouth moist when you are doing your active-labor and transition breathing.

> "We were excited and determined to have a shared, fully conscious and aware prepared childbirth experience, but the apprehension of whether we could do it successfully persisted to the moment Amy went into labor. Amy was most concerned with whether she could withstand the pain, as she had never suffered significant physical pain. I was concerned about whether I could withstand Amy's pain and the sight of the birth; I'd recently fainted at the sight of the X ray of my broken arm. When we viewed the movies in Lamaze class, Amy could barely watch. I kept trying to reassure her by saying things like, 'Isn't that exciting! That's a baby being born!' but I felt no better than Amy. We felt none of those negative feelings when the moment of truth arrived."

Lip balm or gloss to make your lips feel more comfortable. After hours of Lamaze breathing, they will feel dry and chapped.

A stopwatch for timing contractions, or a wristwatch with a second hand if you prefer.

A deck of cards, magazine, newspaper, book, or needlework will help the time pass if you are admitted to the hospital with ruptured membranes and no labor. You could have several hours to while away.

Small change for the telephone so you can give the family an update during labor and spread the good news later. (You won't have access to a private phone until you're in your room after delivery.)

Socks if you always seem to have cold feet. (Mine were always hot and sweaty, but to each his own.)

This book, which I hope gives you solace and direction during the tough hours (even as it helps you enjoy the reward of all your work—the baby—in the weeks that follow).

10

Packing Your Suitcase for the Hospital

WHAT TO PACK FOR THE HOSPITAL

3 or 4 high-cotton-count nightgowns
3 or 4 bras (nursing bras for nursing mothers)
Robe and slippers
Sanitary belt
3 or 4 panties
Toiletries and shower cap
Snack food such as little crackers or nuts
Glazed dried fruits
Birth announcements and thank-you notes
Address book and stamps
A few dollars for the daily newspapers, etc.
Going-home outfit for you and the baby
No valuables

Since it is perfectly normal for babies to come two weeks early, have your suitcase ready in advance.

What will you need for yourself? Nightgowns that, if you plan to nurse, open down the front for easy access to the breasts. You can buy nursing nightgowns with two discreet slits for this purpose but if you are small-bosomed like me, you will find the slits extremely generous. Chatting with visitors in the hospital, I found that guests at the right side of my bed could look clear through the right slit, across both breasts, and out the left slit to the visitors on my left—rather embarrassing to say the least! If your breasts are small, you may want to stitch up the slits partway or look for a regular nightie that unfastens down the front *to the waist.* Many popular mail-order catalogues offer cozy, cotton nightgowns or nightshirts with long front-button closures.

Whether you breast-feed or not, look for nightgowns with a high cotton count when you shop; they absorb more moisture than those made with synthetic fibers. The hot flashes you may have experienced in pregnancy will be more frequent after delivery, and it's not uncommon to wake up during the night soaking wet. Perspiration is one way your body will eliminate the fluids you no longer need.

At night you can wear the gowns provided by the hospital (they can go into the hospital laundry in the morning) and during the day you can wear the nightgowns you brought from home. Your friends and relatives are all coming to see the "radiant new mother"—don't disappoint them!

Pack two nursing bras (see page 289) if you plan to breast-feed or two regular bras if you plan to bottle-feed. Either way, you will need the support.

Slippers with hard soles are a must (intravenous bottles can break and you don't want to step on a piece of glass), as is a long bathrobe. If the hospital's baby-care classes are in a different area of the building, you'll need to be covered as you walk in the public halls.

Pack toiletries of your choice, a shower cap, and thongs for use in the shower (some hospitals recommend them). When you take your hospital tour at the end of your pregnancy, ask about bringing hair dryers, electric curling devices, and so on.

Maternity sanitary pads are usually included in the "daily care pack" supplied by the hospital. Don't be shocked when you see them. They are very large and require a sanitary belt. Your own little sanitary pads, with the sticky backs, are simply not going to absorb enough of the normal, heavy bleeding you will experience in the first week after delivery (see pages 238 and 277). If your baby is born by Caesarean, panties to hold the hospital sanitary pad in place will be more comfortable than a belt.

Leave all valuables at home: rings, jewelry, watches; radios and other portable electronic equipment; expensive books. Fire regulations require hospitals to have unlocked entrances and exits everywhere, and petty thievery is not uncommon. As for money, you will need only a few dollars during your stay, for newspapers or sundries from the gift cart.

If you wear glasses, bring your prescription glasses for labor and delivery, and your lenses for after delivery. Hard contact lenses are usually not allowed in labor in case an emergency Caesarean is needed and you require general anesthesia.

Pack a little snack food—dry roasted peanuts, for example. Most hospitals serve dinner early and it's nice to have a snack with your bedtime juice. Glazed dried fruits (page 51) will help to keep your stools soft and prevent the discomfort of a hard first bowel movement with a very sore episiotomy.

Pack what you need for sending out notes. Babies are not released from the hospital until their birth announcements have been completed and stuffed into addressed, stamped, envelopes ready for mailing! Seriously, you will be so busy the next few weeks that you'll be delighted to have such niceties taken care of before you get home. Better yet, stamp and address the envelopes a few weeks before your due date. If you are thinking, But we want to have them printed!, then print well in advance: "Mr. and Mrs. John Jones announce the birth of Mary/Anne/John/James," bring them to the hospital, and check off what you get! Pack some thank-you notes for flowers and gifts that are delivered to the hospital and send them out right away.

Your going-home outfit can be what you arrived in, but if you feel the urge to burn all of your maternity clothes as you go into labor, remember that what you wear home should be loose-fitting. You'll be able to get into your old, prepregnant jeans eventually— but don't expect them to fit right after the baby is born.

The outfit for your baby can go into your suitcase or your

husband can bring it in on the day you are discharged from the hospital.

That's about it for what you'll need in the hospital. When you are admitted, your suitcase will be taken to your room and you will be on your way to labor and delivery, with your Lamaze goody bag.

PART THREE

Labor and Delivery

We know how labor begins—the amount of oxytocin in the mother's bloodstream rises suddenly and initiates labor contractions—but we do not know exactly why this happens. Some believe that the baby's adrenal gland produces cortisone which in turn causes the estrogen levels in the mother's bloodstream to drop and oxytocin levels to rise. Or it could be that the aging placenta triggers an excess secretion of progesterone and in turn oxytocin.

As inconvenient as it is to have labor begin spontaneously, it seems fitting to have inexplicable forces controlling one of the most important events in life. Scientists may marvel as they observe the wonders of our far-flung universe; it is equally miraculous to contemplate the birth of a child. Not one is ever "routine." Whether it be baby number one or baby number five thousand and one, for those nurses, doctors, and other professionals who are fortunate enough to be in the delivery room, each birth is awesome in its own special way. As a nurse who has assisted thousands of births and a mother who knows the many joys a child can bring, I remember how my eyes would often brim with tears when I slipped each little baby into his father's timid arms.

The process of childbearing is universal, the basic order of events well defined; but for each woman it will be an entirely unique experience. My first labor, for example, was the longest twenty hours in my life, my second an exhilarating three, and my third somewhere in between the two.

What follows is a summary of the normal sequence of physical and emotional reactions to labor and delivery, drawn from personal experiences as a nurse, the shared experiences of my Lamaze students, and, of course, the birth of my own three young children. Do not expect your own labor and delivery to encompass everything described, nor to progress in exactly the same order. Be flexible about your own goals. If you aim for a painless childbirth, you will definitely be proved wrong and may even feel overwhelmed. Better to expect the most difficult labor you can imagine. If you get it, you will be prepared; if you do not, you will be delighted.

As you read through this section of the book, you will find references to the Lamaze techniques where they should be used in labor and delivery; these are discussed in detail in chapter 9. Lamaze is, of course, but one method of coping with labor and delivery; you may have chosen another approach. But learn Lamaze, too. Every one of the couples I have assisted in labor and delivery has found these techniques to be helpful.

11

The Three Stages of Labor and Delivery: A Bird's-Eye View

*T*his chapter presents a summary or overview of labor and delivery, in hopes that it will help orient you to the typical birth process and all it entails.

THE THREE STAGES OF LABOR

Stage I: Effacement and dilation of the cervix to 10 centimeters or five fingerbreadths. Stage I consists of three phases:

Phase One, Early Labor: Cervix effacing to 100% and dilating to 3 centimeters in approximately 6 to 8 hours

Phase Two, Active Labor: Cervix dilating from 3 to 8 centimeters in approximately 3 to 4 hours

Phase Three, Transition: Cervix dilating from 8 to 10 centimeters in approximately 1 hour

Stage II: Birth, with pushing for approximately 1 hour or less
(*Note:* Time approximations of stages I and II apply to first babies; subsequent labors usually progress more rapidly.)

Stage III: Expulsion of the placenta, or afterbirth, taking approximately fifteen minutes

---

Try to picture for a moment what your body will experience with the start of labor contractions and what you can anticipate during the three stages of labor and delivery.

THE FIRST STAGE OF LABOR

This stage is the effacement and dilation of the cervix, easy to envision if you imagine what happens when you put on a turtle-neck sweater. At first, the neck sits on top of your head. Then, as you pull the sweater down slowly, the neck flattens, or effaces, and then as you pop your head through, it opens, or dilates—very much like the effacement and dilation of the cervix during labor.

Dilation of the cervix is measured in centimeters or finger-breadths, one fingerbreadth equaling about two centimeters. When you first arrive at the hospital, your doctor will examine

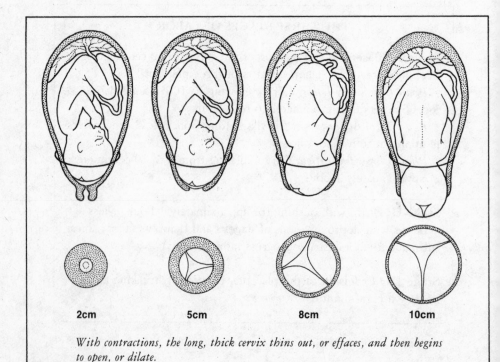

With contractions, the long, thick cervix thins out, or effaces, and then begins to open, or dilate.

you to measure your cervix, saying, "Ninety percent effaced, two centimeters dilated," or whatever his findings may be. At regular intervals throughout the first stage of labor, you will be measured to check the progress of that dilating cervix. Taking the measurements is not an exact science, and it takes some experience to get the feel of it. At New York Hospital, we nurses would find it amusing to observe the new residents who came on to the obstetrical service every July. After doing the vaginal exam, they would carefully walk to the nurses' station with fingers held in the exact position as the dilation just measured, match them up to the measurement chart on the board, and say, "Yes, five centimeters—I knew it was five."

Gradually, due to the uterine contractions, the dilation progresses to its ultimate width of ten centimeters, or five fingerbreadths. At this point in labor, the cervical opening is about four inches wide, or "fully dilated," a phrase I always liked; so concise and full of meaning. In labor and delivery, you would often hear a nurse calling out as she rushed about in the labor room, "Fully, she's fully dilated, is there a delivery room ready? We'll need it very soon." Those words always meant the reward of many long hours in labor and somehow would bring excitement into the air of the whole labor and delivery suite.

And no matter how each particular labor would proceed, it was always interesting to me that *all* cervixes dilated to ten centimeters—weren't there babies born with bigger or smaller heads than that? I always asked myself this same question and then as I began to be with more couples in delivery, I learned that in fact, miraculously, almost all babies have a biparietal diameter (the widest measurement of the baby's head, at about eye level) of 9.5 to 10.5 centimeters. Of course, if a tiny premature baby were delivered at thirty-four weeks, his head would be smaller, but for the full-term baby, this measurement was almost absolute. Amazing, isn't it! That despite all the individual traits and characteristics, most infants are bestowed with an almost universal head size to fit through the mother's pelvis. Of course the forces of labor also assist in elongating or molding the head; but even if the overall bulk of the baby varies substantially, say by three or four pounds, the baby who weighs six pounds may have a head only one centimeter smaller than the one who weighs nine and one-half pounds!

How long will labor last? If someone matter-of-factly tells you they labored for eight days, you have good reason to question what that means and how they could have survived all that time. No one *ever* labored for eight days and eight nights. It would have killed the mother, the father, the doctor, nurse, and the baby! What probably happened is that there was a bout of false labor on Monday, nothing on Tuesday, Wednesday, or Thursday, another little bout of false labor on Friday, nothing on Saturday, real labor on Sunday, and delivery in the wee hours of Monday morning.

For a first baby, the *average* is a twelve- or fourteen-hour labor, with most of the time accounted for in the first stage of labor. As said before, there is always some lucky woman who has a four-hour labor and someone who has an eighteen-hour labor with a Caesarean birth at the end. You just do not know where on the spectrum you'll fall, but at least you know that there is a predictable sequence to the stages of labor and that you are going to have some variation of it.

Because it is the longest, most tedious, and most painful part of labor, stage one is subdivided into three phases—early, active, and transition—each having its own characteristic contractions.

Phase One, Early Labor

Phase one lasts about six to eight hours for first babies, usually shorter for second babies. During this time, the cervix effaces and dilates to about three centimeters. Contractions are fairly mild, lasting thirty to forty-five seconds, and the intervals between them are usually erratic—five minutes, ten minutes, two minutes, twenty minutes, something like that. You should be able to ignore a big hunk of that time, aware of the cramplike contractions, but able to putter around for the first few hours.

Phase Two, Active Labor

Phase two lasts about three to four hours for women having first babies, and about one to two hours for second babies. (This still gives you plenty of time to get to the hospital even if you live forty-five minutes to an hour away.) In active labor, the cervix dilates from three to about eight centimeters. Contractions gradually become stronger, lasting forty-five to sixty seconds with only a two- to three-minute break between. Rather than ignore them and move about, most women prefer to sit and relax between active labor contractions, semi-inclined in a soft chair or in a bed with pillows between the neck and shoulders so they can capitalize on conserving energy.

Phase Three, Transition

Phase three is what everyone who has had a baby wants to discuss with you. This is when the cervix goes the last, painful distance from eight to ten centimeters, stretching to its utmost, which is why it hurts so much. The baby's position during transition also has its discomforting effect as the head, having entered your pelvis facing your side, now turns to look toward your back. Transition contractions last sixty to ninety seconds and usually you get only sixty to ninety seconds to catch your breath before, *wham-o,* another one hits.

Admittedly, transition is the most painful part of labor, but *it only lasts an hour,* with luck, less. The woman who does *not* know this, having had six or so hours of early labor and four hours of active labor, may well panic when she reaches transition and beg to be put out of her misery. She does not know that the birth, which follows transition, is much, much better and far less painful.

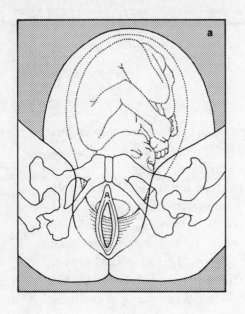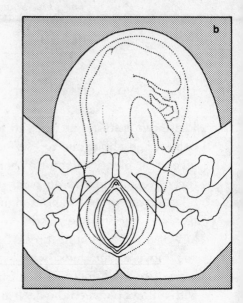

THE SECOND STAGE OF LABOR

This is the birth of the baby. It is the pushing stage. From this point to the birth usually takes about an hour as the baby's head pivots up under the pubic bone and comes right out, his face looking up into the world. Once his head is all the way out, it turns back to look toward the mother's hip and, because the head is the largest part, the rest of him usually scoots out easily.

THE THIRD STAGE OF LABOR

The last stage, which takes about ten to fifteen minutes, is the expulsion of the placenta. With a few very mild contractions, the placenta sloughs away from the uterine wall, the mother gives one more push, and out it comes. Immediately after the placenta is expelled, the uterus returns to the size of a large orange in the pit of the abdomen, shrinking down miraculously after those nine

158

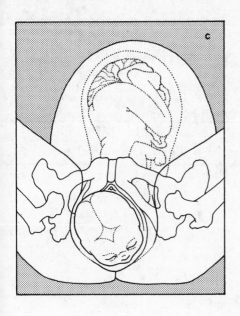

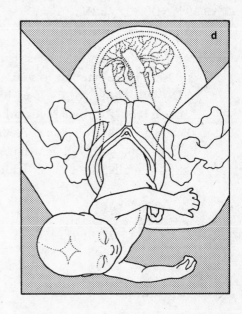

Once the cervix is completely open (a), the baby's head turns to look down as it comes through the birth canal (b) and rotates up under the pubic bone to be delivered (c). Once the head emerges (d), the body usually slips quickly out. Within 10 to 15 minutes the placenta sloughs away from the uterine wall and is expelled (e, f).

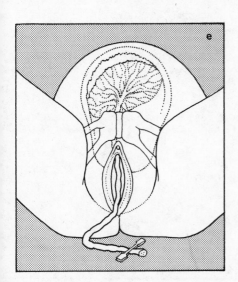

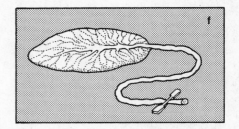

long months. This involuntary process is important because it helps minimize the bleeding where the placenta detached from the uterus.

All of labor and delivery is a gradual progression; once again, remember that everyone will experience something different. As you read through the pages that follow, do not expect all of what is described to happen to you.

Do what suits you best to help you get through it. Use your Lamaze "tools" or whatever other childbirth techniques you have chosen to help you cope. As have the vast majority of women before you, you will manage to give birth to a beautiful new baby—literally, the perfect fruit of all your labor.

12

Stage One, Phase One:
Early Labor

RECOGNIZING THE START OF EARLY LABOR

With or without the signs of impending labor (see chapter 7), around your due date you will inevitably wonder how you are going to recognize labor. If you are worried that labor will start without your knowing it, remember what one obstetrician I worked with for many years would tell his patients, "If you're not sure you're in labor, you're not!" Although this holds true for recognizing contractions, there are other signs of early labor that are not quite so evident and it is reassuring to know how to recognize them.

Show

The first little clue that labor is starting may be your passing of what is called "show." Show is the mucous plug that has been in the neck of the uterus or cervix throughout your pregnancy, acting as a barrier against intrusion. If you pass it, the plug will look like a blob (about a tablespoonful) of blood-tinged, viscous gelatin, in your panties or in the toilet.

Do not confuse show with what you experience after a vaginal exam four to six weeks before your due date, when your doctor checks to see that the cervix is closed and there are no signs of premature labor and you come home that afternoon with cramps and staining and think, "He's put me into labor and I still have four weeks to go." This is neither show nor early labor. All that has happened is that some of the many tiny blood vessels in the neck of the uterus have broken during the exam to cause the staining, and his touching the cervix triggered off a series of strong Braxton Hicks contractions (see page 68). A bath and perhaps a little wine or beer may help them peter out. The plug comes out of its own accord, not because of intrusive activity, and when it does, labor will usually begin within twenty-four to forty-eight hours. Do not, however, hold your breath—several mothers have gone without their plugs for as long as a week! If the mucous plug is your only clue, wait before you call your doctor. Continue with your normal activities, including tub baths, secure that the amniotic sac is intact and the baby is fully protected inside it.

> *"I woke in the night feeling a slight gush of fluid. Nothing further happened, so I waited until morning to tell my husband, who insisted I see the doctor. I tested negatively for amniotic fluid and was told that the baby had still not descended. That afternoon I started feeling very crampy and by ten P.M. the discomfort was fairly significant and did not stop after a glass of wine. We timed the pains, determined a four-minute pattern, and called the doctor. Neither he nor I believed it was labor, but he said to go see the resident. When I was admitted, I was 90 percent effaced and one centimeter dilated. Walking helped me keep my mind off contractions in early labor."*

Ruptured Membranes or "Waters Breaking"

A much more obvious sign of labor than show is rupture of the amniotic membranes. It occurs as the first sign of labor in about

25 percent of all pregnant women. If you hear the phrase "my water broke" to describe the start of labor, it refers to the rupture of the thin, outer membrane of the amniotic sac, the "bag of waters" that surrounds the baby in the uterus, and the subsequent release of the amniotic fluid it contains. Membrane rupture can occur at any time before or during the first stage of labor, usually flushing out the mucous plug when it happens.

The reason why membranes rupture is up for conjecture. One mother was convinced that her baby ruptured her membranes with his fingernail: she felt fetal movement, heard a little *pop* sound, then felt a gush of water. Who knows, this may well explain it.

There is no pain involved when membranes rupture, as there are no nerve endings in the amniotic sac. However, should the membranes rupture in active labor, contractions will intensify because the dilating force against the cervix is then the baby's head rather than the soft amniotic sac, which is like a balloon full of water. The amount of amniotic fluid that comes out when the rupture occurs varies depending upon the size and site of the hole.

> *"The first sign was when Patty woke me up at two* A.M. *to tell me that her water broke, at which point I discovered that there was a pond in our bed."*

> *"One week past my due date, my mother and I were sitting in the park. As I stood up to head home, all of a sudden my water broke and, yes, it ran down my overalls into my sneakers."*

If your waters break in one huge gush on the corner of 57th Street and Madison Avenue, releasing a full two to three cups of amniotic fluid as you wait for the light to change, you will know it. One of the obstetricians at New York Hospital, Dr. Francis

Ryan, always recommended to his patients that they keep a small jar of pickles in their handbag around their due date, anticipating this event. Then, if their water suddenly broke all over the marble floor in Bloomingdale's, they could simply drop the jar so all the fluids would mingle and no one would ever suspect what was really going on. In fact, two researchers found that as membranes rupture, endorphins are often released into the mother's bloodstream so that, as the amniotic fluid cascades down her legs, into her shoes, and onto the pavement, she merely smiles demurely, not minding a bit.

Membranes can rupture high up in the uterus and because the baby's head acts as a plug against the cervix, the flow of amniotic fluid can be no more than a trickle. If this happens, you might think, This is so embarrassing, the baby just kicked me in the bladder and now I'm soaking wet. Or maybe you think it's just a little mucus discharge.

A leak can occur high in the uterus (a), *usually causing only a trickle, or low* (b), *usually followed by a gush. An amnio hook or small orangewood stick may be used to artificially rupture your membranes* (c).

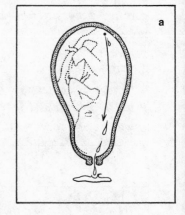

a

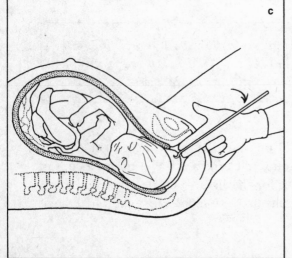

c

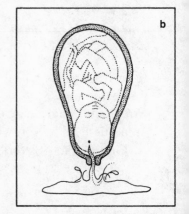

b

> *"I thought labor would feel somewhat like the Braxton Hicks contractions, but that wasn't the case, since the Braxton Hicks contractions were mostly right below my bosom. I actually didn't recognize the onset of labor because it felt like one continuous heavy menstrual cramp, with no start or stop so I couldn't time it—how could it be labor? Also there was a mucous discharge, but it looked smaller and less pink than I'd expected. I went to my doctor in the morning because even if it wasn't labor the pain was getting moderately serious and I thought I'd better check with him. He told me the cervix was effacing, to go home for a couple of hours and come back. We did so, and then he sent us to the hospital."*

With a high, tiny leak that stops and starts, you will need to determine whether it is urine or amniotic fluid that is released. Urine is, of course, pale yellow in color and has a very distinctive smell, while amniotic fluid is usually clear, with a faint odor of clorine or freshly done laundry. If you are at all unsure of which it is, notify your doctor. He can use a little piece of alkaline-acid test paper to diagnose the leak properly in his office. (If the amniotic fluid has a tinge of dark green color, this means that your baby has had a bowel movement in his amniotic fluid, discoloring the water. Consult your doctor at once for him to determine if fetal distress or a breech position may be the cause.)

You may have heard the old wives' tale that an early rupture of the membranes presages a "dry birth, difficult delivery." (My grandmother always claimed that my father's birth was a "dreadful, dry birth!") I'm not sure how this fallacy evolved—perhaps because people believed that if the membranes ruptured, all of the water would drain out and the baby would no longer be wet and slippery but dry and thus would not slide out easily. This could not possibly happen; amniotic fluid is constantly replenished. Even if your membranes rupture and labor proceeds slowly, you will leak fluid constantly and there will still be a big gush right after the baby is delivered.

Call your doctor if your membranes rupture, whether or not contractions have begun. He will probably recommend that you go to the hospital and check in so that the nurses can attach an external fetal monitor to pick up developing contractions.

Your progress from this point will be watched closely, as there are copious numbers of bacteria inhabiting the anal area nearby that would love, via capillary action, to travel up through the vagina and into the uterus to infect you and the baby. Oh, you might think, but I can keep an eye on myself at home and soak up the fluid with a sanitary pad. This would be the worst thing you could do. Even if you have to wear something to soak up the fluid on the way to the hospital, it will be removed immediately after your arrival and you will sit on what looks like a large absorbent pad; a standard minipad only promotes the collection of bacteria and encourages it to travel up the vagina. For the same reason, you should not take a tub bath, use tampons, or have intercourse once membranes have ruptured: these too could introduce infection.

Now, if it is 4:00 A.M. when you call your doctor with the news that your membranes have ruptured, *if contractions have not begun* he will probably want you to try to go back to sleep (you will need all the shut-eye you can get) and come in refreshed in the morning. But if it is 9:00 A.M., the chances are he will tell you to come in.

Half of all women with ruptured membranes will begin labor spontaneously within eight hours; the other half, whatever the reasons, simply do not. If this is the case, your doctor will probably decide to induce you—that is, start your labor contractions with a synthetic drug similar to your own natural hormones.

What Happens If Your Labor Is Induced

The natural hormone that puts you into labor is oxytocin; the synthetic hormone, made at Lederle Laboratories, is Pitocin. Being induced may sound like a handy way to start labor—fitting in with your doctor's schedule, perhaps, or allowing you to go to Florida next week—but convenience is not a valid reason for doing it. There has to be specific medical indication: elevated blood pressure or being two weeks past the due date or, as pinpointed here, no spontaneous labor six to twelve hours after the membranes rupture.

Pitocin is administered slowly through intravenous tubing, and the amount is regulated closely. Within about half an hour after the I.V. is in place, strong labor will begin. The obvious disadvantage of being induced is that you have not had six to eight hours of early labor to get used to the intensifying contractions. On the other hand, had you weathered those six to eight hours, you would be that much more tired. Being induced may seem like an intrusive procedure, but usually when the membranes rupture you are ready for labor anyway, with a "ripe" (slightly effaced) cervix. In this case, although the Pitocin may be needed to start things going, after the first few hours the body takes over, making its own oxytocin, and you progress on your own. However, even if the cervix is not yet ripe but instead is long, tough, and not effaced, once there's a hole in the amniotic sac, infection becomes a serious possibility when there's no sign of labor, and despite the drawbacks of immediately bringing on very strong contractions, induction is usually indicated.

To prepare for the possibility of ruptured membranes, as your due date approaches, it is a good idea to protect your mattress with a rubber sheet or a plastic bag from the dry cleaner. Put it under the mattress pad on your side of the bed; although the amniotic fluid does not stain, you will not be leaving your husband with a squashy, soggy mattress to air out if your membranes rupture in the middle of the night. Keep a hand towel nearby, too. Depending on the amount of leakage, you may need to wear it like a diaper (a truly stunning arrangement, but a little maxipad will be completely ineffectual!) as you make your way to the hospital. One new mother described how she not only used the towel diaper I had recommended but also devised her own plastic "pants" by cutting two leg holes in a garbage bag.

Artificial Rupture of Membranes

If membranes do not rupture spontaneously at the start of labor, they probably will do so later in active labor and thus are left intact if labor is progressing well. But if labor does not seem to be progressing well—if, for example, the cervix is six centimeters dilated and labor begins to peter out, your doctor may gently rupture your membranes with a little orangewood stick. You will feel nothing more than the examination followed by a gush of warm water, followed in turn by strong contractions.

Many doctors prefer to use an "amnio hook" to rupture the membranes, so if you see the nurse hand your doctor a foot-long plastic stick with what looks like a crochet hook at the end, do not become alarmed that the next step is to try to reach your tonsils transvaginally! The stick is inserted in the vagina only about three inches and gently twisted so the little hook will rupture the sac to bring on good, strong contractions (see page 164).

Contractions

Last but not least, contractions may signal the start of labor. Rhythmic, working muscle contractions are the nitty-gritty of labor and delivery: it is because of them that labor progresses and delivery occurs.

With labor contractions, the whole uterine bag contracts and relaxes, contracts and relaxes, although the rhythm is somewhat erratic in early labor. As the uterus contracts, the upper muscle segments get a little bit thicker, pushing the baby down, while the lower muscle segments pull up on the long, thick cervix so that it flattens, or effaces, and begins to open.

Where Is Labor Felt?

Many women who are having first babies are concerned about whether they will know they are in labor and wonder where, exactly, they will feel labor contractions. If you have experienced menstrual cramps, you know not only the exact location but also the sensation of early labor contractions. Both are caused by the opening, or dilation of the cervix (although in the case of menstrual cramps, it's just a tiny amount of opening to allow the flow of your period to pass through—nowhere near the size of a baby's head).

If you are thinking that because you experience excruciating menstrual cramps you will therefore be able to tolerate the toughest labor contractions with ease, I have some discouraging news for you. The reason most women have severe menstrual cramps is that they have a "tough" cervix that has difficulty dilating, even that one or two centimeters needed for the first day of their period. For birthing a baby, the dilation required is so much greater that there's almost no comparison. On a more encouraging note, if you usually experience sharp menstrual cramps, once the cervix has dilated fully to deliver your baby it takes many years for it to shrink back down to the tight, tough cervix you had before you were pregnant. Consequently, you will probably never have another menstrual cramp again!

If you have been fortunate enough to have missed the experience of menstrual cramps, imagine instead a severe gas pain, centrally located, low in front and just behind the pubic bone, striking about an hour after you have eaten a rancid tuna fish salad for lunch and just prior to an awful attack of diarrhea! That's more or less what an early labor contraction feels like, and although some women feel labor begin in the back and radiate forward, most women feel it as I have described. Obviously, you won't fail to recognize it!

Those who have never experienced labor may assume, incorrectly, that the pain is felt in the entire uterus as it contracts or squeezes down to push the baby out. Actually, the pain of labor is felt only in the dilating cervix, stretching to a full ten centimeters to allow the baby to pass through; that's where the nerve endings that cause the pain are concentrated.

Whatever kind of labor you have, you must use the pattern of the contractions to your advantage; and you can count on the breaks between them. There will *always* be a break. At one point, for example, you might get a contraction that lasts sixty seconds, followed by a respite of three to four minutes, then have another sixty-second contraction, another three to four minutes' respite, and so on.

Hold fast to this idea that there will always be a break because it is the one characteristic of labor that will help most to get you through: knowing that the contraction will last only sixty seconds, or even ninety seconds, and then you *will* have a pain-free interval. It may be shorter than you would like, but definitely there will be a break. You may hear someone tell you, "But I *never* had a single pause between my contractions." This may have been the perception, but it's just plain inaccurate. That woman probably remained so tense and tight between contractions, anticipating the next one, that she never recognized her breaks for what they were.

Contractions seem to have their own distinctive pattern for each woman, right from the beginning. In one woman, they peak in ten seconds and stay up there, while in another they intensify much more gradually and then drop off quickly from the peak. Some women even have a little double peak—the contraction starts to relax and then peaks again before it actually goes completely down. In this case, usually there is a much longer break before the next contraction begins.

Whatever the individual pattern, the *timing* of the contractions will be fairly predictable for everyone. That is, they usually start out lasting thirty to forty seconds each and progress to sixty to ninety seconds each. Almost *everyone* starts her labor with contractions that are shorter, with relatively long intervals in between, and progresses to the stronger, longer, less-break-between contractions as the active and transition stages develop.

Is What I Feel Real Labor?

This is a valid question when you first experience early labor contractions. You might think that if you feel *regular* contractions, you are in labor. That's not necessarily true. You could have regular contractions every five minutes for two hours—and then they might stop. This is false labor. The difference between false and real labor is *progression:* in real labor, contractions must intensify—in other words, they last longer, come more often, and get stronger.

The best way to tell if you are really in labor (after the "dip

"*I went into labor around ten* P.M., *but it did not really affect me until I woke up at one* A.M. *Then I packed (the baby was five days early), woke my husband up at two, and after taking showers we were at the hospital at three with my contractions five minutes apart. Ted was born at nine forty-five* A.M."

and sip" test for false labor, page 105) is to time your contractions for at least one or two hours *before* you call your doctor. (This is for first babies—seconds come much faster.) If you call him the moment you think you are feeling a contraction, you will not be giving him any useful information to assess your situation. So, if contractions begin and your membranes have not ruptured, wait those one to two hours and time the contractions.

Of course, your doctor may tell you in advance when he wants to be called and you certainly will want to follow his advice. He knows your individual case. Perhaps your cervix was completely effaced and three centimeters dilated in his office yesterday and while he feels things may go quickly, he has said nothing to you for fear you will be disappointed if they do not. Whatever your situation, you do as he suggests. However, if at the end of your pregnancy he hasn't yet told you when to call him, ask him to give you these instructions.

On the other hand, as difficult as it is to restrain your excitement when labor begins, do not call your parents or your best friend and tell them you think you are going into labor. Do not call them *at all* until you can report that you have a lovely baby. If you get them involved too early, all they can do is stand by helplessly for the next dozen or so hours, plagued with worry.

"*Even when we got to the hospital and the doctor confirmed we were really going to have a baby, we couldn't believe it. You'd think after nine months we'd be ready—but I don't think anyone is—at least until you hold that little bundle in your arms.*"

Once contractions have started, in tandem perhaps with the appearance of your mucous plug, the rupture of membranes, or any combination of the three, you will know that this is the start of labor and that the first stage of labor, the effacement and dilation of the cervix, has officially begun.

EARLY LABOR

In early labor, contractions are usually mild, lasting 30 to 45 seconds, and patterned erratically, with intervals that range from five minutes to twenty minutes as the cervix effaces and dilates to about three centimeters. Early labor lasts anywhere from six to eight hours for women having first babies. To conserve energy and whittle down the time, your goal is to ignore the first four or five of those hours. While you may feel cramps or something going on, as long as you keep yourself busy and distracted, you will not think too much about it.

If contractions begin at night and you are awakened by what seems to be a strong, painful one followed by a good twenty-minute interval before the next one hits, try to go back to sleep. I know you are probably thinking, Forget that, I'll be so excited I'll want to get up, get dressed, get packed, and get ready to go have a baby! Your activities won't speed things up, so if it is at all possible to go back to sleep, do it. Your biggest enemy in labor is fatigue, so even if you doze on and off for twenty minutes at a stretch over another three hours, it will be worth it.

If napping is out of the question, lying in the darkness, clutching the bedsheet and watching the clock as you wait for the next contraction will make them feel much stronger than they probably are. You'd be better off slipping quietly out of bed without waking your husband, sipping an ounce of wine, and taking a bath. (If your membranes have ruptured, remember, no bath—you can take a shower instead.) You need time to evaluate your situation and assess whether what you feel is real or false labor; keep busy with a shampoo, shave your legs—you may be in the hospital for the next few days—and after that you can determine whether the contractions have intensified, remained unchanged, or petered out. If they seem to have progressed, awaken your husband.

If contractions begin during the day, after you have ruled out false labor, call your husband and ask him to meet you at home.

Gentlemen, your job at this point is to give your wife moral support and, if need be, calm her down. If she awakens you at 3:00 A.M. as she is puttering around the apartment, packing her suitcase and whistling a jolly tune, try to get her back into bed. On the other hand, if you are awakened by the sound of commotion in the bathroom and find her sitting on the bathmat, hair sudsy from a shampoo, doing the transition breathing you learned in childbirth classes and crying between contractions, then you need to help her get dressed, call the doctor, and get her to the hospital, p.d.q. (The latter rarely happens, but you should be so lucky to have a four-hour labor!)

You may have the proverbial friend of a friend who thought she had to go to the bathroom and out came the baby instead. I know one couple who went to Chinatown for a fabulous twelve-course birthday banquet two days after her due date. They enjoyed their dinner and the festivities, but she and her husband both awakened during the night with a common complaint of gas pains and diarrhea. They called her doctor, who assured them that if both were suffering from the same discomforts, it couldn't possibly be labor.

As the night progressed and her husband was able to rest more easily, she continued to have these "gas pains" from the Peking duck. Finally, at about 5:00 A.M., she awakened her husband to say, "Please, dear, take a look below, something is not right!" Sure enough, he could see the top of the baby's head beginning to emerge. He called the doctor and fortunately reached him at once, and as he related the story, he said, "I can see the top of the baby's head, no, I can see most of . . . No, he's out! The baby is out, on our bed—what do I do now?!" Both mother and baby were fine and their doctor gave them instructions until an ambulance arrived to take them all to the hospital. Later, at their Lamaze class reunion, they introduced their baby as "Peking Duck."

Again, if it all goes that easily and that quickly, be delighted! But your chances of having a baby like that are probably one in a million; if you are like the majority of women, what will probably happen is that even after you have stayed home for what seems a long enough period of early labor and finally arrive at the hospital, you will still be in a much earlier phase of labor than you thought. It may even be too early to be admitted and you could be sent home to wait.

When I became pregnant with my first baby I had been working in labor and delivery for eight years and certainly did not want to arrive at the hospital too early. I went into labor at about one A.M. and felt just awful—throwing up every hour or so alternating with attacks of diarrhea, with contractions that seemed very strong coming on every four minutes. Finally, at about six A.M. when I just couldn't stand it any longer, I said to my husband, "I think it's time to go to the hospital; I must be five or six centimeters by now." Off we went—but guess how far dilated I turned out to be? Two centimeters! Terrible! Of course, to be nice to a long-time employee, they said I could stay, but how I wished I had gone home, where it is better to throw up in your own toilet, and be in your own cozy bed, sipping your own ginger ale with your husband close at hand! *Never* will a hospital be as nice as your own surroundings.

Early labor has been aptly described as the Entertainment Phase—a term created by Elisabeth Bing, an extraordinary and delightful woman and one of the founders of the Lamaze method in this country. Literally, this is the time for you, gentlemen, to *entertain* your wife! Divert her attention. Do something, anything that will keep her mind off what she is feeling. You are not permitted to keep detailed lists of contractions or, for that matter, ask her anything about what's going on: "It's been five minutes, are you sure you don't feel anything starting? How about in the back? Maybe *something* is beginning?" Instead, take a walk or go to the movies, preferably a suspense or adventure film. You can always leave the theater or, if contractions get stronger and she wants to start her childbirth breathing techniques (see page 124), she could do so while she's watching the screen. People nearby who have had babies would probably smile softly, while those

> *"The doctor told us the day before Christopher was born that he would be surprised if the baby came soon. We headed out to our country place two hours away thinking nothing would happen. How naive! In the middle of the night we were driving back to New York with me in labor!"*

who haven't would either be oblivious to it or just think you were practicing some new kind of relaxation exercise.

After your outing, you will want to stay close to home and call your doctor. He'll probably encourage you to come into his office between his scheduled appointments so he can examine you and find out exactly where you are in labor. Unfortunately you don't have this option if contractions begin at night, and although you cannot look inside your body to see just how far along you are, knowing how to cope with labor will give you the confidence to stay home as long as possible.

Author's Note: Be ready to begin Breathing Technique #1 (see page 125) when you feel you need it—ideally at the end of early labor or when, as they say, you can no longer walk, talk, or joke through a contraction.

Tip for the Coach: If your wife begins her breathing techniques at home, help her find a comfortable position in which she can relax and conserve energy. Keep in mind that when those strong contractions begin to come with frequency, she will probably forget a lot of what she has learned and will depend on you to coach her through labor.

Remember, gentlemen, if your wife is one of those lucky women who will experience a fast, driving labor of, say, four or five hours, she won't let you keep her at home. When you gently say to her, "Let's not go to the hospital just yet; there's a good movie starting in twenty minutes," and she responds with "I'm going to the hospital and I'm going now, with or without you!" as she rushes to the door, then grab the suitcase and humbly second the motion with "I'm coming! Let's go!"

Many women experience nausea and diarrhea in early labor, probably the body's way of clearing the decks so it can focus exclusively on one major activity at a time. In addition, the digestive tract slows almost to a halt, which is why most women do not feel hungry during labor. While you should not eat solids, it is important to keep drinking clear fluids, and you can eat a little Jell-o if a semi-solid texture is what you want. Because of its salt content, broth might make you thirsty and should be avoided.

Everyone experiences certain events in life that stick securely in the mind, even years after they occurred. I will never forget those early hours in labor with my first baby, feeling pretty miserable physically, but absolutely elated; in some ways loving my large pregnant tummy and voluptuous breasts, but also wanting to deliver and be rid of them; ready for labor, I thought, but scared. Through my myriad emotions, somehow my husband, lover, and more important, my best friend, stood by me, never left my side. Those early hours remain so special to me—being together, seeking a cab at six A.M., teaching another woman being admitted in labor how to do her breathing (she hadn't taken any classes) even as I tried to cope with labor in the admitting office by doing my own breathing exercises. I remember my husband laughing softly at this and saying, "You just can't take the nurse out of you, can you?" It was nice to share that laugh—we all needed it that morning.

CHAPTER REVIEW

SIGNS OF LABOR

Show: loss of "mucous plug," a viscous, tablespoon-size blob streaked with blood, passed from the vagina usually about 24–48 hours prior to the onset of contractions

Rupture of membranes: resulting in the loss of a gush to a trickle of slightly chlorine-smelling, amniotic fluid; may or may not be followed by contractions

Contractions: felt at first as erratic, cramplike contractions (much like menstrual cramps) that progress or intensify, becoming stronger, lasting longer, and/or coming more often

COPING WITH EARLY LABOR

Go to a suspenseful movie to keep your mind off contractions
Take a relaxing bath and drink some wine or beer to determine
   whether it's real labor
Drink only clear fluids once contractions begin to progress
Catnap between contractions to stay well rested
Get your husband home from work to keep you distracted
Don't begin to Lamaze breathe until you can no longer walk, talk,
   or smile through a contraction
Call your doctor to discuss your situation once you've timed con-
   tractions for a few hours
Don't tell your friends and family you're in labor—they'll only
   worry
Practice your relaxation techniques during early contractions

13

Be Ready for Back Labor,
Should It Occur

"*B*ack labor" can occur *at any point in labor,* depending on
the baby's position. Some women experience it from start
to finish, some for a few hours, others not at all. However, since
25 percent of all laboring women have back labor to some degree,
you need to know how to cope with it.

I have heard back labor described more than once as "a kick
in the back by a horse!" The pain lingers between contractions,
too, so that until the baby either turns his head into the proper
position or is delivered, there's always discomfort. Fortunately,
should you experience back labor, there are relief measures that
have proved helpful. It is useful to first understand exactly how
the baby's position can cause this kind of uncomfortable labor.

Earlier, we saw how the baby changes positions as he passes
through the mother's pelvis. The normal presentation of the baby's head is in the well-flexed position, looking toward the mother's back (see opposite). Although he enters your pelvis looking
toward your side, his head gradually turns to look at your spine
in order to pass through your bony pelvis in the most efficient
way. Normally, as he delivers, he pivots up under your pubic bone
and with wide-open eyes looks up into the world.

This almost universal sequence of a baby's head entering the pelvis sideways, turning, and then pivoting at delivery was for generations an enigma in obstetrics. Today, with accurate examination in labor, the reason for this precise maneuver is well understood. The widest diameter on entering the pelvis is sideways, but deeper into it, two bony prominences on either side put the widest diameter on a vertical plane. The entire maneuver is a perfect demonstration of physics in action: forcing an object through the pathway of least resistance.

Seventy-five percent of all babies pass beautifully through the pelvis in this fashion, but for the baby whose head is in the occiput posterior position (the back of the baby's skull to the posterior side of the mother) the progression is quite different. He enters the pelvis properly, but then his head begins to turn so that his face is looking up, toward the pubic bone, instead of down. Usually the head of a baby in the posterior position is not very

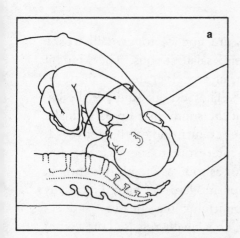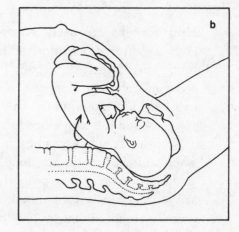

(a) *A normal presentation. With an occiput position* (b) *your baby will be facing up, exerting pressure on your back, but will hopefully rotate into the proper positions* (c, d, e) *as labor progresses.*

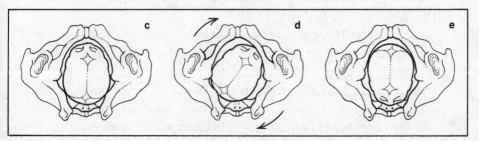

well flexed. This, and his position, are what produce "back labor": his head presses against the sacrum with each contraction.

Although during labor one out of four babies assumes the occiput posterior position partially or completely, only one out of ten actually delivers in that position, looking right up into the doctor's face. (These babies are often referred to in the delivery room as "sunny side up.") More typically, a baby in the posterior position will suddenly turn his head (probably due to a forceful contraction), and just as suddenly all back pain will go away.

Some babies get stuck in the posterior position, perhaps because the mother's pelvis cannot accommodate the head for delivery in this position and contractions aren't forceful enough to help him to turn. If this should happen to you, your doctor may decide to use forceps at the time of delivery to gently turn the baby's head, rather than having you labor for hours without making progress.

How forceps are used. Forceps are not ice tongs. Bill Cosby gives a better description of them: salad spoons. The kind of forceps used for a first baby's head are elongated in shape to accommodate that elongated head. They do not squeeze the baby's head but rather, in the case of the sunny-side-up baby, make space around the baby's head so he can turn and can be delivered.

With sunny-side-up babies, it is interesting to see what happens when a forceps rotation is done, for as soon as the head is turned, at the *very moment* it is properly positioned, the baby practically shoots out like a cannonball, confirming that he was, indeed, literally caught in that spot. When he is finally released, he comes through with ease (for more on forceps, see page 234).

Vacuum extraction may be used to turn a sunny-side-up baby (see also page 234).

Although as labor progresses most babies correct their position without assistance by the time of delivery, it is reassuring to know that forceps or a vacuum extractor are available to minimize trauma to the baby if needed by correcting his position or speeding the delivery. If your delivery warrants their use, be glad they are available and trust your doctor's expertise in this decision.

COMFORT MEASURES FOR BACK LABOR

If back labor occurs, there are several measures that you can try.

For many women, **counterpressure** is effective, with the help of the coach. Get into a comfortable sitting position in bed or on a chair. Gentlemen, make two fists, slip them behind your wife's back, and press hard where it helps. She'll tell you exactly where to press ("a little higher on the right," "more toward the center") and then she will probably say, "Press harder, *harder!*" Just when you feel your fists will pop through her belly, a little smile of relief will creep across her face and she will say, "Perfect. Now keep it that way, please!" You'll probably be so delighted to be able to offer her this relief, you would gladly do it forever. But as the time passes and your arms and hands become so tired that you just cannot sustain the pressure any longer, you will need to substitute something for them.

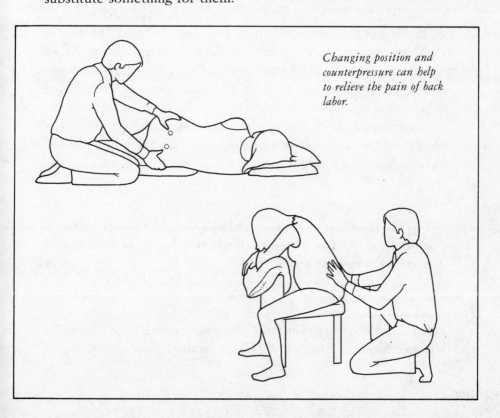

Changing position and counterpressure can help to relieve the pain of back labor.

Gentlemen, use tennis balls—two of them—to replace your fists behind your wife's back when you need to rest your arms. They will not offer quite as much counterpressure as your fists, but at least they will offer some. One mother commented, "The balls didn't help at all, but the round side of the can was perfect!" Along with the balls, then, pack a hard tennis-ball can in your Lamaze bag (page 143) should you want to give that a try.

The degree of counterpressure that's required to offer relief in back labor is intense—you might have bruises on your back the day after delivery, but they will quickly fade.

Cold or heat application may also bring relief. When back labor occurs in early labor, heat seems to be soothing until contractions become sharp; then cold seems more helpful, numbing the area.

A hard, cold pack also offers counterpressure. The best kind of cold application to help relieve back pain is the freeze-it pack or ice pack, a plastic rectangular slab about the size of a paperback book filled with a blue petroleum-based substance that, when placed in the freezer, absorbs the cold and then stays frozen for six to eight hours. (Keep it in your freezer until you are ready to go to the hospital, then pack it in your Lamaze bag.) The cold is numbing and the hard surface provides counterpressure. Avoid using cans for ice packs—the metal edges are uncomfortable—and be sure to wrap the ice pack in a hand towel before tucking it in behind your wife's back.

Sometimes a **change of position** to remove the weight of the baby from the spine can offer relief. Lean forward over a desk or chair or lie on your side with your top leg propped up on a pillow.

Tip for the Coach: With the baby's weight off her spine, give your wife a vigorous back rub or exert counterpressure where it hurts.

If every other position fails, try getting down on all fours. If you are thinking, Forget it, I'll never do that, especially in one of those skimpy little hospital gowns that will expose my bottom—never say never! If that position relieves the pain of back labor, you won't mind the awkwardness of it a bit.

Acupressure seems to be effective for some women. There is a spot on the inner side of the heel, just above the sole and directly down from the ankle bone that, when slowly pressed, sends a stimulus along the nerve pathway utilized by the lower back as it sends a pain message to the brain. If slow, rhythmic pressure is applied to this spot on the heels, the pathway is utilized to its fullest capacity, blocking the pain stimuli from the lower back.

You must locate that spot on your heel before labor begins. Poke around the inner heel area until you feel a sudden, sharp twinge, almost like the sensation you feel when you hit the funny bone at your elbow. Show your husband where it is and, once you have it, gentlemen, stand at the foot of the bed, a thumb on each spot, and slowly and *firmly* press, then slowly and completely release, press, release, in a steady rhythm. (It usually takes a good two to three minutes worth of strong, pulsating squeezes, working both feet, to bring relief, so don't give up before then.) The fingers on the outside of the heel exert some pressure, but the thumb points are to be where the most pressure is exerted. If you have a backache one evening (after a long day sitting in an office chair, for example), let your husband try this acupressure technique and see if you feel any relief. Many couples swear by it not only for back labor but also for any other kind of low-back pain.

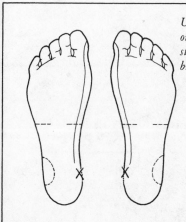

Using acupressure points on your feet, applying slow, strong pressure may also bring back labor relief.

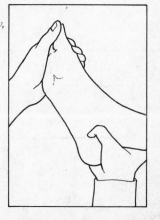

CHAPTER REVIEW

WHAT TO TRY FOR BACK LABOR

- Counterpressure
  partner's fists
  forceful back rub
  tennis balls
  tennis-ball can

- Cold Application
  freeze-it pack

- Change of Position
  lean forward when sitting
  lie on the side with top leg bent up
  get down on all fours

- Acupressure
  direct, slow, pulsating pressure on tingly heel spots

14

Stage One, Phase Two: Active Labor

*A*s labor progresses the mild, aching contractions of early labor give way to the sharper, stronger contractions of the second, or *active,* phase of labor.

In active labor, contractions are usually three to five minutes apart, timed from the beginning of one to the beginning of the next. They usually last about sixty seconds and feel quite sharp and painful at the twenty- to thirty-second peak. During this phase, which lasts about three to five hours in women having first babies and one to three hours with subsequent babies, the cervix is dilating from about three centimeters to about eight.

There will be no fanfare to signal the onset of active labor, since the whole of labor is a gradual progression, but you will know you are there because when the contractions become stronger, they also become sharper.

Gentlemen, try to keep your wife relaxed at home and doing breathing technique #1 until she is well into active labor. It would be best to arrive at the hospital when she's five or six centimeters dilated.

Author's Note: Evaluate your Lamaze techniques. It would be great if you have been so well entertained during the first phase of labor that you haven't even started to use your breathing tech-

niques yet; but if you are like most of us mortals, you have probably been using slow-paced chest breathing, Lamaze Technique #1 (page 125), for several hours and find that now, because it no longer seems to fit the pattern of the contractions, it's barely helping. It is time to move on to modified-paced breathing, Lamaze Technique #2, page 131.

Watch for signs of hyperventilation as you do the breathing. This happens when the body is deprived of carbon dioxide, and it can leave you feeling light-headed and dizzy. (For remedies, see page 128.) Gentlemen, your wife could hyperventilate in labor without realizing it. You will know this is happening if all of a sudden she begins complaining of painful cramping in her fingers or toes. Quickly remind her to cup her hands over her nose and mouth, or give her a little brown bag to hold over her mouth, while you vigorously massage the appendages. Those cramps can be dreadful!

It is usually in active labor that you begin to feel flushed and start to perspire, working hard with the contractions. Some powder or cornstarch as you effleurage (see page 127) will be soothing. When I was in nursing school, we were taught that talc was not to be used because it contained asbestos. Cornstarch was preferred until it was found to be a good medium for bacterial growth—so talc was suddenly back in favor, having lost its bad reputation by then. Today it's claimed that bacteria grow in cornstarch only when accompanied by moisture. I say use whatever you like!

During the beginning of the active labor phase, you will probably still be getting ready for the hospital, packing or rearranging the final items in your suitcase (see page 147), sipping ginger ale, and stopping to do breathing technique #1 or #2 (pages 125 and 131) when a contraction hits. Be sure to keep your bag of supplies for labor (see page 143) separate from your suitcase, as your suitcase will be going to your room and you won't see it until after you deliver.

By now you will probably have spoken to your doctor, maybe several times, especially if early labor has been slow to progress into active labor.

Let us say you are having good strong contractions, perhaps

the beginning of active labor, it is the middle of the night, and your doctor tells you it's time to come in. Let me warn you about taxicabs in large metropolitan cities like New York or car services in the suburbs, before you make the mistake of telling them to be quick because you are about to give birth to a baby. When I worked nights in labor and delivery, most of the couples I admitted had the same complaint, "We couldn't get a taxi! There were plenty of them but none of them would stop for us." It did not take much to figure out why this was so. Cab drivers know as soon as they see a *very* pregnant woman clutching a slightly nervous, impatient-looking gentleman, who in turn clutches a small suitcase, that the destination is clearly the hospital, and rather than chancing a delivery in the back of their taxicab, they speed off into the night. To avoid being passed by, gentlemen, your wife needs to stand unobtrusively in the doorway of the nearest building while you, working solo at curbside, secure the cab. Get partway in, hold the door open for your wife, and have her get in. If you happen to glance at the driver's face as your wife does her breathing you'll probably see panic, and it will probably be the fastest taxi ride you will ever experience.

> "*When we got to the hospital the resident examined me and said I was dilated one-and-a-half centimeters, the amount I was dilated four days earlier. I was hoping to be five centimeters. She also said they were probably going to send me home. I thought I was doing so well up to this point, remaining calm and breathing and thinking I was halfway there, then when she told us this I thought I couldn't go on. I thought I could never do it and I wanted to cry. The doctor said we could stay and in two hours I would be examined again and if there was no change we would go home. When it was two hours later, the resident examined me and said she couldn't believe it. She had to examine me again to see if she had made a mistake. There was no mistake. I was seven-and-a-half centimeters and we were going upstairs. By the time we reached the labor room, I was ten centimeters and the doctor said three pushes and the baby would be out. I was shocked.*"

Gentlemen, en route to the hospital, your wife may decide she doesn't want to have this baby after all. That's normal. Encourage her to use her breathing techniques, support her efforts, and get her back on the track again. She now depends on your support and encouragement.

CHECKING IN AT THE HOSPITAL

Your first stop when you get to the hospital is the **admitting** office. All of your preregistration should have been completed in the final weeks of your pregnancy (usually by your doctor's office staff), but in case there might have been a mixup, have ready your medical insurance card and whatever papers you may have concerning your admission.

I highly recommend that you and your husband have a tour of the hospital at some earlier point during your pregnancy. Not only does the tour help make the hospital real, and therefore less intimidating, but it also helps eliminate the stress of having to find your way to admissions—you'll know exactly where to go when the time comes.

Admissions will need to register you before you proceed to the prep room or the labor-and-delivery suite. If it's difficult to cope with labor during admission procedures, don't worry about what people think. Simply say, "Just a minute, please, here's another contraction," and go right into your Lamaze breathing.

After admission information has been recorded, you'll be taken to the prep room where you will remain (many hospitals hook you up to a monitor) for about half an hour to an hour to evaluate the nature of your contractions and whether to send you home or up to labor and delivery. If your membranes have ruptured, you may have to ride a wheelchair, especially if the hall floors are marble. This is for your protection—and the hospital's—should you leak amniotic fluid onto the floor, slip, fall, break your neck, and sue. If your membranes have not ruptured, you can choose whether to walk or ride.

> *"Bob had missed the hospital tour because of work and when he had to bring the suitcases on his own, it turned out he didn't know where to go. The cab had dropped him off a block from the hospital and Bob proceeded to dash into every building looking for me. Once he found the hospital, he ran up to the eighth floor and couldn't find me. He finally arrived in the first-floor monitor room sweating profusely."*

In the prep room or labor-and-delivery suite, you will be greeted by a nurse who will ask you to undress and don a hospital gown that fastens down the back. Remember to take off your panties! It's difficult to deliver with them on—though it's not *impossible.* One of my students, an elegant French woman who lived on the West Side of Manhattan, went into driving labor at rush hour. She arranged to meet her husband at the hospital across town and quickly caught a cab. About halfway there, she realized the baby was being born. With her wonderful French accent she called out to the driver, "Ze baby is coming in ze panties!" He, unflappable as only a New York cabbie can be, responded, "What do you want me to do, lady, stop and take them off for you?"

In fact, she did have the baby in her panties—a soft, gentle catch for a newborn! If you are ever confronted with a similar situation, simply lie down on the back seat, begin the appropriate breathing, and once he is out and in your panties, scoop him up, wrap him in something warm, and continue to the hospital.

Undoubtedly you will *not* be bringing your newborn to the hospital but will proceed with the normal hospital admission routines instead. The nurse will ask you to give her a urine sample and then settle you into a bed. She will take your blood pressure and temperature, listen to your baby's heartbeat, and ask you some questions about your medical history and the progression of your labor. Remember to ask her to adjust the back of the bed to whatever angle feels best to you.

If your membranes have not ruptured, she will get you ready for your **first in-hospital vaginal exam**—which of course you await with great anticipation, hoping your labor is well under way. The exam might be with your own doctor or it may be with a resident if your doctor is not available. Put the soles of your feet together and let your knees flop apart so the nurse can spray the whole vaginal area with an antiseptic. It is usually cold and often brown, an iodine-base solution. (If you are not prepared for that red-brown color, after the first exam you will think you have hemorrhaged on the pad under your hips, so be ready for what you see. It's a shame no one seems to have been able to come up with another color!)

If your membranes have ruptured but labor has not begun, the vaginal exam will probably be postponed until you are in good labor.

Use your Lamaze breathing techniques (page 125) when you have your vaginal exams during labor and try to keep the rest of your body relaxed.

During your exam you will hear what by now are the familiar terms referring to the effacement or flattening out of the cervix, in percentages, and its dilation, in centimeters. You will also hear, perhaps for the first time, the "station" or depth of the baby in the pelvis, expressed in terms of from minus-four to plus-two, which means centimeters either above (−) or below (+) the two small pelvic spines. (See the top of page 100.)

As your doctor examines you, you may hear the term referring to the position of the baby's head, that is, which way he is facing. LOA is for left occiput anterior; LOP for the not-so-common left occiput posterior (see back labor, page 178). Listen for the position—it'll give you a clue about the kind of labor you may experience.

All through labor, you'll be examined periodically, not always by your own doctor but perhaps by a resident or nurse-midwife instead. Be sure to ask questions (as you did in the exams in your doctor's office) about how things are progressing—in terms that will elicit more than just "fine" for an answer. You might say, "How far dilated am I? What about effacement?" Hearing about the effacement is just as significant a clue as dilation: if your cervix is "paper thin," the dilation will probably go very quickly. If you were only two centimeters dilated, for example, it would be good news if at the same time you were 100 percent effaced! Ask each time about the position of the baby's head; it too indicates how he is progressing. All of this is important information about your labor and gives you clues to how you can handle it. Ask direct questions and you will get specific answers.

Generally, **shaving** the whole pubic area is no longer done. Some doctors request a "mini-prep" or "poodle cut," shaving only the area between the vagina and rectum, where an episiotomy (see page 232) would be done. Do not think that this shaving is something better done in the privacy of your own home. In an effort to be thorough, you would probably shave off more than your nurse would; she uses only two or three short, deft strokes of a disposable razor and it's done. Furthermore, since this is a difficult area to reach on yourself when nine months of baby is interfering with your view, you would probably do your *own* episiotomy while trying to do your mini-prep. Some doctors feel that shaving is altogether unnecessary. If you have your own views, discuss them with your doctor during one of your prenatal visits.

Enemas are often offered at this point. Obviously, if you have just had a good bowel movement or a bout of diarrhea (which along with throwing up are not uncommon at the onset of labor), tell the nurse and the enema will most likely be dispensed with. If on the other hand, you have not had a bowel movement for a while or you know you are constipated, you would be wise to say "yes, please" when she offers it: it is far better to have a small enema in labor than to have to worry about a hard bowel movement over a very sore episiotomy the day after delivery. Also, if you think you may have some natural inhibitions about the pushing urge (see page 225) when the baby is coming through the birth canal, you will feel much more confident during the process if you've had an enema beforehand.

The enema is often a small, disposable one (nothing like the red-rubber enema bag you may have encountered in childhood) or it may even be a suppository, so do not be anxious about it. The nurse will administer it to you as you lie on your left side, and if you feel a contraction beginning, tell her and she will stop until it is over. Once you have taken it, the nurse will show you to the bathroom and be sure that you stay in there a good ten minutes. I've seen many a mother who came zipping out of the bathroom and climbed back into her labor bed, certain that she was finished with the enema—only to find that en route from the prep room to the labor suite in the labor bed (usually right in the middle of a crowded elevator with everyone smiling at the mother-to-be), a strong contraction would begin and the baby's head would push against the rectal wall. She'd frantically realize she was not quite finished with the enema and wanted only to crawl right under the labor bed, dying of her embarrassment.

Some mothers consider giving themselves an enema at home. The problem with this is that you have no idea where you are in labor, and if you were six or seven centimeters dilated and gave yourself an enema, it might radically change the progress of your labor. By emptying the lower bowel and stimulating the uterus through its peristaltic movement, you could all of a sudden find yourself in transition or even close to delivery while you are still at home in the bathroom! If you need an enema at all, get it in the hospital.

Gentlemen, the ten-to-fifteen-minute interval when your wife is having an enema is the perfect time for you to go and eat, unless you feel you must be together *every* moment. (One husband insisted on such togetherness that he went with his wife right into that little stall in the bathroom. Not my favorite idea, but, again, *chacun à son gout!*) A good meal, a trip to the bathroom, a phone call or two now will have you comfortable and ready for spending four to six uninterrupted hours with your wife.

It is important not to go hungry during labor. For some reason, many men decide that "If she's not going to eat, neither will I!" Nonsense. If you don't eat, gentlemen, you really *will* faint, not from the birth but from hypoglycemia! You should plan to get out of that labor room every three or four hours. You will *need* to get away. Coaching is exhausting, and a fifteen-minute break for a bite to eat and a moment to yourself will help you return to the labor room a refreshed, *better* coach. Just alert the nurse: "Please stay with my wife until I get back in fifteen minutes." Some couples bring snacks for the husband in the goody bag, but be sure to check with your hospital about their policy on this;

food in the labor-and-delivery unit may not be allowed. It also seems a little unfeeling for you, gentlemen, to spread out the cold fried chicken and deviled eggs while your poor wife isn't allowed to eat and doesn't feel like eating.

The fetal monitor. Even if you have not previously had an electric fetal monitor in place to evaluate labor, once it has been determined that you really are in labor a monitor will probably be used throughout.

Fetal monitors display on a graph the baby's heartbeat and the strength of the uterine contractions. The external monitor is attached with two soft, pliable elastic belts. One holds the fetal-heart pickup disk in position, usually just above the pubic bone; the other holds a disk over the fundus, or top of the uterus, to register the tightening of the uterine muscle.

Sometimes an internal fetal monitor is put into place during a vaginal exam. A small plastic tube is slipped in between the baby's head and the cervix, to record the strength of contractions, and a tiny curled needle, inserted into the skin of the baby's scalp, in turn records the baby's electrocardiogram by way of a soft wire and transducer.

The internal fetal monitor is used only in special situations: if, for example, the baby were displaying heartbeat irregularities or occasional periods of mild fetal distress and your doctor wanted to get a more accurate reading of what was going on. Or, if there were twins, the upper twin might be put on the external monitor and the lower twin on the internal monitor. If a women were so obese that the baby's heart rate could not be picked up externally through her fat tissue, this again might warrant an internal fetal monitor. Whatever the medical reason, your doctor would explain in advance your own need for an internal monitor.

Some couples oppose the use of fetal monitors, claiming either that the belts are uncomfortable and confining or that the staff pays more attention to the monitoring equipment than to the mother. Having worked with monitors for many years now, I do not feel that either of these complaints is warranted. Belts have been perfected and can be adjusted to any size mother. Transducers and electrical monitoring components of these machines

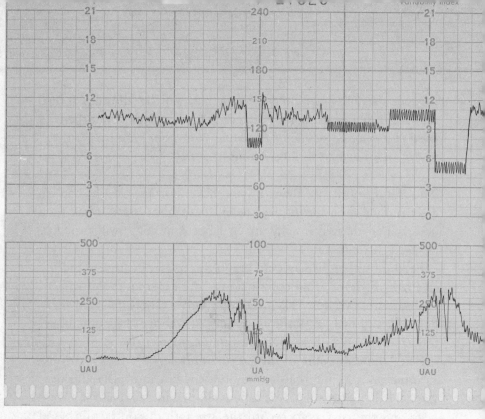

This monitor printout shows good active labor contractions with a fetal heart rate in the range of 120 to 150 beats per minute.

have also been perfected so that a mother can be in any position she wishes, and if her membranes have not ruptured she may walk from the bed to a nearby chair, as there is about six feet of wire from machine to mother. Newer equipment utilizes transistor components that are wireless. I've never seen anyone pay more attention to a machine than to a mother; but if you feel this is happening to you, be sure to tell the nurse.

The advantages of using a monitor far outweigh the minimal inconveniences involved. Most physicians routinely use them, when available, to be able to closely monitor what's going on with the baby. In the past, nurses could do nothing more than listen to the baby with a fetoscope about every ten minutes. If fetal distress should occur during the interim, the baby could be in distress for as long as ten minutes before it was recognized by the staff. With the monitor, distress is evident immediately.

It is probably true that with the increased use of fetal monitoring, the Caesarean birth rate in the United States has also in-

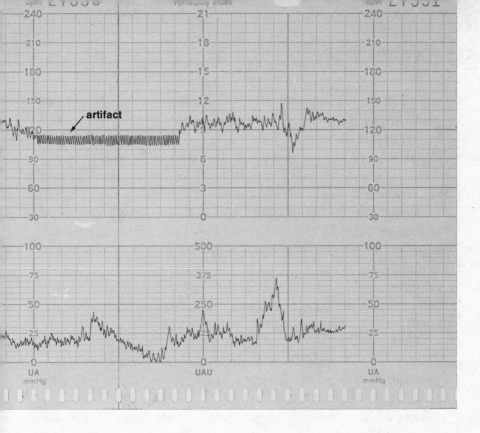

creased. When fetal distress is picked up, it is not always easy to determine exactly how much distress there is or exactly when a Caesarean is the best option. Your doctor will watch your baby's reactions to labor carefully. He may take a drop of blood from the baby's scalp transvaginally (similar to a finger stick you may have had) to help determine the extent of your baby's distress, should it become apparent. If there is still some question, he may ask for another physician to consult with him. The normal fetal heart rate is between 120 and 160 beats per minute; certainly if a baby's heart rate plummets to 60 beats per minute he should be delivered at once. But when a milder form of distress is exhibited, when it is not a matter of life or death, there is no way to know exactly what the effect of stress in labor will be on a baby—whether he's receiving adequate oxygenation, whether his intellectual capacity in later life will be diminished. The fetus can certainly tolerate lower levels of oxygen than an adult, which is undoubtedly one of nature's protective mechanisms, but when, *exactly* when, is the lowest level of tolerance reached? American obstetricians are sometimes criticized for acting hastily, or out of fear of potential lawsuits; I do not believe that is true. Although I have worked at only two hospitals, I have been with over five thousand couples in labor and delivery, and the decision to do a Caesarean section has never been taken lightly.

On the other hand, no matter how badly you may have wanted to deliver vaginally, if there's any question of fetal distress adversely affecting the baby's well-being, either now or much later in his life, there should be no hesitation about revising your own priorities and choosing the safest course, which may be Caesarean delivery. But certainly you take it as it comes, appreciating the monitor for bringing the baby's condition to everyone's attention.

Gentlemen, fetal monitors are of great assistance in coaching. The stylus on the machine begins to rise as the contraction begins (sometimes even a little before your wife begins to feel it), then peaks and declines. One woman in labor wanted her husband to tell her nothing about the contraction except when the peak was over, and I could see that he often said "The peak is over" before it really was. It had a wonderful calming effect and she coped beautifully with that cue.

One last word about monitors: be sure to ask the nurse to give you a basic understanding of yours. Monitors are only machines; they are not infallible and they are definitely capable of malfunctioning. While it is perfectly normal to see the baby's heart rate dip slightly after each contraction, you should not panic if all of a sudden the digital light on baby's monitor stops flashing, the "artifact" light flashes, and the stylus goes berserk. It does not mean something dreadful has happened to your baby; rather, the machine needs to be readjusted. The audio button can be turned up so you can hear that little *kerplunk, kerplunk* of the heartbeat. If that distracts you, the sound can be turned down.

> *"I watched the fetal monitor and could see the progression of the actual labor, the rise of the contractions, and Patty and I started breathing together."*

"Labor and birth were very intense. I expected the labor to be longer. I didn't need the stopwatch, as I could read the monitor across the room and gauge the length and the peaks of each contraction." (Father)

ARRIVING ON THE LABOR AND DELIVERY SUITE

Once you are admitted into the labor-and-delivery area and the fetal monitor is in place, you will probably feel more relaxed and better able to handle your contractions. Chances are, you will be in your own labor room with your husband; but the rooms are not soundproof, and it can be disconcerting at first to hear a woman in the labor room next to you moaning or groaning or even yelling. Remember that each woman will have a different reaction to labor, some of it influenced by her own cultural background. One woman may have been taught that she should never scream, but instead should "bite the bullet," while another may use a scream or a yell to "act the way she is supposed to."

Some hospitals require that once you are in good labor, glucose water be administered through tubing into a vein in your arm. Although the IV is started with a needle, the needle is then removed and a tiny, flexible plastic tube, the size of a half-inch-long pencil lead, is left in its place and secured by a piece of tape so you can move your arm freely.

For many years, *intravenous glucose* was not routinely begun until a woman had been in good labor for about eight hours. This was too long to wait, judging from its beneficial effects, once started. The way it transforms most women from a state of limp exhaustion to one of renewed vitality always reminded me of watching a time-lapse film of a blooming flower: from quiet bud to brilliant blossom in twenty minutes. I see no reason to object to this intravenous drip, although some women do, claiming it's not necessary. Certainly the fluid and glucose can only help you to keep up your energy and cope with labor. Aside from the initial needle stick, it's painless.

There is another good reason for the IV. If a true *emergency* Caesarean birth were necessary, which is rare but can happen, the intravenous would already be in place, a ready route for anesthesia. When time is crucial, a gain of thirty to ninety seconds (the time it would probably take to start the intravenous) could really make a difference.

The intravenous is usually started when you are in active labor, four to six centimeters dilated, and it stays in until an hour or two after a vaginal delivery, in case there should be excessive bleeding immediately postpartum. While heavy bleeding is not a usual occurrence, if it should happen, some Pitocin could be put directly into that intravenous drip to help the uterus contract and control the bleeding. Once the medication and fluid were absorbed, the IV could be removed. In the case of a Caesarean birth, the intravenous stays in longer (see page 259).

Once you are in good labor, your doctor will stop in at frequent intervals, depending on his schedule that day, to see how you are doing. He may be away for one to two hours to do a hysterectomy, come by for fifteen minutes, then be off again, this time to the office to see a few patients for an hour, and then back again to you. Once you are eight centimeters dilated, he'll be there until the delivery, but in the meantime, it's the nurse whom you will count on for what you need during those long hours of labor. Most women develop a close rapport with their nurse, and there is good reason to expect this. Because labor and delivery is a critical-care area, the nurses on duty are usually highly skilled as well as sympathetic.

Talk to your nurse; let her know what helps you most. She will not only be there for your general welfare as well your baby's, but she will help you with the breathing and give you, gentlemen, guidelines as to how best to help your wife.

Gentlemen, coaching your wife in active labor is not easy. The signs of fatigue soon become apparent, and she may be feeling discouraged that she's not progressing as quickly as she had hoped. You must support her now; encourage and compliment her and try to anticipate her needs.

> "*I was there coaching, wetting washcloths: the all-around utility infielder. Also, artist. Barb and I forgot to pack a picture to focus on, so I had to reproduce sections of the Sistine Chapel on a paper towel.*"

Ice chips are usually available and might be a welcome refreshment.

For many women, a washcloth becomes the most treasured item from the Lamaze "goody" bag—dipped in cool water and held against the forehead or lips where it can be sucked a bit to wet the throat. Just be sure the washcloth you bring from home is an old, well-worn one. Before going into labor with our first baby, I bought a bright new orange one at the five-and-ten and packed it into my Lamaze bag, thinking it would be a cheery reminder of my husband's college colors. When I needed it in labor, my husband dipped the washcloth in cold water and laid it across my forehead. First the orange dye ran everywhere; then when I put it against my mouth, it tasted dreadful, probably still full of "stay fluffy" chemicals that had never been washed out. When I asked one of the nurses for a disposable washcloth, the only kind available, it tasted even worse.

As transition approaches, gentlemen, you will notice that your wife has more and more difficulty coping with the stronger and longer contractions. Help her to adjust her breathing. Talk to the nurse about how to make your wife comfortable; maybe she can suggest something you have not thought of. Remind your wife that she's well beyond the halfway point now—she's terrific and in a few hours she'll be a mother!

Tips for the Coach for timing contractions:
Listen for your wife's cleansing breath
Check your watch or stopwatch and begin timing
Watch her, give her encouragement and pointers
Remind her to: focus on her spot; keep her breathing

light, rhythmical, and not too fast; effleurage or keep
hands relaxed in lap, palms up
As you hear her take her final cleansing breath, say,
"Contraction over—take a deep breath, you did a great
job, now relax"
If there's a monitor, tell her when you see the contraction
begin to subside

CHAPTER REVIEW

COPING WITH ACTIVE LABOR

Assume a comfortable position between contractions to conserve
energy
Try to stay relaxed
Go to the hospital if you're not there yet
Post your focal point (page 126) at eye level
Discuss comfort measures with your nurse:
Need another pillow?—Try lying on your side—Rinse your
mouth—Wipe your face with a cool cloth—How about a back
rub?—Put some lip balm on your lips—Powder your neck and
tummy to feel refreshed
Discuss your progress with your doctor
Remind your husband to take a short break to eat and get away
Adjust your breathing to the pattern of your contractions
Watch your contractions on the monitor if it helps make the time
go faster
Remember to urinate every few hours

You're doing great—you're halfway there!

15

Medication in Labor—It's There if You Need It

*I*f you are feeling great in labor, well in control and in need of nothing more than some encouragement, that's fabulous. On the other hand, as contractions become sharper and stronger, you may feel the need for some kind of medication to help you relax or to "take the edge off." Be honest with yourself and ready to discuss it with your doctor or nurse, who can help you make decisions with the added dimension of professional experience.

Ideally, medication should be a joint decision. I think you should feel perfectly free at any time in labor to say, "This is hurting a lot more than I imagined. Is there medication available for me?" But in asking the question, you must also be ready to accept the answer: "It's too early. You are only one centimeter dilated and we really can't give you anything right now."

Gentlemen, if it's too early to consider medication, help your wife by reviewing your childbirth techniques and other tactics for coping (listed at the end of chapter 14) and see if they cannot be adjusted to further help her along. This should be your first option, ladies, certainly before taking medication. Do everything you can with your "Lamaze tools" (page 116) to better help you cope. Change your position or vary your breathing. Maybe a quick, vigorous back rub between contractions would enable you to relax a little better, or moving your focal point closer, or

> *"I refused to take any drugs during labor or birth. I wanted to feel what borning a human was like. I didn't want it muffled through some drug. I didn't want to wonder at age eighty-five what it felt like; I wanted to know in my bones what centuries of women have known. So you might say I was highly motivated in approaching the pain. I also had an excellent coach in my husband, who was willing to see me march through this particular line of fire as far as I wanted to go. He too gave birth to our daughter."*

speeding up your breathing a little. You can always consider medication if other measures don't alleviate your distress.

Certainly the more you know how to help yourself and the better prepared you are to handle labor, the less medication (if any) you will need—and the least amount is, of course, best for you and the baby. But keeping in mind that in a group of ten women having first babies there will probably be only two who have *no* medication, it's far better to judge the pros and cons of Demerol and epidural or caudal anesthesia at the end of your pregnancy than in the midst of active labor when you are coping with powerful sixty-second contractions coming every two or three minutes. Then, if the time comes in labor when some medication seems to be a suitable option, you'll be knowledgeable and ready to discuss your situation with your doctor, husband, and nurse.

When you think of relieving or reducing pain in general, there are three ways to do it: general anesthesia, local anesthesia, or analgesia.

If you have ever had general surgery, a tonsillectomy or appendectomy, for example, you were probably given a **general anesthetic,** such as sodium Pentothal, which put you to sleep for the duration of the procedure, and when you woke up in the recovery room, you had no memory of the surgeon's making the incision or performing the operation. This is what most people think of in connection with anesthesia.

In childbirth, because it would take away labor by totally relaxing the uterus, the use of general anesthesia is limited to Caesarean births and usually only to emergency Caesareans. So if your mother or mother-in-law has told you she had a "general" as soon as she arrived at the hospital in early labor, and found out the next morning when she awakened that she "had had a lovely baby boy," let's clarify that misconception now.

In the nineteen forties, fifties, and even the sixties, a medication called "twilight sleep" was frequently administered to women who wanted to be "put out" in labor and/or delivery. Uneducated concerning every aspect of childbirth, they found the progression of their labor as it intensified to be so painful that by transition they were ready to quit, thinking birth would be even worse, and thus begged to be "spared the agony."

Given by injection, twilight sleep is not a general anesthetic at all but rather a combination of Demerol (a relaxant) and scopolamine (an amnesiac). Those ladies who were given twilight sleep experienced all the sensations of the contractions and reacted to them, were awake throughout the process—in short, felt all the pain of labor and delivery—but afterward they forgot it. They simply *forgot* that they were ever in labor or delivery at all!

If you should choose to be "put out" during labor, twilight sleep is probably what your doctor will prescribe, because a true general anesthetic such as sodium Pentothal would, as mentioned before, simply stop your labor. Once you've received the injection of twilight sleep you will function on a subconscious level. Between contractions, the scopolamine will probably make you babble about things that are on your mind or the Demerol will put you to sleep. One mother I was with years ago routinely gesticulated through labor; when I asked her what she was doing she responded, "I'm filing." Another mother would look over at me and say, "Add more white. Not enough, dear. Better." For nine hours, she told me to stir this stuff. The next morning when I went to see her she looked at me suspiciously, as if she were thinking, "I've seen you somewhere before." I explained who I was and said I just had to ask her what the yellow-and-white mixture was. "Ah," she replied, "you mean the paint for the baby's room? The painters don't have the color quite right—but how did *you* know that?" So whatever it is that's on your mind, under the influence of scopolamine, you discuss it.

When a contraction does come, you react to the pain, but you would probably describe what you felt as severe gas pains. One mother who had had twilight sleep, would, with each contraction, sit bolt upright, cross her legs tailor fashion, and turn to me with a serious expression and say, "Excuse me, miss, but do you have any Kaopectate?"—a very appropriate comment when one is functioning on a subconscious level and feeling pressure on the lower bowel.

Twilight sleep was extremely popular for a while, but it is not used very much today. Too many women either felt an eerie void concerning the hours of their labor and delivery or remembered bits and pieces of what they described as a terrible nightmare. All one mother registered after her labor was over was that she wasn't pregnant anymore. Another woman, believing she was actively participating in a tennis tournament all through labor, had to be restrained from smacking her hand hard into the cement wall next to her labor bed. The next day she could remember nothing except that she had had one arm "tied down." It's gruesome to recall only fragments from the subconscious—and certainly much better to be "present," aware and coping and able to say, later, "Yes, it did hurt but my husband coached me through my breathing techniques," or "I had the epidural," or whatever. At least the experience is a "real" part of you instead of some strange, dreamlike episode lost in time.

There is yet another consideration: the nursing staff generally has no problem being with a woman who is in twilight sleep, but it's very upsetting to see someone you love experience pain and react to it subconsciously by strange behavior or constant disjointed conversation, such as talking about yellow paint for nine hours. Therefore, if twilight sleep is the medication you choose, your husband will probably be asked to go to the visitors' room and perhaps check in every hour or so to see how you were progressing.

Today, local anesthesia seems to be the choice of women who

> *"The low point of labor came about three and a quarter hours after labor began. Demerol had been administered to Amy but it had not yet taken effect. The pain seemed unbearable and inescapable. Amy suggested she might prefer to be 'knocked out' or given a spinal. The labor nurse, the attending resident, and I discouraged her. The feeling passed in about five minutes."*

want to remain awake but free of pain to witness the birth of the baby. A full discussion of local anesthesia follows, but let us take the options as they come and first consider the use of analgesics, as this may be all you really need (if anything) to help you along.

Analgesia is a systemic relaxant that reduces pain—does not eliminate it—while you are awake. Nothing is numbed. Aspirin, Demerol, and morphine, for example, are analgesics.

The analgesic used most often in labor is Demerol. Demerol is a synthetic narcotic that gets into your entire system and into the baby's system as well, although in a filtered form. If you are given Demerol too early in labor, contractions will just peter out. If you get it very late, at the end of transition, by the time it is absorbed the baby will be the one to experience the relaxing effect intended, not you. If an analgesic is needed, Demerol is best administered in active labor so that the mother benefits from the effect but it then wears off before birth and neither she nor the baby are sleepy. Ideally, the baby should be alert and wide awake when he starts to breathe on his own.

Demerol is available in varying dosages of anywhere from 25 mg. to 100 mg. and is injected either into the muscles of your buttocks or into a vein in your arm. Since an intramuscular injection takes five to ten minutes to reach full effectiveness and remains in your system for about two hours, it would be the preferred route for a woman in active labor.

Demerol does not eliminate the pain of the contractions. It only takes the edge off and, more important, helps you relax.

Tip for the Coach: Watch your wife closely in active labor. If you notice that she lies tense between contractions, anticipating the next one and unable to relax no matter how much encouragement you give, probably what would help her is a small amount of Demerol.

There are certain circumstances in which the beneficial effects of Demerol in labor are immediately evident. I've seen women in good, strong labor, with contractions every two to three minutes lasting sixty seconds, who get to five or six centimeters and just seem to be *stuck* there—contractions still coming but everything else on hold—while they lie in the labor bed tense all over. There is a reason for this. No matter how prepared you are for labor and delivery, it is still a stressful experience and your body responds to it by producing adrenaline. This normal defense mechanism is, unfortunately, a cervical constrictor—just what you *don't* want pumping through your body during labor! So with Demerol to relax her and decrease the adrenaline production, the mother who was stuck at five or six centimeters often opens to ten centimeters in one hour, whereas it would probably have taken three without the relaxant.

When the possibility of medication is being considered, your doctor will first examine you to see how far along you are and decide what, if any, medication would be helpful. If it turns out that a little Demerol is in order, it is important to let your doctor or your attending nurses know how you generally react to medication in an effort to determine how much of it should be administered.

If you've ever had Demerol post-operatively, the dose you got was undoubtedly intended to help you fall asleep. In labor, that will not happen during contractions. You may fall asleep *between* contractions and that might sound like a lovely idea, but the problem is that instead of being aware of the beginning of the contraction, getting on top of it, doing the breathing, coping with it, feeling like you are in control, you awaken from a deep drug-induced sleep at the peak, with a lightning bolt of pain and no time to get on top of it. You've *got* to stay on top of your contractions. One woman who did get a little too much Demerol and found herself falling asleep made up a system with her husband that seemed to work well. He watched the monitor closely and as soon as he saw the stylus of the fetal monitor begin to rise, indicating the beginning of a contraction, he would say firmly and loudly, "Contraction begins." Not only would she wake up just in time, but because they had practiced with that cue, she would also start right in with her breathing.

> *"I never changed my breathing—always a pant—and it got difficult even doing that. I had Demerol for about half an hour and all it seemed to do was give me a headache behind my eyes."*

If you are exhausted, have a horrendous cold, or know that you're always knocked out for the day when you take a mere aspirin, you should *tell the nurse.* These factors influence your reactions to the drug, and it is far better to get a little less Demerol than to get so much that you fall asleep between contractions.

Demerol may be contraindicated in your situation. If you were suddenly to go into labor when you were thirty-six weeks pregnant, your doctor would probably say, "We won't be able to give you any Demerol because you will deliver a baby who is small and whose lung maturity is not that of a full-term infant. There will undoubtedly be some breathing difficulty due to his prematurity and so, regardless of where you are in labor, we don't want to take any chances of depressing his respiratory efforts by making him sleepy."

Local anesthesia, numbing the body from the waist down, is another method of pain relief in labor. Administered by injection, it blocks the nerve pathways that transmit pain signals to the brain from the pelvic area, and has virtually no effect on the baby. The obvious advantages of having local anesthesia are that it won't make you groggy or sleepy, affect the progress of your labor (if

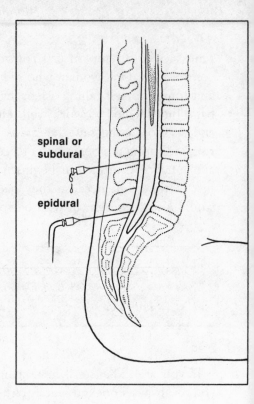

spinal or
subdural

epidural

*With an epidural the needle does not
penetrate the dura as with a subdural
or spinal.*

given at the proper time), or dull the baby's natural resources at
birth.

There are several ways of administering local anesthesia: by a
saddle block, spinal, or subdural (the "three S's") or by an epidural
or caudal. Each requires special skill. The difference between the
two groups has to do with the depth the needle penetrates into
the spinal column.

The spinal cord is protected by a tough, fibrous coat called the
dura. With a saddle block, spinal, or subdural, the needle penetrates the dura as it injects the anesthesic agent. You may have
heard that one of the aftereffects of a spinal is a "spinal headache."
No one knows why this happens. Perhaps a few drops of spinal
fluid leak out of the tiny hole that remains when the needle is
removed and, because the spinal-fluid system is very sensitive,
the minuscule change in pressure results in a headache. Today
the needles used are ultrathin, and the chances of experiencing
this unpleasant aftereffect have been drastically reduced by taking

a little blood out of the arm and injecting it at the spot where the needle penetrates the dura, sealing that tiny hole.

With the epidural or caudal anesthesia, the needle does not penetrate the dura, but instead enters the epidural space between the muscle layer and the dura. Both the epidural and the caudal are administered below the spinal cord, so the needle cannot damage the spinal cord. Of course, there are nerves in the area, and if the needle touched one, you would feel that "funny-bone sensation," with a twinge going down into your legs.

The caudal (explained below) lasts about an hour and is usually administered at the very end of labor, while the continuous epidural can be started in women who are dilated at least five or six centimeters (four to five centimeters with second babies) and in good labor—any earlier than that would risk slowing down labor.

To gauge whether you are far enough along for an epidural, your doctor may do an internal exam at the peak of one of your contractions. Uncomfortable as it may be, this is the best time to get the widest cervical measurement as the baby is pressing down hard on the cervix.

Although the continuous epidural is started with a needle, the needle is withdrawn and replaced with very fine, flexible plastic tubing about the size of a pencil lead which is taped to the back so it will stay in place. The tubing is soft and pliable, and you can lie on it in a comfortable position without blocking the flow of the anesthesia. With a continuous epidural, more medication can be given every hour, if needed, which would probably be the case if you were five centimeters dilated and had five centimeters to go.

As the epidural begins to take effect, a tingling sensation begins in the toes, feet, legs, and moves gradually up to about navel height. Once you're numb from the waist down, you can move your feet at will, but if you tried to stand, you'd fall down. The legs are heavy and floppy; as one mother described it, like tree trunks.

The great advantage of an epidural, caudal, or spinal is that with a difficult delivery or even a Caesarean birth you can still be awake at the birth.

The greatest disadvantage is that there is no urge to push. When the cervix is fully dilated, most women feel a sudden, overwhelming sensation that makes them, almost involuntarily, want to bear down and push the baby out. Without that sensation, pushing can be ineffective.

Some women who have epidurals require forceps deliveries because they are unable to push properly, but this does not have to be the case: it may be difficult to push well, but it can be done and you can certainly give it a try. Frequently, the epidural is timed to wear off just as the pushing (which is a *much less* painful stage than transition) begins, and that urge to push returns in full force.

There is often a slight drop in blood pressure while you are anesthetized epidurally, which could mean a slight decrease in blood flow to the placenta. For those women who have an elevated blood pressure at the end of pregnancy, this may actually be beneficial. In any case you will notice the nurse monitoring your blood pressure closely.

If the epidural sounds like the perfect solution when labor becomes more than you bargained for, remember that it may not be appropriate for you—if you've had back surgery, for example, or a back injury.

Epidural anesthesia will not usually be given with a sunny-side-up baby (see page 101), either, because when the muscles in the pelvis are relaxed (as they would be with an epidural or caudal), they cannot assist in turning the baby's head, and your doctor may want to wait for this to happen before he gives you any anesthesia.

Finally, epidurals (and caudals) are not always effective. The one I had with our first baby offered wonderful relief for three hours and then it just stopped working—as hard as the anesthesiologist tried, by "jiggling" the tubing and administering more medication, it never did work again. After the baby was born and the tubing was removed, a small kink was discovered; unseen until then, and undoubtedly the source of the problem.

Some women find that while the epidural brings pain relief on one side, the other side is not affected by the anesthetic at all. Or there is a "hot spot" of pain, apparently due to the medication spreading unevenly over the area. In that case, you may be tilted

> *"After having contractions every two to six minutes for fourteen hours, I was naturally quite interested in whatever medication I could get. The nurse in the downstairs labor room said I couldn't get any medication until I was in the* upstairs *labor room and I couldn't get to the upstairs labor room because there was a delivery of triplets that was occupying everyone on the floor. I wanted to throttle that nurse! Eventually I did make it upstairs and, to whomever invented the epidural, thank you, thank you, a million times,* thank you!"

a bit in the hope that gravity will move the medication into the desired area.

A caudal is similar to an epidural, but it is administered by injection lower in the back, at the base of the spinal column. One injection lasts about an hour. Thus, if you're eight or nine centimeters dilated with only an hour or so to go before full dilation and pushing, a caudal may be the preferred choice. It might also be given in anticipation of a difficult forceps delivery (see page 234).

A paracervical block can also be given for pain relief. As the name implies, this local anesthetic is injected into the cervix, at four locations, to numb it. Obstetricians need special training to perform this technique, which must be done quickly and efficiently during a vaginal exam—though not usually after eight centimeters' dilation because the cervical edge is too thin at that point. Since the pain of labor is felt in the dilating cervix, with a paracervical block you would be virtually pain free for one to two hours. There is often a very slight and temporary slowing of the baby's heart rate for a few minutes after administration, perhaps indicative of the medication getting into the baby's system, and for that reason some doctors prefer other medications.

Whatever kind of local anesthesia might be available for you, if this form of pain relief seems appropriate, the anesthesiologist will inform you of everything that could possibly happen during the procedure; as you sign the forms you will probably feel as if you had donated your body to medical research. Finally, the cervix is always measured immediately before medication is administered to be sure you are not fully dilated and thus no longer need it, because at full dilation, the pain of labor diminishes rapidly.

> *"I thought I would be able to tough it out without any drugs, but found I wanted the epidural the moment it was offered!"*

As you look ahead toward your own labor and try to assess your options, remember once again that it is never going to be just what you envision and yet you can count on the hospital nurses, with their experience and care, your doctor, and, of course, your loving husband—you'll have all these people to help you get through labor with the least amount of discomfort. Your individual needs are their primary concern, and it is important to keep this perspective. No one is going to try to overmedicate you. One father was so concerned about this that the moment the nurse would come closer he'd exclaim, "She doesn't need anything! She doesn't need anything!" No nurse is going to come up at the peak of a contraction with a gigantic syringe in hand and say, "Okay, dearie, last chance. Do you want medication or not?" Instead, if you ask for a pain reliever, she will probably encourage you to take the lowest dosage. She won't say, "You took those childbirth classes, so just keep breathing. Nothing for you!" No one would be that sadistic. Know your options beforehand and, should you need to choose, do what's best for you (and your baby).

16

Stage One, Phase Three: Transition

Now the contractions are getting stronger, coming fast and furious, and they are pretty terrible. I remember one mother saying, "Fritzi, those contractions in transition were not like waves at all, they were like a hurricane!" That's just what transition is like: a hurricane. You barely have time to catch your breath (sixty to ninety seconds) before another contraction hits—that, too, lasting sixty to ninety seconds.

Transition marks the third and final phase of the dilation of the cervix when it stretches the final, torturous distance from eight to ten centimeters to let the baby's head out of the uterus and into the birth canal. Transition may feel like the worst hour of your life, but at least you know that it lasts only that one hour, or, it is hoped, even less.

As the contractions of active labor intensify, there are several signs and symptoms that transition has arrived. Be prepared to recognize them.

Backache. If you look at a diagram of the baby's position during transition, you will see that his head is pressing directly against the mother's spinal column, which inevitably produces a backache. (See *e*, on page 9.) *Everyone* experiences a low pressure backache in transition, even those who have been fortunate enough to have had none until this point in labor.

Use some form of counterpressure or the freeze-it pack from your Lamaze goody bag (page 143) rather than a change of position to cope with a backache now. If you move around from your side to your back or vice versa, one of those powerful contractions might catch you off guard and overwhelm you.

Rectal pressure. During transition, the baby's head presses against the rectum, making you feel as if you are ready to have a bowel movement. I have been with many a woman who urgently asks for the ladies' room in transition, despite the enema she had earlier; rectal pressure, whether from a baby or a bowel movement, *feels* like a bowel movement. As transition progresses, the persistent pressure will give way to the much more forceful early urge to push, but this comes later, at the very end of transition.

Vaginal bleeding. Until now, you may have been leaking clear amniotic fluid or have seen the mucous plug, or both, but there has been no bleeding. In transition, however, you will see some bright red bleeding, or what the nurses humorously refer to as "a good bloody show." This is perfectly normal, a good sign that the cervix is *almost* fully dilated and some of the tiny blood vessels it contains are rupturing as the baby's head is coming through.

Nausea. Not all women, but enough so that it is considered normal, feel nauseated during transition and might even throw up at the peak of a contraction—not exactly what you need at this moment of time, to say the least. Usually, it is a momentary occurrence—not like the nausea of early pregnancy or the flu, but instead a sudden wave of nausea rising at the peak of a contraction when it creates pressure under the stomach. The nausea lasts for five to ten seconds and then it's gone.

If you feel nausea coming on at the peak of a contraction, quickly tell your husband, "I'm going to throw up" so he can grab one of the little kidney-shaped, white plastic dishes available and hold it for you to throw up in.

If you haven't eaten for a while (which will probably be the case because you are at least a few hours past early labor) and you do throw up, remember that stomach juices are green. This is normal. Do not think to yourself, "Oh, my heavens, on top of everything, now I have some sort of fungus." You are merely seeing what is normally in your stomach when you haven't eaten for eight hours.

After throwing up, you will be very tempted to sink back down on your pillow, rinse out your mouth, have your husband comfort you—but you can't do that right away. If you let go in the middle of one of those contractions, you will absolutely be overtaken by it. Instead, before you take care of yourself, you must try to distract yourself (Technique #3, page 136, is recommended) until the end of the contraction. *You've got to.*

Gentlemen, if you are now thinking "I'm not sure I can handle all this," I assure you, you can. It's just hard to picture yourself— or your wife—in such a situation when up until now, you may never have had anything more than the unpleasant task of cleaning up after a pet, for example. The intense involvement you will have with your wife in labor will leave you no time to consider your own reactions or feelings. Just as she is using every fiber of her being to cope with labor, you, too, will rise beautifully to the occasion and never give it a second thought, even if she throws up for the fifth time into that little white plastic dish you're clenching.

The shakes. Everyone gets "the shakes" about an hour after delivery, but some women get them in transition, usually with quivering leg muscles, due to fatigue. If you get them in transition, ask the nurse to pull the side rails up on the bed so you can lean your legs against them, or put some pillows under your knees. The quivering occurs when you are making the muscles work; it stops if they are at rest.

Irritability is a sure sign of transition. If, gentlemen, until now your wife has been relatively even-tempered during labor, do not be surprised if she suddenly becomes impatient with your efforts to help: when you approach her with the washcloth, she shouts, "Don't touch me with that!" As you offer her the mouthwash

> *"I had a vaginal birth and it hurt more than I expected, but I felt prepared for it (I just don't like pain!). Knowing that the transition stage lasted only about an hour helped, and that it was almost over when I was pushing. Yes, I screamed a lot, but two hours after the birth, my husband and I were eating Chinese food. I was starving!"*

spray she always liked, she yells, "Get that stuff away from me!" Feeling a little dejected, you sit down, and with the next contraction you watch the monitor and tell her when the contraction is peaking. But rather than encouraging her, it simply elicits the response, "Why don't you get out of here!"

Don't do it, gentlemen! Don't leave her. She may sound as if she truly wants you to go, but because she is in the worst part of labor, trying to get through terribly painful contractions, anything—even the touch or sound of someone she loves—is too much of an intrusion on her concentration. Don't try to discuss it with her, commiserate with her, or jolly her. All of that is out of the question in transition. With the next contraction, she will probably demand that you give her the washcloth or mouthwash—just what she didn't want you to do during the last one. Take your cues from her and help her stay on top of those contractions as best you can. It is very rough, but the end is in sight.

There was only one time in all my years as a nurse that a woman had the self-control to be able to say to her husband, when she was eight centimeters dilated, "Now I can't talk anymore; this is when I'm supposed to become a monster"—until she was fully dilated about forty-five minutes later, she never uttered a word! I stood there in disbelief at her control, wondering what, if anything, she was trying to prove to herself. When I was in transition, every time my husband brushed against the bed I wanted to kill him. "Don't touch the bed!" I would snarl, feeling a little better that there was an outlet for my anger.

If, gentlemen, she is really treating you badly, take it as a good sign that the worst is almost over.

Despair. As transition progresses, gentlemen, you can anticipate the moment when your wife really seems ready to quit. She may begin to cry; she may say vehemently, "I can't take this anymore! Help me!" This is normal, and as desperate as she sounds, it means she's almost there—the cervix is reaching full dilation. Quitting is not an option.

> *"The low point was about half an hour before I could start the pushing. There was no break between pains. I was overwhelmed and I had no idea when it would be over. The nurse kept putting the monitor on and I kept pushing it off. They examined me periodically and I just did not want to be touched. Luckily it didn't last too long before I could start to push and was home free."*

Lamaze technique: In transition, contractions usually start off so forcefully you barely have time to take a quick cleansing breath before starting the breathing. Breathing Technique #3, page 136, seems to work best for transition. It's the most rhythmic of all the breathing techniques, with a pant-blow pattern that you can vary yourself for distraction *or your coach can vary for you to mimic.*

Do not effleurage. Instead, tuck your hands down in the groin area and give a little counterpressure there, or sit on your hands and put counterpressure on your coccyx (tail bone), whichever brings some relief.

Tip for the Coach: Breathe loudly so that she can mimic you. Make her look into your eyes as you firmly encourage her to breathe with you. Convince her that she can do it.

As you are trying to cope with the painful, ninety-second contractions of transition, you will suddenly have that seemingly uncontrollable early urge to push. You may not be aware of it at first, because your concentration is focused on the intensity of the contractions. But you, gentlemen, will notice it right away. Your wife's face will turn bright red and you will undoubtedly think, "Oh, what's happening now?" What you're seeing is her body's response to the baby's elongated head pressing on the vaginal walls and the rectum.

When the narrow crown of the little "cucumber head" comes through a cervix that is not quite fully dilated (let's say it's at nine centimeters), it elicits an overwhelming sensation of wanting to bear down. It is not yet time to do so. If you push against a cervix that is only nine centimeters dilated, you will put about thirty-five pounds of pressure behind the baby and against the cervix, which may either swell up or tear. So you want the cervix to dilate that last little bit before the pushing starts. Since about 50 percent of women get an early urge to push before full dilation, you need to counteract it with forceful blowing.

Lamaze technique: When you feel the early urge to push, breathe in and blow out forcefully until the urge subsides; then return to Breathing Technique #3, page 136.

The urge to push, the first time you feel it, will just be for five seconds at the peak of a contraction, and then you might have two contractions with no urge, and then you feel it at two peaks for five seconds each. When it really gets to be an overwhelmingly forceful sensation, you usually *are* fully dilated.

Once when I was describing the pant-blow pattern of the breathing used for dealing with the early urge to push, one of the fathers in my Lamaze class asked, "But we *will* have a hospital professional there with us at that point, won't we?" sounding as if he feared he'd be coaching his wife through labor alone on a deserted island. Yes, a labor-and-delivery nurse to guide you throughout, offering support, encouragement, and constructive suggestions that you may not have thought of for handling labor, and a doctor will come in frequently. Communicate with your nurse all during labor, asking questions and telling her how you feel.

If you feel the urge to bear down, immediately *tell* the nurse so she can get your doctor in there to examine you. With luck, he will say, "Yes, you are fully dilated, it's time to push!" However, he will probably say, "No, it's not quite time. Hang in there for ten or fifteen minutes and then we'll check you again."

Now you are through the worst of labor. The cervix is all the way open, your contractions are more like those in active labor, and you are beginning to feel much better about everything. The horrendous pain is behind you. Transition is *over.*

CHAPTER REVIEW

COPING WITH TRANSITION

- Ladies, don't try to reposition yourself—there's no time

- Close your eyes and try to relax between contractions

- Keep the Lamaze cleansing breath short to stay on top of contractions

- Keep your eyes on your husband's during contractions

- Don't panic! This is the toughest hour. You can do it!

- Recognize the early urge to push and notify your nurse when you do

- You're almost there!

- Gentlemen, offer mouthwash spray between contractions, and if she tells you to leave her, don't!

- Exert counterpressure where it's most needed to relieve backache

17

The Second Stage of Labor: Birth

Once the cervix is fully dilated to ten centimeters, most women find that the sensations of labor improve dramatically. The sharp, very painful ninety-second contractions of the transition phase give way to "working contractions" that are usually forty-five to sixty seconds long and come with good two- to three-minute breaks. You are on the home stretch, ready to push the baby down from the mouth of the uterus to the outlet of the vagina and into position for delivery.

The pushing starts in the labor room, in your labor bed, and once the top of the head is visible you are moved into the delivery room and onto the delivery table for the actual birth of the baby (see *e*, *f*, and *g* on page 9). Generally, the pushing you do in the labor room takes about half an hour, with delivery room pushing of about ten or fifteen minutes and then the birth. However, the time can vary tremendously depending on the size of the baby and the effectiveness of your pushing. If you have a little five-pound, eight-ounce baby, pushing it into position for delivery may take you ten minutes. If you have a nine-pound, seven-ounce "moose," which is how my husband described our first son, you might push for two hours, accomplish nothing, and then go to the delivery room for a forceps delivery, as I did, because there's no sense in remaining pregnant for the rest of your life.

> *"In delivery, I will never forget my doctor leaning over the labor-room bed saying, 'There is only one way out of this fix, Kate, and that is to push!'"*

Most women will say "It felt wonderful to push" or exclaim "What a great relief!" This is because the painful dilation of the cervix is now complete and although the pushing is work, it is accompanied by that strong urge to push, which many women describe as exhilarating.

Personally, I thought pushing was the pits. I remember saying to my doctor, "Dr. Ryan, I have a ruptured bladder." And he responded with, "Fritzi, you have worked here for eight years; have you ever seen a woman with a ruptured bladder?" "I know," I replied, "it does not seem likely but, yes, I have a ruptured bladder." In retrospect, because of the size of my baby, maybe he split the pubic bone slightly, and not my bladder.

Whatever the cause, to say that the pushing did not live up to my expectations is an understatement. The irony is that I had been looking forward to it because of all the rave reviews I'd heard, including one glowing description that almost cost me my job. When I was a new teacher at The New York Hospital, my supervisor happened to pick up an extension just as I was on the line with one of my students who blurted out that the pushing "was just as you'd said, Fritzi, a glorious orgasm!" Although I had never used that phrase, I knew I was in for trouble. As soon as I got off the phone, my supervisor called me into her office and in ominous tones requested that we go over the contents of my course before I taught another group. I did so in meticulous detail, and after convincing her that I'd been far less colorful in my descriptions of pushing that my student had credited me for, I was still left wondering whether perhaps there was some truth to this student's description of it. So when my own time to push arrived, I was certainly game—at least at first.

For those who do not care for pushing, and in every group of ten women there will be one or two who do not, since you cannot deliver orally, you have, alas, no choice but to push that baby out through your vagina. Just look to the bright side—you're finally doing something very active, you make real progress, and it's almost all over.

There will probably be about half an hour or so of pushing before any of the baby's head can be seen. The nurse will get you into position and help you get the hang of it, while your husband goes to the locker room and changes from his street clothes into the hospital attire he'll need for the delivery room.

Gentlemen, when you go to change into a hospital scrub suit for the delivery room, take off everything but your underwear, socks, and shoes. Those of you with beards will wear an Arabian Nights–style hood, made out of paper; those without, a paper "shower cap." The scrub suit consists of a top *and* a bottom. I remember one father who apparently assumed otherwise and arrived in the delivery room sporting the hospital cap, mask, *top* of the scrub suit, his own blue-and-white-striped underdrawers, a pair of furry legs, black garters, socks, and his carefully covered shoes.

If you don't see any bottoms, put your head out the locker-room door and ask the nurse to bring some. One size fits all—drawstring waist, fly on the side, pockets for wallet, cuff links, and whatnot. (Keep all your valuables on you!) With the final touches, a mask and shoe covers, you are ready to rejoin your wife.

Years ago, when I had not lived in New York City very long and was quite naive about the mix of people who come through a big city hospital, I told a father to go change and he returned in about ten seconds, still in his street clothes. When I asked him what the trouble was, he produced a loaded revolver and said the scrub-suit pocket wasn't large enough to accommodate his gun. I blurted out, "What do you need that for?" and he responded, "I'm a secret agent." I was immediately suspicious because most secret agents, police officers, and others who are licensed to carry weapons identify themselves as soon as they arrive on the unit and hand over their guns, unloaded, for safekeeping in the narcotics closet. When I informed this gentlemen of the normal procedure, he just handed me the gun, bullets in place, and headed for the locker room. I quickly locked it up and returned to his wife. Between pushes, I asked her what sort of a secret agent her husband was, and she smiled and said he wasn't a secret agent at all but was in the wholesale meat business on Manhattan's Lower East Side—the meaning of which I was left to ponder, having decided to discreetly avoid asking any more questions about his line of work.

Although two-thirds of the women of the world may squat to give birth to their babies, it is not the most comfortable position for most women, especially with a large, pregnant belly putting tremendous pressure on the groin area. Besides being awkward, in this position the force of gravity can add too much pressure at the moment of birth and cause skin tissue between the vagina and rectum to tear, even with an episiotomy.

Once you are fully dilated, the nurse will have you get into position in the labor bed, birthing chair, or birthing bed, semi-inclined at about a forty-five-degree angle with your knees up.

A birthing bed is actually a labor bed that converts to a delivery bed. It's usually placed in what is referred to as a birthing room, which has a cozier environment and less medical equipment than a normal labor room. Birthing beds are quite expensive, but as hospitals replace labor beds, they often try to acquire at least one birthing bed, the advantage being that you need not switch from a labor bed to a delivery table as your baby's head is about to crown. The disadvantage of the birthing bed is that it is relatively soft, with only modified stirrups that can be attached if needed, and may not give the support needed for special obstetrical techniques, such as a difficult forceps delivery.

Birthing chairs are being used in some hospitals and have received mixed reviews. To date they are not padded and their design is such that a mother must stay in one position, which can become tiresome. But they do allow you to push with the force of gravity and then tilt back for a gentle delivery.

When room and bed options are available and several women are in labor, most hospitals usually give first choice to those women having second and third babies. Their labor tends to progress more quickly than with those having first babies; if they choose the birthing bed, more women may get to use it. See what your hospital has and discuss what you want with your doctor, keeping in mind that some doctors are more enthusiastic about birthing rooms than others. But if it means a lot to you—if any option means a lot to you—communicate it in advance to your doctor and by all means, use an approach with him that will set the tone for a reasonable dialogue.

One way to alienate your doctor is to say, "Look. I understand a birthing room [or whatever] is available and I want it no matter what." When I first worked in New York Hospital and Lamaze techniques were relatively new, many women took a combative stance on the whole matter and would come out of the elevator saying, "I demand four pillows, I refuse the intravenous, I am going to squat to push regardless of what position you tell me to be in." By the time they finished, I would want to push the bed right back onto the elevator and have nothing to do with all that hostility. Whereas if they had come in and said, "You know, it would make a world of difference to me if I had another pillow," it would have been a lot easier on everyone. Doctors and nurses are human too, and, like anyone else, are much more responsive to a reasonable attitude. Some doctors are somewhat set in their ways, but things do eventually change in obstetrics.

One last word on birthing beds and birthing rooms: I don't think they are the "be all and end all" of delivery. While it might be nice to stay in the same bed for both labor and delivery, making the move from one bed to the other is done on one level and it's really very easy. A birthing room may be a little more attractive than a delivery room, with a private bathroom and telephone, but

> "My squeamishness was overcome by the sheer excitement of the birth. All the leaking bodily fluids, all the stretching, pushing, grunting and groaning, and all the intimidating instruments paled in comparison to the twin tasks of helping Amy deal with the pain and helping her push out our baby."

it's still a hospital room. If that's what you want and can get it, fine; if not, in my estimate, it's not worth a battle.

THE PUSHING BEGINS

Remember that the sensation of pushing is going to be the same as if you were having a bowel movement—you might not have expected this, and it might create a certain amount of confusion, which is normal. We are conditioned from the age of two to control our bowels and we are taught that moving the bowels anywhere but in the toilet is a mistake, an "accident." We are also conditioned to expect privacy—an element that is sorely lacking at birth. So here you are, a grown woman with what feels like the largest bowel movement you have ever had in your life, in a strange hospital bed with nurse, doctor, and anesthesiologist standing over you and your husband vigorously encouraging you to "push it out!" Under ordinary circumstances, you would cross your legs, tighten your buttocks, and never *dream* of allowing such a bowel movement to come through and land on the bed. The irony is, of course, the "bowel movement" is the baby and you must now forget about all your previous conditioning and inhibitions and *help push him out.* (Another good reason the small hospital enema at the beginning of labor is worthwhile: when you push, it will be a lot easier to say to yourself, "Well this *must* be the baby; my bowels are definitely empty.")

Some experts go on at length about how you should not push rectally, you should push vaginally. I can assure you that it is the very rare individual who is able to tell the difference between the two. Maybe you are so gifted; if so, when it comes time for the pushing, go to it and push vaginally. But if you are like the vast majority of women, you will find that birth is in fact a rectal sensation—perhaps earthier than expected but no less exhilarating in the great relief it brings.

Use your Lamaze expulsion techniques (page 139) for this stage of labor. To make positive gain and prevent the baby's head from slipping back, push only at the peak of a contraction and hold your breath as long as you can with each push, taking a very *quick* replenishing breath to push a second and third time.

I've always thought the sequence of labor to be poorly planned: the active stage (the pushing) should be in the beginning when you have the energy, the passive stage (the labor) at the end, when you are tired. No such luck. You have been in labor twelve hours, you are absolutely exhausted, and now you are compelled to push with all your might.

Of course your nurse will be there to guide you along, helping you conserve your energy by encouraging you to push only at the peak of your contractions and stay in a comfortable, relaxed position between them. She can tell where you are by looking at the fetal monitor and at your face—she *knows* when you are experiencing a contraction because you will grimace, not really from the pain but just from working hard, and she will encourage you to hold each breath as long as possible. (Some women work so hard at the pushing that they actually break a few tiny blood vessels in the face, but these disappear a day or two after delivery.) With contractions typically lasting about forty-five to sixty seconds, three good pushes with a breath between each is usually about what you can get out of each of them. If the contractions are shorter, the nurse might say, "We only have time for two breaths, so let's do it that way." Or if the contraction is longer, she might say, "Take another breath and push, let's not waste it!"—always trying to help you make some headway.

Gentlemen, there may come a time when it seems that your wife cannot manage one more push. Give her all the encouragement you've got to keep her going—she *can* do it. Give her progress reports. Tell her when the baby's head is beginning to appear—first "a dime's worth," then "a quarter's worth," and so on—to give her a new burst of strength.

If you are not making sufficient progress with the pushing, the nurse may suggest that you change your position a little bit: hook your feet on the side rails of the bed, perhaps, to give you more support. Try whatever she suggests.

Finally, when about a silver dollar's worth of the baby's head is visible, the nurse will say a phrase that will be music to your ears:

> *"The lowest point was moments before birth, the overwhelming fear that something might go wrong. Then when his head popped out, an* overwhelming *sense of relief."*

"It's time to go to the delivery room!" This is the moment when you take a long, deep breath and say to yourself, "I've done it. In twenty minutes, I'll have this baby in my arms and no longer in my belly."

The fetal-monitor belt comes off, your labor bed is wheeled into the delivery room, and you are scooted onto the delivery table.

Gentlemen, you can help the nurse guide the labor bed into the delivery room and move the pillows from the labor bed to the delivery table and position them under your wife's head. If there's a back rest on the delivery table, adjust it for your wife's comfort and then stand by her head, where you can offer encouragement and witness the birth with her, looking down over her belly. Stay there. You are not at liberty to saunter down to look over the instruments and discuss the delivery with the doctor!

Most delivery rooms have a mirror, attached to one of the lights, to give you a view of the birth. The mirror image of the vagina can be disorienting, and the view of the bulging anus leaves something to be desired. A better alternative for watching the baby being born is to lean forward with your husband supporting your head so you can see as much as possible.

While you are being positioned, everyone in the delivery room

> *"When I was fully dilated and the doctor told me I could push—that was the high point. I knew the end was near. Finally watching in the mirror and seeing the birth was our most unbelievable experience. My husband cried and I was so pent up with emotion that I couldn't speak."*

> *"The high point was definitely the emergence of our daughter from the womb. It was six A.M., some thirteen hours after my wife and I had arrived at the hospital. We were both exhausted, of course. The immense relief of seeing a healthy child, indeed seeing a child at all, made this about the most emotional moment of my life. Prior to it, the baby was an abstraction; now she was real."*

(the nurse, doctor, and anesthesiologist) will be getting ready for the birth. The nurse will probably cover your legs with wide cotton leg covers, your vaginal area will be washed with a warm brown antiseptic, and a sterile drape will be spread over your legs and abdomen and between your legs—nothing will show but a hole for the baby's appearance. For those unfamiliar with delivery procedures in America, it's a rather strange arrangement. A French obstetrician who observed a birth at New York Hospital exclaimed, "In America, zee babies do not come out of vaginas, zey are born out of zeh hole in zeh sterile sheet!" How perfectly true, we have managed to obscure almost everything but the baby—but that's all you'll be interested in seeing anyway.

> *"At the moment of actual delivery I was so enraptured with the birth that most of it was over before I could believe it. I suddenly realized we were a family. I was the proudest man in the world and still am."*

MEDICATION IN THE DELIVERY ROOM

In the delivery room, a nurse-anesthetist or anesthesiologist might ask if you would like to have some gas—nitrous oxide and oxygen, or what is commonly referred to as "laughing gas."

Gas is often used with a mother who had prior medication that has not been working effectively. In the case of a mother who is delivering a sunny-side-up baby, when she is fully dilated and ready to push, every time she bears down she pushes the baby's head against her own back, causing excruciating pain. Also, for her the pushing takes longer because the baby's head has yet to turn. Needless to say, she is about as interested in pushing as in dying. So for her, a whiff of gas gives an analgesic effect during the contraction so she can push forcefully (which in fact she has to do to rotate the baby's head so it can be delivered) without feeling so much pain in her back.

From the 1940s to the 1960s, nitrous oxide was often given to make women completely unconscious for the birth. For the woman who had made it all the way to the most exciting and wonderful moment of birth to then be deprived of seeing and hearing her baby cry seems unforgivable—inexcusable. It was probably done because, once again, mothers who were uneducated about childbirth mistakenly believed that if transition was awful, the birth must be even worse and therefore begged to be "knocked out" for it.

Since delivery is usually far less painful than transition, be sure your doctor and the anesthetist know you do not want to miss that moment. (Unlike most of those women of a generation ago, you will have your husband with you to second the motion.)

If you do have gas, you will notice that it has a fruity smell and acts as an analgesic, administered through a black rubber mask as the contraction intensifies. Since it is given within minutes of delivery, very little gets into the baby's system. (Rubber masks are also used to administer oxygen to the mother if the baby is demonstrating signs of distress; they too smell slightly of gas, so if you are told you are getting oxygen for the baby, do not let the smell confuse you.)

Again, in a normal delivery you will not be getting enough gas to "put you under." Instead, you will be given carefully regulated whiffs that make you feel dreamlike. Although the first whiff will seem to do nothing, you will notice an effect after one or two more. For some, the effect is more pronounced than for others. One mother kept saying "Giddyap, boy, go!" as she breathed in the gas; as soon as she stopped and inhaled normal air, she'd say, "Excuse me, I was dreaming I was in a horse race." So if you are a little disoriented when you inhale gas, know that as soon as it's taken away, everything will be back to normal.

GETTING THE BABY OUT

While everything else is going on, you will hear your doctor getting ready, too. He washes his hands and comes over with gown and gloves on, to give you specific pushing instructions. He'll say something like, "Okay, let's have a good push," but you will not just push on cue. Instead, you will wait until the contraction comes and then push with it, just as you have done all along. Usually it takes several pushes, and then just at the moment when you have the greatest urge to push that you've ever had, your doctor will say, "Stop pushing." Immediately you blow, taking rapid breaths in and blowing them completely out. This is the moment your doctor is cutting your episiotomy (see below), if one is needed, and allowing the baby's head to be delivered gently with nothing more than the momentum of a contraction.

> *"Birth was thrilling and gratifying beyond all expectations. Our joy was enhanced by the ease of the birth. Ruben was such a good size and in such a good position that he was delivered in the labor room, with just the soft glow of the reading lamp for illumination. We had braced for an episiotomy, but none was necessary. The whole experience was so enjoyable and rewarding that we may do it sooner and more frequently than we had planned!"*

Fundal pressure. If you hear the term "fundal pressure," it would be at this point in delivery, just before the episiotomy is done. Understand what this is, and do not be alarmed by it.

All during the time that you are in the delivery room doing the pushing, the nurse listens to your baby's heart with a type of fetoscope that has long rubber earpieces. She slips the cold metal pickup disc underneath the sterile sheet and onto your abdomen, and listens through the two earpieces, after each contraction calling out to the doctor, "One thirty-six," for example. Then all of a sudden she calls out, "Eighty." But it's coming back up, now it's "one ten," and with the next one she calls out "eighty" again—at which point your doctor will say, "It's very important to have this baby with the next contraction, so I'd like to have some fundal pressure."

What is happening is that the baby is probably tangled in the cord and although that did not cause a problem prior to delivery, now as he is about to leave the uterus the umbilicus is getting tight around his neck or arm, especially as the baby travels through the birth canal. As the cord tightens, the heart rate drops, and so, with your next contraction, the nurse is going to push down on your belly to help *gently* push the baby out. A similar drop in the baby's heart rate can be due to head compression, as it squeezes through the final inches of the small birth canal. In either case fundal pressure may be needed to deliver the baby quickly.

I repeat: do not be alarmed. Many babies (firsts, seconds, and later ones) have the umbilical cord wrapped around them. *Many.* Usually it does not cause a problem until they try to leave the uterus, traveling those final inches through the vagina, and then it starts to tighten up. Fortunately the umbilical cord is elastic—it is a tough, Wharton's jelly tissue that is able to withstand a good deal of pressure as it maintains the baby's supply of oxygen. You may have a friend who says her baby was born with two loops of cord around the neck; say, "No kidding, Sherlock"—this is not uncommon at all. Fifty percent of all babies have cord around the neck or some other part of the body, usually without any sign of fetal distress. If they had shown signs of distress caused by the tightening of the cord back in the labor room, it might have warranted a Caesarean delivery. But because at this point delivery is imminent and the baby is very low in the birth canal, there is no problem getting him out vaginally.

The nurse will act as your coach for the next contraction. You must listen to her; cooperate with her and all will be fine.

Getting into position, she reaches across your belly and posi-

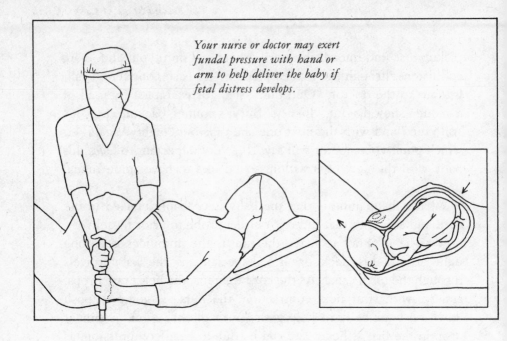

Your nurse or doctor may exert fundal pressure with hand or arm to help deliver the baby if fetal distress develops.

tions her forearm at the top of the uterus, right behind the baby's bottom. When the next contraction comes, you must concentrate on doing the pushing with her. If you stop while she is pushing, it will hurt because she's exerting a lot of pressure on your uterus. If you are pushing together, it won't hurt. The nurse knows you have to breathe. Maybe it won't be at the exact moment you might like to, but you listen and do as she says. She might say, "Okay, push, push, push," as she presses down, and then as she relaxes her arm, "Okay, catch another breath and do it again." As she presses down again, that additional little push does the trick and the baby begins to be delivered. Your doctor will say, "Okay, stop pushing," the nurse will relax her arm, and you will blow, blow, blow, forcefully, while he does the episiotomy.

Episiotomy is a term that you may or may not have heard before; as the baby is about to be delivered, about 95 percent of women having first babies need to have this small incision made in the perineum, the space between the vaginal outlet and the anus. At birth, the whole area between the vagina and rectum becomes very, very stretched, and the episiotomy helps to avoid what could be a very painful, ragged-edged tear.

There is some discussion about the pros and cons of episiotomy and whether they are necessary. In some hospitals, doctors do not seem to be doing as many as in the past. In all the years I worked in labor and delivery, it was extremely rare to see a first baby born with no episiotomy and no tear. You can certainly say, "I don't want an episiotomy, I'll take my chances on a tear," and everyone will abide by it. But I can tell you from experience that a tear can be pretty uncomfortable: with our first baby, I had an episiotomy *and* a tear and I wanted to have the bottom half of my body amputated the evening after my delivery. My second baby was exactly the same size as the first and I had an episiotomy and no tear—with none of the excruciating pain that I felt after my first baby. If you've ever been scratched badly by briars, you know that a clean cut is much easier to tolerate than a jagged one. Just be prepared, if you decide to give it a try without the episiotomy, to take the consequences. Some physicians believe that even if you are able to deliver without a tear, the extreme stretching of the vaginal outlet could lead to a weakening of the area in years to come. With a second or third baby, the tissues are more stretchable and an episiotomy may not be necessary.

In any case, discuss your views on episiotomy with your doctor in his office—*not* when you are in the delivery room and the baby's head is crowning!

For the episiotomy, so he will not hurt the baby's head, your doctor uses a scissor rather than a scalpel to make the cut, but

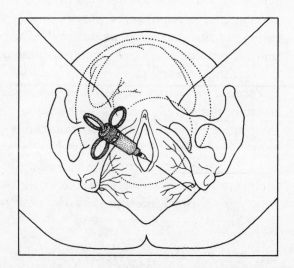

This pudendal block that numbs the whole vaginal area may be used by your doctor in the delivery room.

first you will be given a local anesthetic. Usually he'll inject it into the skin, but he could also inject the medication into the vagina at the base of the two pelvic nerves, creating a "pudendal block" which numbs not only the area of the episiotomy but the whole vagina as well. If he thinks he'll have to do a forceps delivery, he might choose to do the pudendal block to anesthetize this wider area.

Either way, because there is so much pressure on the area at the moment of birth, even without an anesthetic you might never feel the episiotomy at the moment when it is being cut. One mother who heard the little snip, snip of the scissors said, "What are you doing, cutting the baby's hair?" The pressure was so great that she couldn't feel a thing. However, once the baby is out and your doctor goes to sew it up, you would surely feel pain in such a sensitive area. So your doctor gives you the local anesthetic first, to counter the pain later.

The episiotomy is about an inch long, running from the vagina to the rectum. If delivery is by forceps, your episiotomy will be longer and extend out toward your fanny cheek—a "hockey-stick episiotomy"—to allow additional space for the forceps to enter.

Forceps and vacuum extractors. Forceps have been used for many years and acquired a frightening reputation early on, probably because they were not always used appropriately and in some cases caused damage to babies' heads. Today, however, they are used only when a baby is very low in the mother's pelvis, usually just to turn the head or to deliver him quickly if fetal distress is encountered in the delivery room. Using forceps is an obstetrical technique that can assist in the birth if a head is caught in an unusual position that would require additional, long hours before it would turn naturally.

Vacuum extractors are used for the same reasons as forceps, basically, but were not introduced until much later and were first used in Scandinavia. A small suction cup is placed on top of the baby's head, creating a seal to enable the doctor to turn or tilt the baby's head or just to assist as you push.

Both forceps and vacuum extractors leave red marks on the baby's head. But while the skin of a newborn is very fragile, it

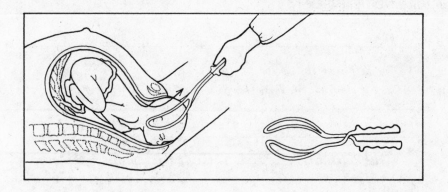

Forceps or a vacuum extractor may be used to assist in the delivery of your baby's head if warranted.

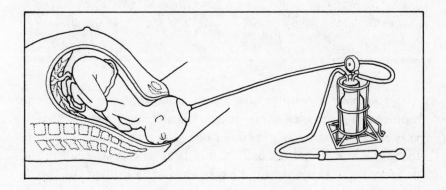

also has fabulous recuperative ability, and within forty-eight hours the marks will have disappeared without a trace. (Plastic surgeons always say, "What I would give to work with newborn skin!" because it heals so quickly and completely.)

Be glad these techniques are available to assist you, rather than necessitating a Caesarean section so close to the time of birth.

Once the head has emerged, most babies slip right out unless they are very big, in which case your doctor may ask for one more push to help deliver the shoulder—and then the rest of him follows *tout de suite.* Your doctor will hold him firmly, place him on your abdomen, and usually then cut the cord.

If the baby is tangled up in the cord, the doctor immediately places his fingers under the tight cord, clamps it in two places, cuts it, untangles it, and then allows the rest of him be born.

The second stage of labor ends—your baby is born!

> *"The best was the doctor putting the baby on my stomach and seeing those innocent eyes. It was love at first sight for me."*

> *"While Patty was in the midst of the final big pushes in the labor room, I remember seeing the top of the baby's head, the hair. I thought to myself, 'This is really happening.' The actual moment when I first saw the baby, I couldn't believe it. I didn't know the sex, and there was his head. He turned and looked at his mother as if to say, 'Is it okay? Can I come out now? Am I safe?' And then he turned back and out he came and right onto his mother's belly."*

If you have a definite idea about what you envision for the moment of birth, tell your nurse. Usually, the hospital staff is very accommodating. I remember one father who wanted his flute to be the first sound his baby would hear. It was so quiet in the delivery room that you could have heard a pin drop as the baby's head crowned, but then just as the baby appeared and his father started to play the instrument, his mother blurted out, "Darling, is it a boy or a girl?" Of course it really didn't matter then, anyway, as the baby's miraculous appearance had already eclipsed the idea of adding music to the moment.

> *"Having a twenty-six-year-old daughter and a twenty-four-year-old son, I was amazed at how exciting and emotional an experience this was for me. When just before noon on Thanksgiving morning they put the little turkey in my arms, I couldn't have uttered a word and I realized that tears were just pouring down my cheeks."* (Father)

The birth is so breathtaking that you will only be able to stare together in awe. It is a moment you will never forget.

"The most interesting expectation that was unfulfilled was that I really expected to be elated, emotional and filled with joy when Alex was born—after all, I felt that way watching the childbirth movies! What I felt was relief, nothing more, nothing less. The emotional high didn't happen until they brought him in the next morning. Then I had the tears, the closeness, the amazement."

Gentlemen, reach out and wrap an arm around your wife; make her realize you are there with her. Usually she has become so involved in the pushing and blowing that it may take her a moment to grasp what's happened. Be prepared to see her happy, crying, laughing, full of joy, or maybe almost in shock, unbelieving. Be prepared to feel these spontaneous emotions yourself. Give her a hug or a pat to show her how great a job she has done, and enjoy the sight of that wet little baby.

"The actual moment of birth was exhilarating. I felt like I'd gotten a shot of adrenaline! When the nurse asked me to move from the delivery table to a bed so she could wheel me to my room, I felt so great I said, 'No need, I'll walk.' She smiled knowingly and said, 'I'll wheel you anyway.' Then I tried to move and my body felt paralyzed. My head was saying, 'I feel great, let's go,' while my body was saying, 'Are you kidding? I'm exhausted.'"

18

The Third Stage of Labor: Expulsion of the Placenta

*O*nce the baby is born, the doctor will lay him on your abdomen for a moment as the cord is clamped and cut, hold him up to give you a good look, and then pass him over to be put in the warmer, where the resident can do a brief physical exam before giving him to Dad to hold.

You will feel a few very mild contractions as the placenta sloughs away—one more push and it comes right out. (See *i*, page 9.) The nurse may press down on your uterus to help you with the expulsion, but if you are up for it you can say, "No, thanks, I think I can push it out myself."

You might ask the doctor to show you the placenta; it's interesting to see, this lobular, fantastic organ that has so carefully filtered waste, given food and oxygen, regulated your baby's environment—in short, kept that baby alive through all the months of your pregnancy. Some hospitals sell the placentas for a nominal fee (about 25 cents apiece) to large medical laboratories for tissue research; we nurses always thought maybe they were just cut up and sold to a shampoo company for much more!

With the placenta gone, there is an open wound in the uterine wall, and to help minimize bleeding, the uterus contracts down rapidly, the muscles clamping off the blood vessels at the site of attachment. In some cases, the bleeding does not stop so readily.

If, for example, a small bit of placenta remains behind in the uterus as "retained secundae," it triggers more bleeding—a protective mechanism to wash out the remaining piece. This type of hemorrhage is rare, but if it does occur, it is usually shortly after expulsion when your doctor would notice it right away as he routinely but carefully examines the placenta to see that it is intact. If a piece is missing, you will be given a local or general anesthetic and your doctor will gently scrape the walls of the uterus to remove the remaining piece.

If you have a large baby or a fast, tumultuous labor and delivery, you might hear your doctor ask for some Pitocin ("Ten units into the intravenous now and for the first two hours after delivery") to help the uterus to contract down and minimize bleeding. Pitocin is not usually given unless indicated, however; the uteruses of most first-time mothers contract down efficiently on their own.

While you are involved with the expulsion of the placenta and the stitching of the episiotomy, your husband can walk over and watch the resident check the baby. Once that's done, your newborn will be swaddled and probably then passed to his father to hold.

Gentlemen, when at last you get your little baby in your arms, hold him cozily and snugly, close to your body like a football, and if he starts to fuss a little bit, squeeze him tighter so he will think he's back at home in the uterus. He'll look into your face with two beady, dark-blue eyes and you can talk to him. "Hi, baby," you say. He'll gaze right up into your eyes, and you will be won over with love and admiration for that little creature.

Ladies, although you can try to hold the baby at that moment, too, it can be difficult: your legs are up in the stirrups and you've got the shakes after delivery. If you are like most women, I think you'll find it's better to wait until your legs are down and you can prop the back rest all the way up before you say to the nurse, "Okay, now I am ready to hold the baby." And when the nurse puts him in your arms, do not be afraid to say, "Unwrap him, please, I'd like to look at him." Don't be like some mothers who furtively sneak a look into the swaddled package that is their baby—three days after delivery. You've waited nine months for this moment . . . *look him over!*

19

The Newborn Baby

*I*f you have never witnessed the birth of a baby, you may be surprised by what yours looks like when he first appears in the delivery room. He won't look gory or very bloody, but he won't look like the placid, pink infant (the one-month-old passing for the newborn) in the baby-food commercials, either. Of course, he will be very wet, and at first he will also look very blue—as blue as modeling clay or an oxford-cloth shirt. It takes a few minutes for his circulatory system to adjust to breathing oxygen, rather than absorbing it from the placenta, and for him to turn pink. You can actually see his color gradually changing, just after delivery, although his hands and feet may remain blue or purple for several hours. Do not be concerned about this. If his feet seem too blue or dark a day or so after delivery, remember that they were inked to take his little footprints (fingerprints being too immature at this stage), and that may be the cause.

The first thing you will undoubtedly check when your baby is placed on your abdomen, just seconds after birth, is whether he can breathe—whether he's alive! It's a mystery how the image of holding the baby up and spanking him to encourage breathing ever came to be the stereotype. In all the deliveries I have seen, no baby was ever turned upside down and spanked. If stimulation is needed, the doctor may rub the baby gently on the back and that's all, much as Dr. Leboyer (author of *Birth Without Violence*) would lead you to believe that rough handling and spanking are standard practice. They aren't.

Some babies are born with mucus or amniotic fluid in the nose and mouth, and a small rubber bulb is used to suck it out. If the excess fluid is down a bit deeper, a little plastic container with a tube called a Delie trap might be used. This method is more prevalent with Caesarean babies than vaginal births because Caesarean babies have not had the full benefit of "Nature's plan": the wonderful, thorough squeeze of the baby's chest in the birth canal, which presses the amniotic fluid and mucous in the lungs out through the nose and mouth. Then, when the chest emerges, because the atmospheric pressure is greater than the baby's inner thoracic pressure, he is compelled to take his first breath—into a set of lungs that has just been squeezed empty. A very clever plan, at that. (To further encourage mucus and fluids to drain out, Caesarean babies are routinely kept tilted head down in the hospital nursery longer than vaginally delivered babies.)

Every baby's **Apgar score** is recorded, with ratings in five categories: heart rate, respiratory effort, grimace, muscle tone, and color. Here is how points are tallied:

- Heart rate: above 100 per minute (2), below 100 per minute (1), absent (0).

- Respiratory effort: regular (2), irregular (1), absent (0).

- Grimace: cries (2), whimpers (1), absent (0).

- Muscle tone: active (2), some (1), limp (0).

- Color: pink (2), blue extremities (1), blue (0).

The best score would be two in each category, obviously, for a total of ten. The baby is rated twice, at one minute and at five minutes after birth. In fact, no baby ever receives a score of ten at one minute. At least one point is lost, for color (you might not think yours deserves *any* points for color, but it's all relative). You will hear the two scores called out, "Apgar: nine, ten" (nine at one minute; ten at five minutes). Or you might hear, "Apgar:

eight, nine" (a point off for color, one off for something else). The Apgar score is a cursory indication that the five areas it covers are functioning. It will not tell you whether the baby will get into the college of his or her choice, tempting as it might be to make your own interpretations!

If this is your first baby, his head will probably be "molded" or elongated due to that twelve-hour squeeze in labor and delivery. The skull bones of a newborn are not yet solidified and can actually overlap if necessary during birth and the fat round head becomes very long and narrow. You may even hear one of the nurses jokingly say, "He's a real cucumber head, isn't he?" Don't be insulted! Nature has just forced a large, round object through a keyhole. I have heard more than one couple with a "cucumber-head" firstborn say to each other, "Oh dear, we'll have to hide that head with one of the baby bonnets we got as a gift—we don't want your parents to see him looking like this!" Take heart. The pointy head will in a few days return to its lovely little round shape.

Regardless of shape, the top of the head may have a bright reddish tinge to it, causing you to think, "Redhead? We don't have any redheads in the family." What you are seeing is not hair coloring at all but a little of the blood from your episiotomy, which transferred to his scalp as he passed over it. The blood will wash right off.

Some babies are born with lots of hair and some are bald as cue balls. Most babies who are born with a lot of hair lose it gradually over the first three months and the new crop that begins to sprout is often a different color and a different texture as well. The newborn baby with the black hair standing on end as if he just put his hand in an electric socket may become a curly-topped towhead before he even sits up!

All newborns have dark-blue eyes—black babies, white babies, all babies—a kind of dark slate blue. If you or your spouse have brown eyes (usually the dominant trait), your baby's eyes will probably turn brown within the first two weeks, although true eye color is not officially confirmed until about four months after birth. Usually it is the gray with green edges, the purple flecks in hazel—in other words, the exceptional colorations—that take the longest to set.

Newborns can definitely see at birth. Their eyes are fully developed, they can see and focus, and they look right up at you immediately after delivery with such a wonderful little gaze that you are smitten with love. After such a look, you would do *anything* for this magical little person!

If some babies seem slightly cross-eyed at first, the muscles will tighten up very soon and then the gaze will become normal. Other babies seem to want to keep their eyes tightly closed at first, much as you would if you were brought out of a dark room into a fully lit one. These little turtles soon adjust, usually in the first minute or two.

Sometimes, because they have been in a funny position, the ears are turned down like the petals of a flower bud. You don't have to pin them back; they will assume a normal configuration on their own.

Due to the trauma of birth, the nose of a newborn is sometimes a little squashed in or pushed over to one side and in a day or two will perk up and straighten out.

On or around the nose there might be little whiteheads, blotches and spots called milia, and even pimples. This "newborn acne" is perfectly normal and should be left alone. The skin that was soaked in amniotic fluid for nine months will soon adjust to the air, and all the little eruptions will clear up. By the time your

"Even before the obstetrician could comment or perhaps even see the baby's genitals, I shouted, 'It's a boy!' The moment he took his first breath, without any prompting, was truly magical. The most emotional moment came when I was holding my son in my arms while my wife slept nearby. It was about five A.M. and all was still. I thought of the miracle of his birth, of his being a boy, of his unlimited potential, and I thought of the man for whom he was named, my father, who had died of a heart attack at the age of forty-eight. I began to cry, praying with all my heart that I would at least be the father to him that my father was to me. I cried until the nurse came to take the baby back to the nursery."

baby is three months old, he will most likely have that gorgeous, rosy complexion that everyone covets.

You might see "stork bites," tiny blood vessels beneath the skin that seem more prominent around the bridge of the nose and eyes when he cries—no doubt visible because the skin is somewhat transparent at first. When it becomes more opaque over the first couple of weeks after birth, these little marks fade.

Lanugo, a soft, usually dark layer of what looks like peach fuzz, may extend from your baby's hairline down to his eyebrows, or from the back of his head, down his neck, and out to his shoulders. About 20 percent of all newborns have this covering, especially babies born early—a brief, albeit humbling, reminder that our ancestors were apes. It wears away in the first week or two after birth. You'll love him regardless, I promise!

Babies born two or more weeks early also have a large amount of vernix on their skin. This substance resembles cream cheese and could well be described as Nature's cold cream, so rich in vitamins, estrogen, and oils that many cosmetic companies have tried to create a synthetic version of it to use in their skin products—to no avail. In the uterus, vernix keeps the baby's skin from becoming waterlogged; in the initial hours after birth, it is believed to insulate the baby and is therefore left untouched until his internal thermostat has stabilized and he's able to keep himself warm. After that, a full bath and shampoo are in order.

If the baby arrives near his due date, most of the vernix will have worn off except for a few traces in the skin folds under the arm or in the groin. If he's two weeks overdue, not only will all of the vernix be gone, but the skin will be as shriveled as a prune, much as your hands might appear if you kept them submerged for a long period in warm water.

Early, late, or on time, all babies' skin peels, usually in the first week, as that waterlogged layer dries out. Don't be alarmed by the peeling. The nurses in the hospital will show you how to use a little lotion or oil to minimize the dryness. It's normal and passes quickly.

All newborns have puffy breasts and genitals. Many a father looking over his baby boy in the delivery room exclaims in awe, "My son has equipment like I've never seen on a man before!"

"I realized that I'd been kidding myself about whether we had a boy or a girl. As soon as I saw Ted's you-know-what, I knew what I wanted. The immediateness with which love for the baby overtakes you—that was easily the strongest emotion of the experience, and possibly of my life."

The temporary swelling is normal, again due to the mother's high hormone level which in part is transferred to the baby.

Baby girls often demonstrate pseudomenstruation. On about the tenth or twelfth day after delivery, there might be a spot of old, brown blood in the diaper—a sign that the hormone level in the baby has finally dropped off to normal.

If your baby was a breech, that little bottom (or whatever the presenting part was) may be black and blue for a few days. Breech babies who kept their legs straight up with the feet beside their head when they were in the uterus are funny to watch after they have been delivered. They keep that position for a day or two, even when they are encouraged to bend the legs down. As soon as they're let go, the legs spring up again. If you have a breech with toes in his ears, take heart: in a few days they'll be down where they belong.

The breasts of a newborn are said to contain witch's milk, whatever that is, and there's nothing to do about them if they are enlarged. Puffiness is due to hormonal stimulation and, along with genital swelling, will subside by the time the baby is four weeks old.

The umbilicus of a newborn often protrudes. You will be able to see clearly where the skin-covered nub stops and the white, gelatinous Wharton's jelly begins. You may have always thought your obstetrician blew it when he "tied" your cord because it was always an "outie" and not a neat "innie." The cord is never actually tied—the only place touched by the doctor (clamped, actually) is the gelatinous part. Before that ever happens, Nature has already bestowed you with more or less belly-button skin, and that's that.

The metal clamp that is initially used on the cord is replaced with a small plastic clamp. The plastic clamp, in turn, can be removed the day after delivery and the cord will already look like a dried-up, healing scab. In the hospital you will learn how to wipe it once a day with alcohol, to help with the drying process. It falls off when the baby is about ten days old; then the skin will look like yours would if you bumped off a scab. The navel may be a little gooey for a day or two, but you keep cleansing it with alcohol and in a few days it will be completely healed. At that point, a tub bath is usually a great source of pleasure for your baby and you (see page 333).

Contrary to the old wives' tale, belly-button binders are *not* necessary. In fact, all babies have belly buttons that stick out, as do their tummies until they are about three years old. This is because their abdominal muscles were split to make a place for the umbilical-cord blood vessels to pass through, and it takes almost three years for the muscles to knit closed and become the flat little muscular tummy of a four-year-old. Do not let anyone try to convince you that your baby has a "milk belly." Instead, nuzzle that delicious little round belly while you can before it gradually disappears.

Pigmented skin areas or Mongolian spots are particularly evident on black babies, usually seen across the lower back, bottom, or upper thighs. Their location is proof enough for all who believe (and would love to have you believe) that "this is where the doctor beat the baby." Thank goodness you were there and awake during the birth and so can respond, "Don't be silly, I was there and he did not!" These marks usually fade gradually over the first few years of life.

Black babies also look quite fair-skinned at birth, and it takes as long as a few weeks for the pigment to settle evenly throughout the baby's skin layer.

Fingernails and toenails at birth are different from what they will be later. The part that is grown out is attached to the skin underneath and the side edges of the nail begin to grow out first, before the part at the center. The nail edges become pretty sharp and the baby can inadvertently scratch his face with them if they are not clipped. (There are "baby nail scissors" on the market, but they are so dull they couldn't cut anything. Instead, bring your own little nail scissors or clippers to the hospital and when the baby is asleep just hold his hand firmly and gently trim the edges.) The toenails look like someone has been nibbling on them for the last six months and usually do not need to be trimmed until the baby is about a month old.

If you happen to deliver a premature or preterm infant (at less than thirty-eight weeks), your baby may be quite tiny and need to be put into a warm isolette to protect him from infections, given oxygen if necessary, and probably fed by a small flexible tube inserted through his nose directly into his stomach until he is strong enough to suck. (Breast milk is especially valuable for these babies, as they're more suspectible to infection than full-term infants. Ask your hospital about an electric breast pump to express your own milk for him.) Feel free to spend as much time as you like next to his isolette; have the nurses explain cleanliness routines so you can touch and pat and hold your baby—this will be comforting for mother, father, and baby alike.

> *"The most exhilarating moment was first seeing his mouth open and watching him shaking his arms and legs. It was the first realization that he was truly alive."*

What a wonderful, warm, contented feeling fills your body during those first minutes after delivery. You're relieved that it's all behind you, and respect for your own mother (and for all women who have ever given birth) has just multiplied a hundredfold. Emotionally, you feel very close to your husband, and thankful for his help, encouragement, and steadfast presence. You wonder how women could ever go through birth alone!

How do you feel toward your new little baby? After the long, pregnant wait, now that he's here, he's probably not exactly what you had in mind. Is this little creature really yours? If you had not seen him come out, you might not believe he's the one who's been growing inside you for nine months.

Remember that if his appearance does not live up to your expectations, that's perfectly normal. It doesn't mean that you

> *"There he was, a living creature we had created. He cried very little and before I knew it, I was holding him and he, with those little eyes, was staring up at me. What a feeling to look at our little one. He is the single greatest accomplishment I have ever achieved."* (Father)

will love him any less than you would if he'd been exactly what you envisioned. It's very rare to get that gorgeous little pink Gerber baby you want to cuddle forever. That feeling will grow. I always wanted a small baby, one with some red highlights in his hair, and I'd never envisioned the one we got—a whopping big baby with jet-black hair! Whenever I felt a twinge of disappointment that he wasn't quite as I'd hoped, I'd clutch him tightly to my bosom and hug him, overwhelmed with love and loyalty, and guilty that I could have any negative feelings about this little fellow who, thank God, was perfectly formed and healthy. "My heavens," he must have thought, "she has quite a squeeze, this mother of mine!"

Many couples who have never paid much attention to children before having their own describe a kind of "universal parenting instinct" after delivery—loving, or at least caring for, all children. Maybe this is Nature's final touch at birth, helping to ensure that the newborn will get all the nurturing and love he needs to thrive and grow.

> *"When the baby was born and we heard her cry, it was just another baby crying, but then I realized it was* our *baby, and when she was placed in my arms, she suddenly became our little child. We were a family."* (father)

20

The First Hour After Delivery

*I*n the delivery room will be your obstetrician, a resident obstetrician who will assist delivery and help take care of the
baby, the nurse who has been with you in labor and delivery, and
the anesthesiologist or nurse-anesthetist, if needed. That's all. You
shouldn't be misled if you see a movie in your childbirth classes
that shows twenty people in the delivery room; they're all there
only because they hoped it would be the beginning of their movie
career.

If there *were* a problem with your baby, you can bet there would
be a pediatrician in there right away. (If you have a choice about
where you'll deliver, consider a hospital that has a good perinatal
unit. It's to be hoped that you won't need it, but it's nice to know
that proper care and facilities are just down the hall. The perinatal
staff is trained and equipped to take care of newborns, some like
little sparrows, who need all kinds of special treatment. It's almost
a science in itself.)

Sewing up the episiotomy after the placenta has been expelled
takes about ten or fifteen minutes, which seems like a long time
considering that the incision is only about an inch long. But there
are several muscle layers to work with, and your doctor is also
examining the cervix, making sure that there's not too much
bleeding and the muscle is contracting. If it seems to take forever,

for distraction ask the nurse to adjust your back rest so you can see your husband with the baby.

If it's twins, once the first baby is out, your doctor normally will not wait the half hour or so that it takes for the uterus to shrink enough to push the second baby out; he will get him out right away. While the uterus is shrinking down, sometimes the cervix shrinks down too; if it closed, you would have to go through the painful process of its opening up again for that second baby. So your doctor puts on a long-cuffed glove and gently reaches way in to get ahold of the second baby, saying in effect: "Sorry if you want to stay in there a little longer, but we're taking you out." If the second one's head is right at the open cervix, head first, your doctor's fingers and some fundal pressure will encourage the head to come out. Usually, however, your doctor will locate the feet (which are easier to hold on to than the head) and deliver the second twin as a breech.

As each twin is delivered, a bracelet immediately identifies Twin A and Twin B, with corresponding clamps for cord A and cord B. The one large placenta or two separate placentas are sent to the lab to determine whether your twins are fraternal or maternal—even with different-sexed babies who are not identical, they still like to examine the placentas.

Most women get the shakes once the placenta is expelled. These tremors are due partly to the sudden departure of the baby, placenta, and amniotic fluid from the system, and also to muscle fatigue. If you feel chilly as you shiver, ask your nurse for a blanket; you may want to wait until the shakes have diminished before holding the baby. They usually last about an hour.

Infant-parent "bonding" is a much-discussed phenomenon these days, so father, mother, and baby now "bond." Studies once claimed that babies and parents who were allowed "bonding time" immediately after birth developed a special, stronger relationship than those who were separated for a few hours or more at birth. Imagine how that made the Caesarean mother feel or the mother whose baby went straight to intensive care! The conclusions of those studies have been invalidated. Although it seems obvious that any time spent with your child is worthwhile, I don't believe there is any one hour that is going to make or break your relationship in this lifetime. Certainly, you and your husband should bond with this baby—what a marvelous time—but don't be guilt-ridden if he is whisked away to the intensive-care unit for a medical problem: there will be thousands of hours ahead of you to be together, and it's wise to keep what happens in the delivery room in proper perspective with life's other requirements.

If the maternity wing is busy, you might be encouraged to "bond quickly" so the delivery room can be ready for another couple in twenty minutes. But however long it is, ideally there will be some relaxing time together, mother, father, and baby, to bask in the glory of the whole experience. (If you are inclined to try to breast-feed, I urge you to wait until you are settled into your room; see page 270.)

As you study and examine your new little baby, the nurse will check the size of your uterus and whether there is bleeding. She'll take blood pressure, pulse, temperature, and respiration readings, and then she will turn her attention to the baby, giving him his first medications, just before he goes to the nursery.

First he will have some form of prophylactic antibiotic to prevent gonorrhea of the eyes. Some hospitals use an antibiotic salve, others use silver nitrate solution drops, and others use an injection of penicillin. You may be thinking, I certainly don't have gonorrhea and my baby doesn't need that. It may be true, but the only sure way to know whether you have it or not is to grow a culture. In most states it's a law that all babies have the preventive treatment; that's probably just as well, since a baby who is born over a vaginal mucous membrane that has active gonorrhea will have irreversible eye damage within twelve hours. This happened once at New York Hospital: when a mother who delivered at home came to the hospital about six hours later, we saw that the baby already had what looked like a cataract on the right eye.

If your baby is treated with silver nitrate solution drops, be prepared to see blue all around the area the next day. Your baby does not have a black eye, nor is he wearing eye shadow. The coloration is from the silver in the solution, which has tarnished in the air, and it will rub off.

Some hospitals give babies an injection of vitamin K to help develop their blood-clotting factor, which is immature in the newborn. This would minimize bruises that might be forming due to the trauma of birth. It's interesting to see your baby's reaction to this injection in the delivery room. When the nurse gives it to him (in the thigh because the thigh muscle is meatier than the bottom), the baby will let out nothing more than a little peep-cry. But when he gets his first DPT booster shot at the pediatrician's office two months later, he'll scream bloody murder and shake for ten minutes. The contrasting reactions confirm that the nervous system is not fully developed at birth, which is probably nature's way of protecting the newborn from the rigors of his ordeal. Think what kind of a headache you would have if your head had been squeezed for twelve hours into a cucumber and you could feel it to the fullest degree!

This dulled reaction to pain is also why a circumcision (see page 281) can be done without anesthesia when the baby is a couple of days old but not when he is two months old.

The baby gets a white plastic "Identa-band" bracelet around the wrist, with your hospital number and name on it. You can snip it off when you arrive home.

Two sets of his footprints are taken. You can ask for one copy to tape lovingly into his baby book; the other is for his permanent hospital records.

Either in the delivery room or in the nursery, the baby will be weighed for the first time. The nurse may give you the figure in grams (3,420 for example) and while you may feel as if you had delivered a 3,400-pound baby, ask for the translation into pounds (seven pounds, eleven ounces in the example given).

If your blood is Rh negative, find out your baby's blood type after delivery. Occasionally a baby will be Rh negative like you, but since your husband is probably Rh positive (the blood type of the population at large, and the dominant trait), you will probably have a baby who is also Rh positive. If he's Rh positive you will receive an injection of Rhogam within seventy-two hours. Rhogam is a batch of antibodies that, when injected intramuscularly, prevent the body from making antibodies. It tricks your body into thinking, These antibodies are already floating around and don't need to be made. If your own antibodies are allowed to build up prior to a subsequent pregnancy, they will "attack" a subsequent Rh-positive baby.

In fact, if you are Rh negative, you should have Rhogam if you have an amniocentesis, an abortion, a miscarriage, and at twenty-eight weeks of pregnancy—whenever there's a chance that the blood cells of the fetus have been introduced into your system—as well as after your Rh positive baby's birth.

With the routine procedures in the delivery room completed, the baby is ready to go to the nursery, usually in a kind of metal box that might look like an incubator but is really just a warm, protective container to transport him safely through the public areas of the hospital. When he arrives in the nursery, he will be put under the warmer until his internal thermostat adjusts to the "world outside." It may be one, two, or three hours before you see him again, depending also on what time of day or night it is and whether or not you have chosen to have rooming in (page 273). The hospital staff will do their best to get the baby to you as soon as possible—but inquire about your hospital's policies.

Just before you leave the labor and delivery area, your nurse will give you a refreshing sponge bath, check your vital signs, and firmly squeeze down on your uterus to make sure that any blood clots that may have accumulated are out. This can be quite uncomfortable, but it is important, so do some of your transition breathing for that five or ten seconds.

You may feel mild "afterpains" for about two or three days after delivery, as the oxytocin in your body continues to help the uterus contract down. Afterpains are more common when you are breast-feeding the baby, due to the release of oxytocin during nursing, and women having second or third babies have stronger afterpains than those experienced by women having first babies.

Now begins treatment and care of that episiotomy. The nurse fills a surgeon's glove with crushed ice, wraps it in a cloth or Handiwipe, and puts it against your stitches. It feels good and it also helps to prevent swelling.

With the glove in place under the sanitary pad (a rather bulky arrangement), you are moved out of the delivery room on a stretcher and into the labor room or recovery room, where you get a final check of blood pressure and temperature, and then on to your room.

Your husband is now off to get the celebratory dinner, either from outside or perhaps from the hospital cafeteria, for you to share in your hospital room. The floor nurse will probably have some food for you, but you may want to get something special for this memorable occasion. If in the delivery room your husband asked what you wanted to eat and you said, "Two large Cokes, that's all," you'll both be sorry later. You have done a big, big, job, probably the most physically demanding job of your life, and you have not had any food for the six, ten, twelve hours of your labor—your body will need to be replenished!

Gentlemen, plan for the celebratory dinner to include enough food for three hungry adults. When you return from the Chinese restaurant around the corner with mooshu pork and all the trimmings, your wife will be ready to devour everything, mustard packs included!

21

The Caesarean Birth and Recovery

S ince one or two women out of ten will give birth by Caesarean section, I think it's well worth being prepared for the possibility. Oh, that won't happen to me, you might think, my pelvis is the right size, the baby is in the right position, and besides, I'm in great physical shape for labor. Well, it *might* happen to you even if it's difficult to imagine. Of course, your doctor may have informed you that a Caesarean will be necessary for a specific reason. Even then it takes time for the reality of this idea to sink in.

Some women feel that they, themselves, have failed, so great is their disappointment not to have had a "normal" delivery. When women tell me this after their Caesarean birth, I encourage them to see it from a different viewpoint: another, more vital issue is at stake—the delivery of a healthy baby endowed at birth with his natural, God-given potential. That, unquestionably, is far more important than the route of his delivery.

Midwives in the nineteenth century prayed for an alternative to difficult vaginal births; they knew how much inevitable sorrow would be spared. Today, those prayers have been answered in the perfection of the Caesarean. Only 12 percent of all Caesarean deliveries are done because the baby experiences fetal distress and needs to be delivered immediately. In these cases, the Cae-

> "After about twenty hours of labor (counting from the very first pang) and two hours of pushing, we had a Caesarean because the baby was just too big to come out, even though I was fully dilated. I initially resisted the Caesarean because after so much labor and concentration I wasn't totally thinking straight and I had this funny feeling that I'd get a different baby with a Caesarean than I was supposed to get with a vaginal delivery. My husband, the labor nurse, and the doctor, and the wearing off of the epidural convinced me otherwise."

sarean is so welcome a birthing alternative that the parents involved usually never feel a twinge of disappointment about how their baby was born. However, when a Caesarean birth is not nearly as unexpected or dramatic—that is, in the remaining 88 percent of all Caesareans—parents may then have a harder time coming to grips with the need for a Caesarean birth. In any case, a healthy baby, *not* a vaginal birth, is the ultimate goal for all, and it should be yours, too.

Reasons for Caesarean delivery are varied, as are individual hospital statistics. If the large medical center in your area has a Caesarean birth rate of 20 percent and the small community hospital has a rate of only 12 percent, do not assume that by changing hospitals (from larger to smaller, in this case) you will avoid a Caesarean. The large center, where equipment is probably more sophisticated, may attract a larger number of "high-risk" expectant mothers who more often need to be delivered by Caesarean. Your own doctor will explain your situation and specific needs to you. Since 88 percent of all Caesarean births are done for reasons other than fetal distress (which could occur at any moment in labor and to anyone), you will probably know well in advance if you will have one.

The leading cause for a Caesarean birth is *cephalopelvic disproportion:* the size of the pelvis is too small for the baby to pass through. This may be due to the "natural architecture" of the pelvis, to a very large baby, or a combination of the two. Pelvic disproportion is quite common in the United States, "the melting pot of the world," where nationalities mix and babies who inherit their father's stature are planted in mothers from a race with characteristically small frames. This discrepancy was prevalent after World War II when many American servicemen brought back Oriental wives who almost always required Caesarean sections to deliver their large, half-Caucasian babies.

Although quite rare, preeclampsia, toxemia, and other medical conditions in the mother may warrant delivery by Caesarean if continuing the pregnancy or waiting for labor to begin spontaneously could put the mother or baby in jeopardy. A vaginal infection such as genital herpes, in which a baby delivered over a herpes lesion could pick up a life-threatening infection, would warrant a Caesarean.

Placenta previa, wherein the placenta completely or partially blocks the cervical opening, is another risky situation in which the Caesarean may become a valid option. However, if there is only a marginal or partial covering, a vaginal delivery is possible. Bleeding in the second trimester usually indicates placenta previa and warrants a sonogram (page 26) to determine the exact position; if the cervix is completely covered by the placenta a Caesarean will inevitably be done, usually at the onset of labor. (Sonograms always show the location of the placenta, so if you have one with amniocentesis, for example, you know its position at that point and don't have to worry about it.)

Another reason for a Caesarean might be the baby's position; an unusual presentation—breech, for example, or transverse (lying across the pelvis)—might prohibit a vaginal delivery.

"We knew that we would have a Caesarean—the baby was a 'floating breech' and two weeks overdue. As to my husband's being there, we both decided against it. He fainted during our amniocentesis, and that was enough of an embarrassment for one family to endure! It took me a long time to get over my disappointment that we would not have a normal delivery, but there was no getting around the fact that it was a high-risk situation."

There are other indications as well, including one described simply as the "failure to progress," where for unknown reasons the cervix fails to dilate even after ten to twelve hours of contractions.

If you have an emergency Caesarean, you will be given general anesthesia. For a scheduled Caesarean, however, a local anesthetic is preferable because it allows you to see the baby right away and assures a speedy recovery. With more and more hospitals permitting fathers to be with their wives in the operating room should she have a local anesthetic, many couples find sharing the experience and seeing the baby right away to be just as meaningful an experience as they'd hoped for with a vaginal birth.

Gentlemen, if you are uncertain about being present for your wife's Caesarean even if the doctor permits it, rest assured that you will not actually be watching the surgery. A small screen obscures your view of your wife's incision while you sit by her head, talk to her, and hold her hand.

If your initial reaction to being awake is, Hmm, for major surgery? I don't think I care much for that, I encourage you to think again. First, the recovery from a Caesarean delivery is substantially easier if you do not have the additional strain from general anesthesia. Second, if your doctor will permit your husband to be with you, to distract you from hearing the call go out for scalpel, clamps, and other necessary instruments, you can easily focus away from the procedure until the baby is born. After the birth, which is relatively the shortest part of the whole procedure, you will probably be given a relaxant (it's not given before because it might affect the baby) and be so involved with seeing the baby for the first time that you'll have enough distraction from thinking about the operation. If fathers are not permitted in the operating room at your hospital, the anesthesiologist or nurse will be with you to explain what is happening and to distract you. Usually they are so experienced in assuming this role that you will get a first-rate running commentary as the operation progresses, if that's what you'd like, or they will simply give you candid reassurance about what is happening.

If you know you will be having a Caesarean before the onset

of labor, your doctor will explain how to prepare for it and give you guidelines for eating, drinking, coming into the hospital, and so on. You'll be shaved—not just your pubic hair but the whole abdomen as well—and set up with an intravenous drip of glucose water fed through a tiny needle or tube into a vein in your arm to assure a good supply of fluids during and after surgery since you will not be eating or drinking in this period. The IV also provides a route for medication, including Pitocin if it's needed postoperatively to minimize bleeding. The intravenous usually remains in place for one or two days after the operation, until you are taking fluids by mouth.

Usually one good epidural (see page 209) will get you through the Caesarean without any additional medication; obviously your doctor will make sure it's working before he starts. It lasts for about an hour and wears off very gradually, so there is no danger of feeling the operation. If you should become aware of pressure becoming more intense on the right side, for example, say so and you will be given more medication. If that does not work and you say, "No, I'm still aware of that area," then you might have to be put out with a general anesthetic, but that is unusual.

> *"Birth was ten times easier than what I'd expected. I ended up having a Caesarean after eight hours of labor, but only the last two hours were hard labor, and then I had to be put out because the epidural didn't work. I woke up a little later and had given birth relatively painlessly, it seemed."*

The whole operation takes about an hour, but the baby appears in the first fifteen minutes or so. As your doctor removes him from the uterus, you might feel quite a tugging sensation, depending on his or her size. It's not painful (remember, you're numb from the waist down), but it is a definite sensation of

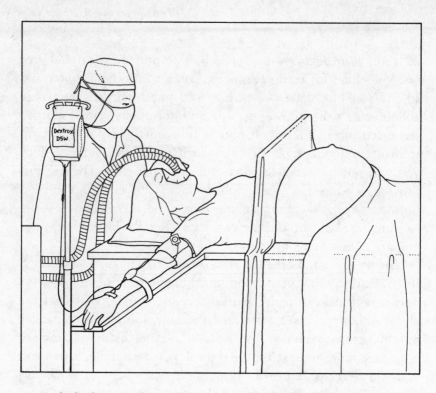

Under local or general anesthesia, the incision is made and the baby is delivered. The placenta is removed and uterus and skin sutured.

something being yanked. Contrary to what some women imagine, delivery by Caesarean is not like having the doctor open a zipper and reach in with his two hands to easily lift the baby out. The uterine incision is only about four or five inches long, not much wider than the birth canal, and it requires deft maneuvering and some effort to get that baby out and leave you with a fairly small incision as well.

And what will you see of this little baby who's making such an abrupt appearance in the world? As with babies born vaginally, he'll look very blue. But he'll have more of a chance to look very beautiful, too, because if he's a scheduled Caesarean, his head will be perfectly formed and as round as can be—he's experienced none of the trauma of labor and a vaginal birth. When one mother's family came to the hospital to see her one-day-old, nine-pound, six-ounce Caesarean baby, she said it reminded her of a scene in an old Hollywood movie. As everyone peered through

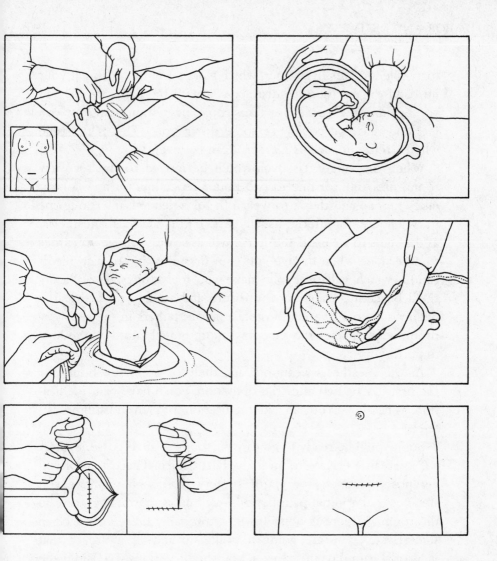

the glass window of the nursery at all those little vaginally delivered babies with their elongated heads and squished features, the nurse smiled and held up the whopping big, perfectly formed "Baby Smith" for them to see—looking for all the world like the two-month-old cast as the "newborn."

Other than head formation, the Caesarean baby will have the same newborn characteristics as other babies (for details, see chapter 19).

Once the baby is out, the stitching-up process takes a good

forty-five minutes to an hour, which will pass more quickly if your husband can be there to distract you with the baby. If not, and you begin to feel restless or claustrophobic, tell the staff how you feel and that you could use some distraction. (This is the time when a relaxant such as Demerol can be given.)

When the surgery is over, you'll be moved to the recovery room, probably for one to two hours depending on how long it takes for the anesthesia to wear off: for a general, it's about one to two hours; for a local, usually less. If you had local anesthesia, as it begins to wear off the nurse will ask you to move your toes to determine when to give you your first injection of pain medication, which will probably make you feel groggy. Periodically she'll be taking your blood pressure and asking you to breathe deeply and cough. Some hospitals permit fathers in the recovery room, which makes the time pass more quickly until you're able to go to your room.

As the anesthesia wears off, and then for every few hours for the first day or two after the operation, you'll have pain medication, as needed. (You can take medication for pain and still breast-feed.)

Soon you'll be ready to go to your room. If at all possible, after a Caesarean a private room is the best choice. The Demerol you get postoperatively for major surgery is enough to make you sleep over the initial pain period—as long as there is no noise in the room. If there is noise (as most probably there would be in semiprivate), you are going to wake up and be aware of that incisional pain. For this reason, you should seriously consider the private room; many Caesarean mothers say the price difference is well worth the peace and quiet you're guaranteed to get.

THE CAESAREAN RECOVERY

The discomforts of the initial recovery period after a Caesarean can be a shock if you've never had a major operation, but following the good advice and guidance of the nurses will help to get the healing process under way. *You can expect to feel terrible the first day after a Caesarean, so plan for no visitors that day aside from your husband and perhaps your parents.*

It's very important to move your body as soon as you can after surgery. Gas that accumulates in the intestines will be passed more easily if you stand up and walk—it can be extremely painful if you don't. For that reason, you will probably be encouraged to get up and sit in a chair the morning after your operation.

Be sure someone helps you to get out of bed. It may take about six separate moves—bend leg and place it here, bend arm and place it there, et cetera, before you can actually say you've made it to your feet. Pain medication half an hour before getting up the first few times will be a big help.

For most Caesarean births, a low abdominal incision is usually done to avoid cutting through the working muscle of the uterus, as well as to allow you the option of wearing a bikini later on. Usually the incision is made just above or just inside the pubic hairline, and in about six months' time it is almost invisible. When you finally get the chance to look down at it, probably when your doctor comes by to examine you and remove your dressing the first day after surgery, you may be taken aback at how primitive the whole thing looks. The stitches are knotted about half an inch apart, with thread ends sticking out every which way (or your doctor may have used "staples" or tiny metal stitches), and it is perfectly natural to think that with one good twist everything will come undone. It won't. The healing process is miraculous, and already the tissues in the abdominal wall and the muscles under it are weaving back together.

> *"I'd say the worst part was the pain of the recovery. Once the painkillers started wearing off, I was in agony. I thought that I'd be able to make it through the night sleeping and woke up in unbelievable pain at about two A.M. the first night. Then I got medication and could sleep. The first step was a killer also. The high point was holding Roddy in my arms for the first time although I was numb from the breasts down."*

Ask your doctor or the nurses when you can take a shower: cleansing will help you gain some confidence to overcome your exhaustion and pain, and it will feel good to take care of yourself in such a pleasant, familiar routine.

After a Caesarean, many women find full-cut underpants more comfortable than a belt to hold the sanitary pad in place. Although bleeding after a Caesarean is often not as heavy as after a vaginal delivery, pads will be necessary for the first two or three weeks.

If you have ever heard the expression "it only hurts when I laugh," you will find it taking on new meaning after a Caesarean. Most of the pain comes because the muscles that usually crisscross the abdomen were cut during the operation, and where ordinarily the simplest task went unnoticed beforehand, now every cough, deep breath, and yes, good laugh not only make you wince, but at first can make you feel as if you were struck by lightning. Blowing up a balloon would be sheer torture (were you aware that the muscles in your abdomen are involved?), but in fact it is just the kind of exercise your muscles need most, so do not think the nurses are being sadistic when they encourage you to use your abdominal muscles.

Health insurance usually covers a week's stay in the hospital, and I would encourage you to stay the full time allotted for a Caesarean birth. You may prefer the thought of going home to your own cozy bed, but recovering from major surgery while caring for a newborn is not easy and the extra days in the hospital will give you more stamina and confidence. Having your mother, sister, or a good friend stay with you for about two weeks will make your recovery easier. Caring for a newborn in addition to recovering from major surgery is a difficult combination. Just be sure the person you choose is someone you feel comfortable with and enjoy.

Attitude is crucial to the progress of your surgical recovery. After the operation, particularly if it is your first bout with surgery, you may have to coax your body to do things it does not want to do. Lying back in bed and groaning for three days, even if that is exactly what you feel like doing, will only make your physical condition worse. Of course the nurses will help you, but you have to find your own motivation to recover. Difficult as it is to get out of bed when the very muscles you need have been cut and stitched back together, you *must* do it. The sooner you do, the faster and ultimately easier your recovery will be.

Perspective also helps to get through a Caesarean. Remember that it has gotten your baby out of a jeopardizing situation and safely into your arms, and the sooner you recover, the sooner you will enjoy this healthy new little person. Whether they delivered vaginally or by Caesarean, most women need time to see the "bigger picture" of life as a parent to understand just how small a price the pain of childbirth is to the whole experience. Difficult as the birth and its recovery might be now, difficult as it is to envision things getting better, the discomfort and pain of a Caesarean birth will fade away just as your love for your new little baby will grow, as will any disappointment that you may now feel.

But for now, once you are settled into your room, concentrate on your recovery and let your husband get involved with the baby. Your spouse, who may or may not have exercised his role as your coach in labor, is in fact now called upon to perform the double duty of caring for both you and the baby, particularly if you chose rooming in (next chapter). The nurses will help too, of course, but many women recovering from a Caesarean find great happiness, humor, and distraction in watching their husband hold the baby and tend to her needs while they are not yet ready to do this. This is an extra, positive aspect of the Caesarean—that special, early intimacy between father and baby.

Remember that the decision to deliver by Caesarean was beyond your control and casts no reflection on your abilities as a woman or your potential as a mother. Talk to your doctor about your options for future births: there may be a good possibility you can deliver vaginally with another child; if not, that's fine, too. Like most women, your childbirth experience will probably, in time, be remembered not so much for the actual event as for its marking the beginning of a new, dynamic dimension in your life—a family.

PART FOUR

Postpartum Days in the Hospital

For most couples, whatever the route of delivery, the postpartum days in the hospital are very special—filled with excitement, joy, and relief in the wake of those anxious days prior to labor and delivery. In time you may very well forget the minutiae of the birth itself, but remember exactly the face of your favorite nurse and the small details of how she ministered to your needs in those postpartum days, especially if you had a Caesarean section, or sat with you as you tentatively put that baby to your breast for the first time. You might vividly recall what was on your bedside table, so neatly arranged, after images of the rest of the surroundings blur.

I remember the comments of one new mother at a Lamaze class reunion. She had had a difficult labor with an ensuing Caesarean. Beaming a smile down at the baby in her arms, she described the moment when the hospital pediatrician came into her room the morning after she had delivered, stood next to her bed, and stated in his clear, official voice, "Mrs. Jones, you have a *perfect* baby girl." She felt so happy at that moment that she thought her heart would burst.

Savor these all-too-fleeting hospital days—they bridge the ordeal of birth and the reality of getting home to assume the new responsibility of being a parent. That, too, will be a time filled with excitement and joy, but with the nurses easing you into the routine of caring for the baby, the dinner hour shouldered by the hospital and perhaps shared by your husband (another mother commented on how she could have lived on those institutional meals forever, since after all, they'd been served to her!)—all is right with the world.

22

New Mother and Baby, Settling In

YOUR HOSPITAL ROOM

In what now seems light-years away, you made the choice of having a private or semiprivate room. If you went on the hospital tour during the last weeks of your pregnancy, you were able to compare the two kinds of rooms and judge for yourself. But that was when you did not know what your actual birth experience would be, and many hospitals allow you to change your mind about your room choice if you speak up about it just before you leave the delivery room.

In most hospitals, *semiprivate* in the postpartum unit means anywhere from two to four beds to a room, with adjoining bath. This situation is perfectly fine for most vaginal deliveries, in my opinion, and in fact has real advantages because it is useful to chat, share experiences, and learn what you can from the other mothers during what are going to be three or four seemingly short days in the hospital. In all fairness, if you choose semiprivate, you will not know who your roommates will be and you could wind up with three women with whom you have nothing in common except maternity. On the other hand, you might be sharing the room with your best friend or some of the women from your Lamaze class. Since there is usually a big turnover in maternity wards, the chances are you would find pleasant company among the other new mothers, at least for part of your hospital stay and possibly for all of it.

Fathers are welcome in semiprivate rooms during visiting hours and sometimes at other times during the day, but usually, so there is some morning privacy, not before about nine A.M. Especially if you are a Caesarean first-time mother, the *last* thing you want to see on the morning after surgery is someone else's husband smiling at the foot of your bed or even in the corridor.

Insurance coverage may influence your choice of a private or semiprivate room. Most insurance companies pay for four twenty-four-hour periods for a vaginal delivery, seven for a Caesarean. If your insurance does not pay, I recommend that you go home. For what *one* day in the hospital costs for you and your baby, you two could have a wonderful three-day stay at the Plaza Hotel, include your husband, and have better room service in a much more tastefully appointed room!

If your coverage includes four days, there are several good reasons to stay in the hospital for all of them—and I urge you to do so.

Your milk comes in on that third or fourth day, and it is reassuring to have the nurses there to help make sure the breast-feeding goes well. Chances are, you will also have your first bowel movement. (If you delivered by C section, you're not allowed to go home till you've passed that milestone.) And no matter how much you look forward to getting home, quiet nights of blissful, uninterrupted sleep are, at least for the time being, going to be rare if not nonexistent; you'll be getting up two or three times a night to tend that baby. Although you may opt for night feedings in the hospital, it is an entirely different ball game to have a nurse come in with your warm, cozy, freshly diapered little baby, gently pat you, and say "Time to nurse, Mother Smith." You latch him on the breast—five minutes on this side, five minutes on that side—then signal the nurse. She takes him away, burps him, changes him, and puts him back to bed. Fabulous!

But when you are at home and awakened out of a deep sleep to the unfamiliar sound of a wailing infant, you will think, "Whaaat is that? Where am I? *Who* am I?" And you roll yourself out of bed, find the crib, stumble to your feeding place, grope around to get the baby on the nipple, nurse on one breast, burp him and change his diaper, and by the time you get finished nursing on the second breast, he will be sleeping soundly—and you will be wide awake, turning on the late late show. One extra night's sleep in the hospital, even with night feedings, is very beneficial to prepare for coping at home. In case you end up with a Caesarean and your hospital coverage includes the first seven days after delivery, find out if it's for semiprivate only and you have to make up the difference if you want a private room.

When you arrive in your room, the nurse will help you into your bed (wonderfully soft compared to that stretcher), check your vital signs, and feel the top of the uterus to be sure it is firm and well-contracted. If not, she will massage it to encourage contraction and minimize bleeding. Use your transition breathing if this hurts.

She will also check your episiotomy stitches and, if needed, offer you a new ice pack. Ice-pack treatments are effective for about twelve hours to help prevent swelling; after that, you should start using heat: taking a hot shower, doing your pelvic-floor exercises (page 75), moving around to encourage circulation to the area.

Once you're settled in, you will be encouraged to stay in bed for the first four to six hours after delivery. This is an arbitrary number, but it helps your circulatory system to readjust after the birth. If you leap out of bed two hours after delivery, you will be so dizzy that in thirty seconds you will be flat on the floor. Even after waiting awhile, 90 percent of newly delivered women feel faint the first time they stand up, so when you are ready, make sure someone is there to help you. After that, you can come and go as you please.

Approximately an hour after delivery, your husband may rejoin you in your room with **food.** In addition to being famished, you will probably crave water. I was so thirsty the night after delivery

"*All the way down to my room I worried that I'd seen only three fingers on each of the baby's hands. My husband tried to convince me that everything was normal, but I pleaded, 'Just go to the nursery and have a look at her for me.' So he went down the hall and had the nurse hold Lily up behind the glass. When he returned, I asked fearfully if all her fingers and toes were there. 'I stopped counting at ten,' he laughed, and gave me a big hug. Only then did I relax.*"

that I grabbed the ice-water carafe off my bedside table and guzzled the whole thing. It was more refreshing than anything I had ever tasted in my life!

A large rush of adrenaline courses through your system and your thoughts are racing even though your body is exhausted. It's nice to share this time with your husband.

Gentlemen, reach into your Lamaze bag and get out that split of champagne to toast the event. The champagne not only gives you a chance to celebrate, it also helps you unwind a bit, giving you both a chance to relax and then get some rest.

As you and your husband are eating your meal together and getting used to the idea that you are proud new parents, your freshly bathed baby is warming up in the nursery, lying swaddled up and on his side to allow any mucus or amniotic fluid to drain out of his nose and mouth, adjusting his own internal thermostat, most likely asleep in the aftermath of birth.

Some women find that they are completely preoccupied during the "celebratory meal" by a painful episiotomy, especially if it was for a very big baby or a forceps delivery, both of which require a relatively large incision. If you are very uncomfortable, ask the nurse for some medication to help reduce the pain. Usually it will be a combination of two light analgesics such as Darvon and aspirin or Tylenol, but you may need something stronger, a narcotic such as codeine, for example. It all depends on the size of the incision. If you had a forceps delivery, you have that hockey-stick episiotomy which, instead of being one inch long and straight, is three inches long and curves out to your fanny cheek. Mine felt as if it went from my vagina to the nape of my neck and I remember that when I finally did ask for pain medication, my nurse said, "We wondered how long you would last. You have a very big episiotomy and a tear as well." No wonder I felt so miserable! (Remember, you can take medication during the first three or four days after delivery, as colostrum is made during pregnancy.) After engorgement, take no medication without consulting your doctor.

If it is codeine you take in those first twenty-four hours, keep in mind that narcotics are constipating, and you will need a slice of your glazed dried fruits that evening.

An hour or so after your meal together (now about two or three hours after delivery) you will drift off to sleep, exhausted. If it is the middle of the day, your husband may want to stay with you. If it is the middle of the night, he may go home, as exhausted as you are, and return in the morning.

When will you see the baby again? This depends on whether or not you have chosen rooming in, as well as what time you came down from the delivery room.

Rooming in means that the baby stays in your room most of the day, in a little bassinette on wheels, and returns to the nursery at night and during visiting hours. Of course he needn't be with you constantly; you can take him back to the nursery, or request that the nurse take him, any time you wish. But in general, he can stay with you longer during the day than the baby who is not rooming in and returns to the nursery after each feeding.

I would encourage you to have rooming in because a baby's first few days of life are delightfully peaceful. They are asleep more than awake (recovering from delivery), are not too interested in eating (full-term babies utilize the extra fat stores nature bestows before birth), hardly need changing or cry—it isn't until you get home that all hell breaks loose! With rooming in, the routine in the hospital is wonderful. When you feel so inclined, you can reach over and take the baby out of the bassinette for a cuddle and an inspection, put him back and take a quick shower, take a little nap together—sheer bliss. You get a head start in baby-care experience, too. You learn that it's normal for babies to breathe with grunts and groans—thus sparing yourself from sitting up all night when you get home, thinking he's dying when you hear these sounds. If you are in a semiprivate room you can gather information as nurses answer the other mothers' questions about rashes, crying patterns, nursing, and whatnot, and may get some useful tips from a roommate who's an experienced mother.

> *"I loved going to the hospital each day to see Patty and the baby. The nurses allowed me to stay late each evening and we would sit quietly talking about the baby and the whole experience. It was also great to look into the nursery and to watch his face, to hear his cry, to wonder what he was thinking and feeling."*

GETTING INTO THE HOSPITAL ROUTINE

Hospital routines may vary slightly, but because of the nature of institutions, there will always be what might be called a typical day, with events unfolding in rapid succession somewhat like the following:

Awakened at 8 A.M., you have from 8:00 to 8:30 to do everything you planned to do for yourself that day. At 8:30, the breakfast trays appear. At 9:00 A.M. it's time to feed the babies. You have two full hours, which may seem like a long time, but if you have never fed or burped a baby, changed a diaper or wrapped a baby up, it really does take a full two hours.

At 11:00 it is off to classes: mother care, baby care, emotional development of the newborn, whatever you might want to attend. Back by 12:15 P.M. when lunch trays arrive. Eat until one o'clock and then it's time to feed the babies. Feed the babies from one to two, and at two o'clock it's time for class, this time breastfeeding, formula preparation, and so on, then back to your room. At 3 P.M. the visitors start arriving. (Babies go back into the

> *"The second day in the hospital I went into the nursery and started wheeling out someone else's baby by mistake. You'd think a mother would know her own baby!"*

nursery during visiting hours to limit their contact with people other than parents.)

By the time visiting hours are over it's 4:45 P.M. Then from 5:00 to 6:00 it's baby-feeding time again. You eat from 6:00 to 6:30 P.M., when visiting hours start again and all the babies return to the nursery. Visiting hours until about 8:30 P.M. And at 9 o'clock?—time to feed the baby again! Feed the baby from 9:00 to 10:00, then collapse into bed exhausted.

Whatever the variation, the routine day is not unlike being on a merry-go-round—but you can always skip classes and take a nap if that is what you need most.

> *"For me, the experience of childbirth caused a momentous change in my perception of my wife, whom I had known as a girlfriend, new bride, wife, and now, in the space of a few dramatic hours, mother. I felt proud of her and deeply grateful that, through her, we had been transformed into a family."*

Helping Your Body to Recover

The nurse on duty will help get you get started with the routine care of your body; she'll also assist you with the care of your baby. Listen closely and ask questions—your time in the hospital will be over before you know it. (Those who have a Caesarean and a longer stay in the hospital also have the advantage of more time to absorb the information and expert advice of the nursing staff.)

Routine care of your episiotomy should include rinsing the area after you go to the bathroom and patting it dry with a soft tissue. Some hospitals supply numbing sprays or creams that offer temporary relief. As you run your fingers gently along the episiotomy, you will feel the little stitches tied in knots. On the fourth or fifth day after delivery, the part of the stitches inside the skin has been absorbed and the knots fall away. Do not be surprised if you notice several of them on your sanitary pad.

If you find that your episiotomy is still very sore after the twelve-hour period when you used the ice packs, try some of the following relief measures:

- Pelvic-floor or "elevator" exercise: to increase circulation to the area (see page 75); start doing these regularly as soon as possible after delivery

- Warm sitz baths: Soaking your whole bottom in a warm bath soothes the area and promotes healing; ask the nurse to explain the bath procedure to you

- Hot showers: Allow the warm water to run down over the episiotomy and suds the area gently with your fingers—not a washcloth, as that could catch on the stitches; rinse well when you shower

Sitting on a rubber ring (similar to a child's inner tube) is discouraged because it keeps you sedentary when your main goal should be to increase circulation in the sore area. Some physicians believe that these rings actually increase the chance of cutting off the blood supply to the pelvic area because they exert pressure when you sit on them.

Hemorrhoids are another postpartum discomfort. Eighty percent of women who have a vaginal delivery develop them due to the forceful pushing of the second stage of labor, which makes the veins at the rectal opening protrude. At first they may be large enough to resemble a cluster of grapes around your rectum and you may worry that you'll be plagued with them forever, but they usually shrink back to their prepregnant size in a few weeks. In the meantime, if you have used home remedies in the past, use them now—or try the following:

Thoroughly cleanse the area and gently apply some numbing, lubricating cream (the nurse can give it to you) to the hemorrhoids. Coat them well and gently tuck them back into the rectum to encourage shrinkage and relieve pressure.

If you find this impossible to do yourself, ask the nurse for assistance. Sitz baths may bring relief for hemorrhoids, but some women prefer cold treatments. For example, a few ice chips wrapped in gauze, dipped in witch hazel, and held in place with a sanitary napkin can be soothing.

Avoid getting constipated. If natural fiber sources are not adequate, ask your doctor about a stool softener.

Heavy, red bleeding, referred to as lochia, is common during the first few days after delivery, and you may even pass a few small blood clots. Some cramping and a gush of bleeding may occur when you are breast-feeding, as breast-feeding encourages the uterus to contract down. After the first few days postpartum, the bleeding diminishes and becomes darker, but many women experience a renewed bout of bright red bleeding on the day they go home from the hospital or during the subsequent weeks at home. It is a sign that you are doing too much and need more rest. Contact your doctor if it persists. First-time mothers often find it difficult to know when to limit activities, and this bleeding can serve as your cue. As it wanes, it will become a pinkish, mucous discharge, and usually will end at about three or four weeks.

If you had a Caesarean, you will not have as much bleeding initially, but will experience more of it, off and on, during the first two weeks at home.

Keep using sanitary pads until the bleeding stops completely, and to avoid the risk of infection, ask your doctor when you can resume using tampons.

Regaining Your Figure

When you look down at the flab and sag of your postpartum abdomen, the sight may well tempt you to despair. You lost ten to fifteen pounds with the birth itself, but you probably have another ten to fifteen to go. Your empty belly still looks almost seven months pregnant. It has an eerie softness and, much as you concentrate on pulling it in, it just won't go. Despite its appearance the day after delivery, the body has fabulous resilience. Do not turn to girdles. The greatest way to make that abdomen flat again is to try to hold it in!

Before having my own children, I would blithely assure the women in my classes that they would have their waistlines back six to eight weeks after delivery. Having had three large babies of my own, I must confess that if you are able to regain your prepregnant waistline before a year has passed, you are my true heroine! Realistically, you'll need almost the same length of time it took to stretch that belly out of shape to get it *back* into shape, and although Mother Nature is concerned that your uterus contract down quickly so that bleeding is minimal, she is not at all interested in your aesthetic form after delivery. Regaining that firm, flat abdomen is entirely up to you.

While breast-feeding helps the uterus to contract down to its prepregnant size, you also need to give your body a big nudge with some simple exercises. The following can be done in the first twenty-four hours after delivery or, if you had a Caesarean, after a few days.

Lying in bed on your stomach not only encourages the abdominal wall to begin shrinking down, it also helps your pelvic organs return to their proper place. Take it slow—this position will feel a little strange at first, after three or four (or more) months of not being able to do it. If you have had a Caesarean, use a little pillow to pad the sore areas, or wait until your stitches are removed if they seem to pull. If your breasts feel tender, roll up a towel and position it under the rib-cage area.

Lying in bed on your back and lifting your head will work the muscles in the abdomen. Rest your head on a pillow and slowly raise it, flexing your feet at the same time. Hold for several seconds and then release the head back down as you point the toes. Repeat this ten times, twice a day.

Begin your full postpartum exercise program (see page 351) when your doctor gives you permission, usually within a few days after a vaginal delivery and two to three weeks after a Caesarean birth. Start slowly, and if you find that your bleeding becomes heavier, stop. It means the program is too strenuous for you. Try again in a day or two, this time less vigorously and with fewer repetitions.

Although you may not be able to pinpoint where excess body fluids remain, you will know from the number of pounds still to go that your body is adjusting slowly, with excess fluids being urinated or perspired away. Remember that it is normal to awaken at night soaked in perspiration or to feel that you need to urinate almost as often as when you were pregnant. This is not the time to try one of those crash diets that you may have used in school. Your body is on the mend and needs a well-balanced diet for repair. If you are nursing, remember that you need very few extra calories daily (see page 308).

Once you are settled in at home, the time you spend caring for your little baby will help you get back into shape. Babies keep you moving, and hard as it is to imagine, that same baby who sleeps so peacefully in the hospital nursery will soon make General Patton look like a drum majorette! A brisk walk around the block or a determined strut across the living room with your newborn (to help him relax and get to sleep) will burn lots of calories and increase your stamina.

If you are breast-feeding, those first few feedings in the hospital are critical to the ongoing nursing process. The more you know about it, the more confidence you will have in this method of feeding your baby (discussed in chapter 23), and I hope you will give it a try.

BABY'S IN-HOSPITAL DAYS

On the third day or so after delivery, your baby will come out to you with a Band-Aid on his heel. This is where he has had a few drops of blood taken for a battery of basic body-function tests such as thyroid and phenylketonuria. Defects in these functions are fairly rare but easily checked; everything is fine unless you hear otherwise.

Jaundice. On that same day, you may notice that your baby's skin has a wonderful, kind of peachy, suntanned look and you'll think, My, he looks handsome today. Actually, the color is the result of what is referred to as infant jaundice, and all babies will have some amount of it. This is because when they are in the uterus they have extra red-blood cells to circulate the oxygen from the placenta throughout their system. But once they are born and breathing their own oxygen (a much more efficient system), those extra red cells are broken down and excreted in a byproduct called bilirubin. Since a newborn's liver is immature and inefficient, most of the excess bilirubin passes through the skin, giving it a slightly yellowish tinge.

Premature babies usually have higher levels of bilirubin, as their liver maturation is even less than a full-term infant's. Early clamping of the umbilical cord is one way to prevent extra blood from pumping into the baby's system, but when it occurs, phototherapy is a simple, routine treatment.

It was found in hospitals years ago that the babies situated near the windows in the nursery rarely had a high bilirubin level: something in the sunlight helped break down and excrete the substance from the skin. If your baby shows a high bilirubin count, which would make him lethargic, he will be a candidate for simulated sun treatment. He will be placed naked in an isolette or warm, air-filled box (wearing a surgeon's mask as a bikini to prevent him from urinating all over the box and two little patches over his eyes so he needn't look at ultraviolet light all day), and when you visit the nursery you'll see him sunbathing under the ultraviolet light as if he were on the beach in St.-Tropez. With this treatment, the bilirubin level drops substantially within twelve hours.

If you are breast-feeding a baby who is receiving phototherapy for infant jaundice, it is important to remember that while the bilirubin level is high the baby will be lethargic and fall off to sleep when you try to nurse him. As the bilirubin level starts to drop, he will become hyperirritable: getting on the breast, suddenly getting off; wanting to nurse, not wanting to. It's very hard to deal with, but you've got to hang in there, first for the six hours of the high level and then for the twelve hours of the decline, or however long it takes until things are back to normal. After that, everything will be fine.

Circumcisions, in most hospitals, used to be done in the delivery room, but it soon became evident that babies were better off put under the warmer right away. If you plan to have your baby circumcised, it will probably be scheduled for the day after delivery or the day before you are going home and will be done by your obstetrician. If you have a religious ceremony in the hospital, your rabbi may lead it, but the obstetrician will probably be the one to do the circumcision.

Circumcisions in the United States are not the routine procedure that they were in the past, when they were done more for reasons of hygiene than religion. Now the issue of cleanliness is obsolete; nearly every house in America has hot and cold running water and soap, so it is the matter of other issues being weighed. Should there be a surgical procedure when it is not essential? (Minor though it is, there is still an element of risk.) And what about psychological considerations? Is his father circumcised? (Later in life, he may want his penis to look like Dad's or his peers'.)

On the other hand, if he is not circumcised, there is the one-in-a-thousand chance that in time the foreskin might get too tight, a medical condition called *phimosis* that requires a circumcision. One Lamaze class father described having it done for just that reason when he was nine. Because it was a big trauma for him then, he heartily recommended the postnatal circumcision!

Whatever your views, talk the issue of circumcision over with your obstetrician, who will usually do the procedure. If you decide to have it done, you must sign a permission consent form—it won't be done without your knowing it.

As for what the baby feels, he certainly will feel something, but while it is being done he seems to show as much of a response to being restrained (which is necessary to keep his hands clear of the area) as he does to the actual procedure. In other words, just as with getting that first injection, he still does not have a fully developed reaction. You certainly wouldn't get the same reaction with a two-year-old!

Once the foreskin has been removed, a little piece of Vaseline-coated gauze will be placed around the edge that was cut; the baby usually urinates this off within twenty-four hours or so. When you do see the circumcision for the first time, remember that circumcised or not, the head of that little penis is normally a deep red color at first and soon settles down to a less intense color. Not to worry.

23

What No One Ever Told You About Breast-feeding

*I*f you were a breast-fed baby, you may love the whole idea and feel completely committed to breast-feeding your own baby. If you find breast-feeding completely unappealing or, as one mother-to-be put it, "absolutely bovine," that's fine, too. In either case, the decision has already been made, consciously or subconsciously, and since all babies thrive whether breast- or bottle-fed, it seems to me that a *happy* mother and baby is the goal, particularly in those early, hectic weeks of adjustment after birth.

For many years it was important to decide before you delivered if you were going to breast-feed because mothers who planned to bottle-feed were often given a male hormone at delivery to discourage milk production. Today the trend is against giving women male hormones, since some women experience rather unsettling side effects from this practice—they sprout a few whiskers or their voice temporarily sinks an octave or two. If you haven't made up your mind definitely one way or another, I recommend that you give breast-feeding a try. If you don't like it, you can always switch the baby over to a bottle; but I've worked with so many mothers who were at first unsure, tried breast-feeding, and loved it that you may end up regretting it if you never try it.

There is a critical, hidden factor to breast-feeding—your confi-

dence. You may think, But what could be easier? Breast-feeding is a natural process—I have a breast and a baby and I'll just put them together. This is perfectly true, but new mothers are particularly vulnerable to minor obstacles that arise during the initial postpartum period. Hormones are in upheaval, fatigue level is high, and to further aggravate the situation, a well-intentioned mother or mother-in-law, especially if she did not breast-feed, may unintentionally undermine your confidence.

When I told my mother that I planned to breast-feed, she smiled approvingly although she had been convinced when she delivered me in 1945 that the new infant formulas just being introduced on the market were better for babies than mother's milk. It did not bother me that we had different opinions on the subject. I had taught so many breast-feeding classes and had worked with so many breast-feeding mothers during the eight years before our first baby was born that I was sure everything would go smoothly. So what if my breasts fit nothing larger than a 32B bra at full nursing capacity—I knew breast size has nothing to do with the ability to breast-feed, and I started nursing our baby with vigor.

> *"Breast-feeding in the weeks postpartum was very stressful—the most challenging on-the-job training I've ever experienced because I felt so responsible for my baby's survival. Once we settled down to something of a pattern, however, it became easier and easier and both of us thrived."*

During the first two weeks, every time the baby let out the faintest cry or whimper, my mother or my cleaning lady remarked, "With those small breasts, dear, he must still be very hungry"—and each time my poor, worried little bosom shrank back in embarrassment. While I clung to the facts—that all you need is a nipple attached to your chest wall to make a go of it; that the baby stimulates the mother's body to produce as much as he needs; that babies cry for many reasons other than hunger—somehow all rational thinking went right out the window and I was reduced to tears. Thank goodness we were in walking distance of the hospital where I had worked and I could take the baby there with me for a pep talk from my co-workers.

Whatever happens, you've got to hang in there with breast-feeding for at least a month. You may have times when you want to give it up, but to throw in the towel at three weeks is too soon. Your body needs a full four weeks to adjust, after that you will have mastered the procedure and will enjoy it.

THE MIRACLE OF THE BREAST-FEEDING BREAST

The simplest way to understand how breast-feeding works is to compare the nonpregnant breast, the pregnant breast, and the nursing breast. While your body prepares for the birth of your

Prior to pregnancy (a) breast cells are undifferentiated. During pregnancy (b) the milk-producing glands and intricate duct system develop to reach maturity while nursing (c).

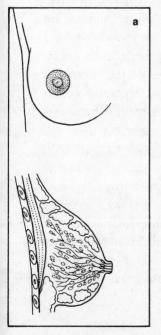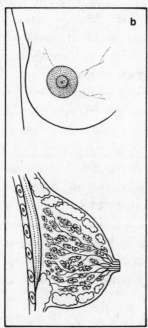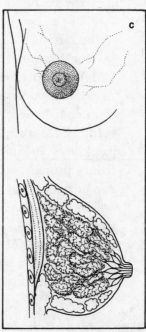

baby, it is also preparing to feed that baby, and the breast changes you have probably noticed during your pregnancy are part of that process.

Before you are pregnant, you have what are called undifferentiated cells in the breast. These cells are stimulated by the hormones of pregnancy to become milk-producing glands, an intricate duct system, and milk sacs or pools just under the areola, accounting not only for the enlarging breasts during your pregnancy but also for the slight sagging you will probably notice after you give up breast-feeding. (Some women mistakenly believe that breast-feeding causes sagging, but whether you breast-feed or not, the changes in the breast during *pregnancy* are what cause this to happen.)

While it may not be readily apparent, the milk sacs are significant in the process of feeding. They sit just under the areola and in order for the milk to be released, the baby has to get a substantial amount of the areola into his mouth and then press the milk sacs with his gums. This triggers the letdown reflex, an involuntary response to the baby's sucking which forces milk down into the milk sacs and out through the tiny holes in the nipple. If he clamps down on just the nipple, it hurts a lot, nothing comes out, and everyone is unhappy—which is why positioning the baby correctly on the breast should be your first objective. You have a few choices for how to do this (see below), depending on the size of your breast and baby; once you've found the right position for him to latch on comfortably and properly, it's easy.

Milk production begins with colostrum, the perfect nutrition for your newborn in the days just after delivery. Since the colostrum your baby gets for the first few days after birth is produced before he's born, there is no risk of his being affected by the painkillers you may be taking during this period. Colostrum is rich in protein, acts as a natural laxative, and contains antibodies and enzymes that help combat sickness in a newborn. The antibodies fight bacterial diseases such as measles as well as some viral infections; the early enzymes help fight intestinal infections.

Humans are the only species in the animal kingdom to produce colostrum; all others begin real milk production at birth. I once attended a lecture by a researcher who proposed that the reason for this is that we are the only animals who do not eat our placentas as perhaps their hormonal content would stimulate early milk production. He then described a recipe for "Placenta Oregano Stew"—ugh!—concocted by a group of people who claim that it's a tasty dish that induces early milk production. I am certainly not suggesting placenta stew for your post-delivery celebration dinner, but in any case it's an interesting theory on milk production!

Although your milk "comes in" three to five days after delivery, "mature" milk may take one to two weeks, perhaps longer, to develop; after that, the milk supply is truly established. Mature milk is thin and slightly bluish, like watery skim milk, and it varies in its components during each feeding. At first the baby gets the "foremilk," which is high in protein and acts as a natural laxative. The "midmilk" is slightly richer, and the "hind milk," high in fats, is much like a rich dessert which satiates the baby and sends him off to sleep with a wonderful contented smile.

You may remember the myth of Romulus and Remus, two abandoned children believed to have been nursed by a she wolf. It's a lovely story, but because wolf milk contains about four times more protein than human milk, it would have undoubtedly killed off the babies after the first few feedings!

Breast size has nothing to do with milk production or successful breast-feeding. If you have always wondered why you were a size 28AA while your friend was a size 38D, the difference has to do with the amount of fat tissue, the globules that appear throughout the breast (see the illustration). It does not matter how much fat tissue you have: small breasts will make just as much milk for that hungry baby as large breasts. Have confidence in those bosoms!

Breast size is one misconception; nipple shape is another. You may, from limited reading, have been led to believe that half of all the women in the world have inverted nipples—and that you are one of them. Erroneous literature may have told you that if you place your thumb and forefinger on either side of your nipple and give it a squeeze and it goes "in," it's inverted. Not true! There isn't a nipple in the world that wouldn't go in with that sort of pinch-maneuver. In all the years I've worked with nipples,

I have seen only two pairs (out of about three thousand) that actually were inverted. They look like an "innie" belly button, and hard as you try, you cannot get a hold on the nipple to try to encourage it to come out.

The odds are that you don't have inverted nipples; but even if you did, it would not be a problem. There are plastic breast cups that can be worn daily in your bra in late pregnancy and during breast-feeding, exerting gentle pressure around the areola and gradually making the nipple become more prominent. These cups also allow air to circulate around the nipple, which toughens them. No one would ever know you are wearing them, unless of course they brushed up against your bosom. Then they'll have encountered their first "iron-clad woman"—no harm done, but a curious surprise to say the least! And if you did have true inverted nipples, after you finished breast-feeding they would remain "outies" like everyone else's.

Preparing for Breast-feeding

There is a good deal of controversy about nipple preparation: some people say it won't do any good, others believe it to be essential. I think it can't hurt to try to toughen them up a bit. Nipples lead a very sheltered and tender existence in our society, and the strong, vigorous suck of a full-term newborn is going to give them quite a jolt. So about four weeks before your due date, I recommend to you the following procedures:

Keep to your usual bath or shower routine, but avoid sudsing the nipples with soap—it dries them out. The nipples will stay clean without extra attention.

After bathing, rub a Turkish towel across your nipples to the point of discomfort but not to pain. This roughs them up a little bit and usually causes them to become a little more erect. After toweling, do some nipple rolling. Hold the nipple with your thumb and forefinger on either side and rotate it gently, which again makes them become a little perkier.

To assist the work of the Montgomery glands in protecting the nipples from getting chapped, take a dab of Massé cream, which is available in any pharmacy (or lanolin or A&D ointment if you want more protection), apply it to the areola and the side of the nipple, and rub it in. It may tell you on the tube to squeeze out an inch for one application, but an inch would cover your entire body. A small dab is plenty.

When you begin breast-feeding, you should continue to use the Massé cream after each feeding to help prevent dryness. You needn't wash it off between feedings (regardless of what it says on the package) because it's absorbed right into the skin if you use only a small dab. At first most breast-feeding mothers are very conscientious about using cream because the nipples are sore, and then as the nipples toughen up they tend to forget about it and gradually do not need it at all.

You may have heard that breast massage, from the base of the breast toward the nipple, is beneficial in preparing for breast-feeding. But if you happen to be the person who is prone to premature labor, you might unknowingly cause this to happen. Breast massage is one of the ways labor is induced in England: it causes the release of oxytocin, which in turn triggers the onset of labor. If you are two weeks overdue, you might consider massaging those breasts; otherwise, I would forget about it as a means of preparing for breast-feeding.

Orgasm and sexual arousal also release oxytocin, and if your doctor tells you that your cervix is prematurely dilated and he does not want you to have intercourse, rather than being concerned about introducing an infection, he may be trying to avoid the chance of releasing that oxytocin. Clarify it with him if it comes up. Otherwise, if everything is progressing well in the pregnancy, I would not worry about it.

Choosing a Comfortable Nursing Bra

With more women breast-feeding today than in the past, bra styles have been greatly improved and you need not settle for a style that appears to be regulation army issue. Look around, and buy two different-styled bras at the end of your pregnancy. Then, about a week or two after delivery, when nursing has been established, you can buy one or two more in the style you like better.

For the large-breasted, underwire bras are the most supportive. I always loved the story one of my students told me about asking to see an underwire nursing bra, only to have her "knowledgeable" saleslady vehemently exclaim, "Not one of those! They curdle the milk!" Absolutely not true, and also keep the following information in focus as you shop.

• *The bra cup* should be about one size larger than you are at the end of the pregnancy, allowing for a slight increase in breast fullness before feedings and also for inserting a small nursing pad to absorb leakage (see page 298). Avoid bras with plastic linings in the cups. This might seem like a good idea for keeping leakage off your clothes, but breast milk is a wonderful medium for bacterial growth, especially if left to sit in a dark cozy area, moist against warm skin, which in turn can lead to a breast infection.

• *The band of the bra* should lie flat just under the breasts.

• *The fastenings* should be easy to undo with one hand so that when your baby is crying and famished, he won't become even more frustrated while you try desperately to release the clasp. Snaps, Velcro tabs, or "fastnuts" (an easy open-and-shut plastic fastening) are preferable to a cross hook which is almost impossible to undo with one hand. (If you do get the Velcro closure, be sure to fasten them before they go into the wash so lint won't stick to them.)

Most women who breast-feed feel more comfortable wearing a nursing bra twenty-four hours a day; for some, it is too constricting. After dutifully wearing my nursing bra all through the night, I found that in the morning my arms were numb, my fingers blue and tingling. Obviously, my small breasts did not need to be strapped into a bra all the time; you'll have to be the judge of your own situation. If you have big breasts and need the extra support, or if your milk leaks and it wakes you up during the night, then you will probably want to wear the nursing bra constantly.

WHAT NOT TO EXPECT WHEN
BREAST-FEEDING BEGINS

If you've taken childbirth classes, you may have seen a film in which a mother nurses her "minute-old" newborn with ease. Do not expect such a performance from either yourself or your baby. I was in the delivery room during the production of one such film and it took an hour or more to get those few minutes of breast-feeding exactly right: nursing immediately after birth is frequently a far-from-satisfying experience for both baby and mother. Generally you'd be better off breast-feeding when you are in a soft bed in your room with lots of time to introduce yourself to this new little person, but if you feel strongly about it, ask your nurse for her assistance and do not feel rejected if the baby isn't interested.

Most babies respond to the first time at the breast in one of two ways. Some are so sleepy or disinterested in feeding that they won't even take hold of the breast (nature has equipped them with extra food stores to allow for this early fatigue or lack of interest in eating). Other babies latch onto the breast beautifully, nurse vigorously for the initial time recommended, and then, when they are taken off the breast, immediately spit up. It doesn't mean that the baby hates your milk. Nature has designed colostrum to help break up mucus or amniotic fluid that may still remain in your newborn's stomach, and up it comes, to clear the system. He then usually proceeds to go right off to sleep, exhausted. All of this is normal.

> *"A precious moment is when Lucia eats. The breast-feeding not only nurtures her but also has a soothing, calming effect. It lulls her."*

NURSING YOUR BABY

Positioning Yourself for the First Feeding

Because your bottom is usually very sore at first, you will probably want to lie on your side when you breast-feed for the first time. Find a comfortable position with pillows in place to give some support to your back, and perhaps with the head on the hospital bed very slightly raised. Settle your baby in next to you and assess the situation. If your breasts are small, use the muscle of your upper arm as a pillow for your baby's head; if your breasts are large, slide the under arm up and out of the way and put the breast and baby together on the bed, facing each other. Bring your baby in closer and hold the nipple between thumb and forefinger at the base of the areola, popping it right into his mouth.

If you cannot get him to face you, stroke his cheek (on the side you want him to turn toward) to stimulate his rooting response. If he keeps his lips tightly closed, touch the tip of his nose with your nipple and gently stroke down to his lips. This will stimulate him to open his mouth. Try to tuck as much of the areola in as you can so that his mouth puts pressure on those milk sacs underneath the areola; your nipple must touch the *back* of his tongue so that he latches on properly. Obviously, if your

Be sure as much of the areola as possible is in his mouth to allow his gums to release milk from the milk sacs or pools.

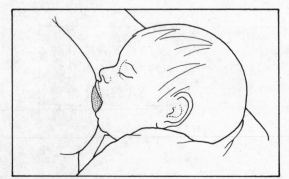
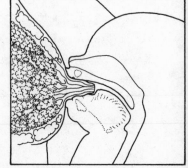

areola is the size of a silver dollar, you won't be able to tuck it all in. (If you have continued problems getting him on, ask for a breast shield to use over your breast for the first minute or two to draw your nipple out.).

If you've had a Caesarean birth, you may not feel like breast-feeding immediately. Don't worry. You can begin when you feel up to it, and because you'll be in the hospital a week, you'll have that extra time to perfect your skills, under the guidance of the nurses, before you go home.

Most women find that sitting in an armchair, on a pillow for a sore bottom, is the best position for nursing in the hospital. Put another pillow behind your back if needed, and if you've had a Caesarean, one or two across your lap to support the baby and protect your incision.

Time the Feedings

When your nurse advises you to breast-feed for five minutes on each side and no more, there's a good reason. If you were to let the baby nurse for an hour (which is tempting when he latches on nicely and nurses vigorously), you would definitely want to amputate your nipple that evening. Even if they've been toughening the nipples in advance, most women need to increase nursing time *gradually at each breast* to prevent soreness:

> 5 minutes, delivery day and the 1st day
> 7 minutes, 2nd and 3rd day
> 10 minutes, 4th and 5th day
> 15 minutes, 6th and 7th day
> 15–20 minutes, 8th day on

The breast is emptied in about the first seven minutes of nursing; you are providing adequate nutrition if that is how long the baby nurses at each breast. If he falls asleep when he is sucking, tickle his feet to encourage him to take the full recommended time at both breasts at each feeding. If your nipples begin to feel sore, stay with the time period you can barely tolerate until you are completely comfortable with it after nursing. Offer a pacifier or glucose water (see below) if he still seems to want to suck. If you have a very active baby, he may eventually want a full twenty minutes at each breast, so the feeding may take about 45 minutes, including burping time. However, many babies will be content with ten to fifteen minutes at each breast at each feeding.

When the recommended time is up, your baby will probably still be sucking vigorously, and you will wonder how to get him off your nipple. You may dote on your "fragile" darling's chubby cheeks, but don't let them fool you. Newborns arrive with muscular suck pads in their cheeks to ensure that they get every drop of milk you provide, and if you simply pull, he will suck that much harder, like a plumber's helper. Just pulling him off the breast is almost impossible, and very painful. To remove him, depress the breast firmly at the corner of his mouth and slip your little finger right in, pushing down on his lower jaw to break the suction. If this is difficult, hold his nose and eventually he will open his mouth to breathe.

Until your milk comes in, a small bottle of sterile plain water or glucose water will probably accompany your baby when he comes to you for feedings. Glucose is the simplest sugar; it's what your body produces when it breaks down proteins and carbohydrates to be used for energy. It is not a food supplement—your colostrum is perfect nutrition for your baby—but rather a little extra fluid to assist him in lasting approximately four hours until his next scheduled feeding. Offer him the glucose water after you finish nursing at each breast. When you get home, you'll be able to be more flexible with his feeding schedule than in the hospital; until then it won't poison him against the breast to take glucose water. After your milk comes in, extra water should be needed only if it is a very hot day and you and the baby are perspiring a lot.

If you think your baby *loves* the glucose water because he guzzles it down rapidly, it's not the case at all. Rather it's because the holes in the nipple are so large that the baby must swallow fast or choke to death!

Burping a Baby

Breast- or bottle-fed, all babies need to be burped. Their mouth does not form a perfect suction cup over the nipple, and they get air in their stomach because they gulp it in along with the milk. The standard procedure during breast-feeding is to try burping the baby after he's nursed on one side and before he's started on the other. With bottle-fed babies, you would try burping halfway through the feeding and again at the end of the feeding. Ask one of the nurses to show you the three positions for burping and just how you should pat or rub his back. A feathery touch is far too light for getting up a bubble.

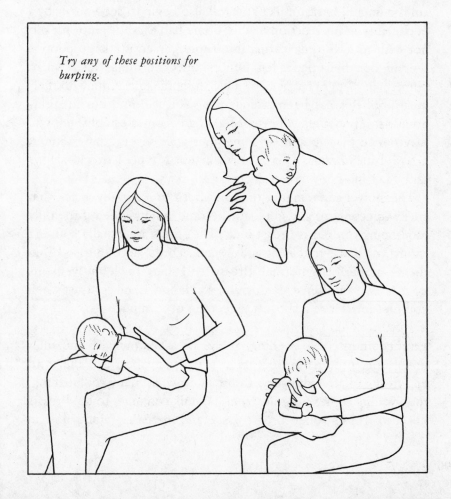

Try any of these positions for burping.

Sometimes it may be helpful to begin each feeding with a minute or two of burping, as there is often a residual bubble from the last feeding that needs to come up before you start. One of my babies would dive in and nurse nicely for two or three minutes and then become restless, making funny loud humming noises. He had an uncomfortable bubble inside, but when I would try to take him off the breast and burp him, he became furious because he was still hungry and didn't want to be interrupted. I realized I just had to be firm about it and say, "No, honeybun, you must burp first!" and burp him; otherwise the situation would just get worse: the bubble would get buried so deeply that it would give him intestinal gas later, making him even more unhappy. Watch your baby as he feeds and try to sort out his needs as he eats.

You will probably notice that your baby has a bowel movement during each feeding, due, as mentioned, to the laxative effect of colostrum and breast milk. You will also begin to see your baby's personality in his reaction to this. Some babies, the "gluttons," do not wish to have their eating interrupted, even if a large poop is seeping out their diaper leg. Others, the "gourmets," insist on an immediate diaper change and cannot fathom continuing with their meal until this has been attended to. You will find out his preference soon enough. As breast-feeding becomes established, you may notice that your baby sometimes goes several days without a bowel movement. This is normal, too. My pediatrician always said, "Let me know when it's been ten days!"

The bowel movements of a newborn are initially black and sticky (meconium) and gradually become yellow-green if the only food being offered is breast milk. The stools are usually soft and runny and have mucus strands, slime, curds, and "birdseed" in them—all perfectly normal. Breast-fed babies' bowel movements do not have an offensive odor, and you'll notice the contrast when you first introduce a substitute feeding of formula.

Engorgement, the swelling of the breasts which accompanies initial milk production, occurs at some point between the third and fifth day after delivery. Contrary to what many might think, the swelling comes not only from the milk coming into the breasts but also from swollen breast tissue and increased blood flow in the veins. It usually takes about twenty-four to forty-eight hours for the milk to begin flowing freely.

It's important to watch for early signs of engorgement to alleviate the discomfort as much as you can, relieving the pressure of milk in the breast by encouraging the letdown of milk by nursing as soon as possible.

Early signs of engorgement include a tight, tingling, warm sensation in the breasts. If you notice this feeling but decide to ignore it and sleep through the night without taking the baby for the next two feedings, by the next morning you will have won the watermelon contest at the state fair. Your breasts will be so full and painfully tight that the nipples will be pulled flat and the baby will have a difficult time latching on. Take the baby for night feedings as soon as you are up to it, preferably for at least one feeding starting with the night after delivery.

If you think to yourself, Middle-of-the-night feedings, forget that—think again. In a hospital, the night feedings are delightful. As described earlier, it is the nurse who brings out your baby, swaddled and burped, freshly diapered and ready to feed. All you do is nurse for five minutes on each side and alert the nurse to trundle him back to the nursery so that you can go back to sleep.

If engorgement sneaks up on you and your breasts are very full, take a hot shower or put a hot, wet washcloth or heating pad over the breasts for five or ten minutes before nursing to help relax the duct system. Or have a glass of beer or wine ten or fifteen minutes before nursing. Long ago, professional "wet nurses" received a lager of dark German ale daily as part of their compensation, in the belief that the hops and yeast it contained would encourage the milk to flow. What probably happened was that the light alcoholic content of the beer relaxed the nurse's duct system and the hops had nothing at all to do with it. Gentle massage from the base of the breast toward the nipple may also assist the letdown reflex. This same massage and then pressing the areola with thumb and forefinger can result in manual expression of some milk if the breast is very full and the nipple too flat for the baby to get hold easily. Some women bring their own little breast pump (see page 301) to the hospital with them in anticipation of engorgement, but you can also ask the nurse to show you how to manage hand expression if you are painfully engorged, or request a breast shield to use over your nipple if it is pulled flat by the fullness. After your baby has nursed with the shield for a few minutes, the breast will be softer, the nipple more erect, and you can put the baby directly onto your own nipple with ease.

Once you are over that day or two of engorgement, you will never have such a tight, hot, uncomfortable feeling again. The swollen tissues shrink down and your breasts become smaller, probably about the size they were at the end of your pregnancy. This does not mean your milk supply is diminishing, but only that the increased circulation to the breast during engorgement has subsided. Your breasts will be slightly larger when full (just before a feeding) and slightly smaller just after a feeding.

It's a marvelous feeling when that milk comes in and your baby begins the first "real" feedings. As you pop the nipple into his mouth and he begins to suck, you'll probably notice a tingling, prickly feeling from the base of the breast toward the nipple when the milk lets down, and a warm sensation just as you begin to hear your baby drinking and gulping, his beady little eyes riveted to your face the whole time!

Leakage. Most women don't have a lot of leakage when they are breast-feeding, but there is a little sometimes because breast-feeding is a psychological involvement as well as a physiological involvement. The leakage seems greater in the first few days of breast-feeding, as the letdown mechanism adjusts. The baby's chomping on those milk sacs will trigger the letdown response, but the release can also occur due to psychological stimuli—the sound of a baby's cry, yours or someone else's, causing milk to leak from your nipples. Some women start to leak from just thinking about their baby; for others, the letdown mechanism is tighter and they have no leakage. (If you find you don't leak at all, don't worry—it does not mean there's no milk.) Sometimes, when the baby nurses on one breast, the other one thinks it's nursing too and starts to leak; or when you have an orgasm you may leak again, due to the release of oxytocin. (If you have difficulty with pumping the breasts [see page 301], grab the pump if you can when you feel the letdown response and collect some of that milk!)

If you're wearing a silk blouse and walking down the main street in town when you feel your breasts tingle, signaling the letdown response, you can discreetly try to apply direct pressure to the nipples and get your mind off the baby. As a further precaution, to prevent wet spots on your lovely blouse, wear nursing pads in your bra. Disposable nursing pads are readily available in pharmacies. If you find them a little too bulky under your clothes, try the one-size-fits-all reusable cotton pads (see page 381 for mail-order information).

BREAST-FEEDING AT HOME

When you first get home, you're going to have a baby who wants to nurse every two and a half hours *from the beginning of one feeding to the beginning of the next.* That means that if you start feeding at 9:00 A.M., nurse one breast until 9:15, change the diaper, burp the baby, get him on the other breast at 9:30, nurse until 9:45, change the baby, burp him, it's 10:00 A.M. At 11:30, you're going to be starting again!

You must accept in your mind that during the first four to six weeks at home you're going to do nothing but lounge around and breast-feed. That way, you won't put yourself through a lot of frantic unhappiness. If at ten o'clock you say to yourself, "There, I've fed the baby and now I'm going to quickly get downtown and exchange that little infant stretch suit and then I'm going to

"As much as I hated being up at one and four at night, once we were settled together, rocking and nursing, looking down at those two little bright eyes that never left my face made me forget quickly that lost sleep."

zip over to the deli to get a sandwich and be back in time for the next feeding," you'll drive yourself crazy! Just decide that for the first six weeks you're going to do nothing but mother. Gradually, the baby will begin to stretch the time out between feedings, you'll have more sleep at night, and you can get a few things done. But not right away!

The Relief Bottle

I recommend that you not offer a relief bottle of breast milk or formula during the first two weeks after delivery. You and your baby need to work out your own "supply and demand" system of nursing, and a relief bottle can get in the way if it is introduced this early. If you "let nature take its course," you will also be able to tell in those first few weeks what the baby's natural feeding pattern is going to be, at least in the early part of breast-feeding. Most babies seem to average out nursing time to ten to fifteen minutes per breast per feeding. Those who are not terribly inter-ested in sucking may nurse only a total of fifteen minutes, which will probably be the minimum time, and then you must offer seven minutes at each breast. Other babies want to nurse for forty-five minutes. Offer twenty minutes at each breast, no more, and then give a pacifier for the extra sucking.

Many books show a rather blissful picture of a husband giving the baby a bottle in the middle of the night, and you may have already decided that since he's halfway responsible for this baby, why not now have him get you halfway out of it—at least in the wee hours. Usually this plan does not succeed, and the relief bottle at night may be no relief at all. Once when I was very tired I said to my husband, "Why don't you get up for the night feeding and give the baby a bottle?" Fine. I didn't hear him get up at two A.M., when the baby started to cry, but I did awaken with uncom-fortably full breasts when he climbed back into bed at three, whispering as he drifted back to sleep, "The baby did beautifully, took five ounces and will probably sleep until seven." I lay there bug-eyed for the next two hours, trying to go back to sleep, my breasts getting more and more uncomfortable as I wondered anxiously when the baby would be up again. Finally, at five o'clock, my breasts were so large that I got up and pumped them, which took about an hour, jumped back into bed and sure enough, the baby woke up at seven. I'd had one hour of sleep! So while nursing at night might seem disruptive at first, pretty soon it barely registers at all—you are able to go on automatic pilot and your body seems to compensate for the sleep interruption.

About two weeks after your delivery day, I believe it is essential to plan an evening out with your husband, which would be the ideal time to give the first relief bottle of either your own milk or formula. Commercially prepared formula is available today in sterile "nursettes," ready-to-go bottles that require nothing more than unscrewing the cap, putting on a nipple (preferably the Nuk brand, which is designed to mimic the shape of the mother's nipple when the baby is sucking) and collar, and warming the bottle slightly under tap water to emulate the mother's 98.6-degree breast milk.

Some babies are very cooperative and will take a bottle of your breast milk or formula without balking. Others simply will not. If the baby resists the bottle and becomes fussy, which triggers your letdown reflex, you begin to leak and the baby then knows for sure that there's something much better behind that blouse and will have nothing to do with the substitute being offered. The harder you might try to give it, the more resistant he becomes, so you have your husband give it a try, and you escape to the bedroom. Unfortunately, that's not far enough. He knows you're still there in the house or apartment, and he *still* resists. It's not until you *really leave* that he somehow realizes there is no choice and he takes the bottle beautifully. Try it. But if it does not seem to work, then you can express your own milk.

Pumping the Breasts

You might be one of the exceptions, but most people are not too successful with manual expression and find the breast pump a better alternative. To pump milk you must first trigger the letdown reflex. Pumping should not be painful, but the first two or three times you use the pump, it will seem a very awkward, perhaps unpleasant task. Whether you want to continue with it depends on how much you really want to take a break from feeding. (Remember, too, that babies are much more efficient than pumps at expressing milk, so do not expect to get a full relief bottle after one time with the pump. You will have to keep collecting milk throughout the day(s) before you plan to use it.)

Even if you do not use it for the relief bottle, I think it's a good idea to keep a breast pump on hand; you never know when you might need it. One night the baby might nurse beautifully at the right breast, but no matter what you do, refuse to take the left breast. With the pump you could empty the full breast and freeze the milk for an evening when you're going to be out, or simply throw it out. Suppose you know you're going to miss two feedings, or that you've got to go out for the whole day. Missing one feeding is not too uncomfortable, but by the time you miss the second feeding, you may be miserable. In that case, take the pump with you, find some privacy, and express the milk. You'll feel fine and, again, you can either save the milk for the baby or dispose of it.

With the breast pump, many working mothers can continue breast-feeding after their maternity leave is up. One of my colleagues at New York Hospital fed her babies breast milk until they were eighteen months old. She was so proficient with the pump that she would express her milk in three minutes flat, store it in the refrigerator, and take it home for the next day's feedings.

When we had our first baby, the only breast pump available was the rubber-bulb type. It was excruciating to use, and I was so discouraged with it that I decided to invent a breast pump based on the siphon effect. After a good deal of trial and error, I came up from the basement with my first finished product, beautifully packaged and labeled Kallop Breast Pump. My husband's only comment was: "Couldn't you have used your maiden name on those pumps?" He needn't have worried—the plastic Kaneson Marshall breast pump, made in Japan, soon arrived on the scene. It works beautifully, like a syringe. The milk collects in the plunger, which can be converted to a feeding bottle. Nowadays small, battery-powered electric breast pumps are also available.

Sterilizing Breast Milk

If you plan to keep the milk for longer than 36 hours, it should be sterilized and frozen to prevent bacterial growth. To do this, take an eight-ounce bottle, pour in what you have pumped of your milk (three ounces, for example) and loosely screw on the nipple, collar, and cover. Stand the bottle in a deep soup pot with a washcloth in the bottom so the bottle doesn't jiggle, add two or three inches of water, cover the pot, bring the water to a boil and let it boil for ten minutes. This assures sterility of bottle, nipple, lid, cap, and milk and is referred to as the terminal method of sterilizing. Allow the bottle to cool and then place it in the freezer. You can continue to add collected, sterilized, chilled milk to that bottle in the freezer until you have enough for a full relief bottle.

Breast milk can be kept frozen for several months. A few hours before you plan to use the relief bottle, take it out of the freezer and thaw it gradually in the refrigerator or at room temperature. About ten minutes before giving it to the baby, warm it up in a bowl of hot, not boiling, water. The water should be deep enough that all the milk is immersed, but the bottle cap should be out of the water to prevent water from getting inside. (Remember to tighten the cap before you place the bottle in the water.)

I think you should offer a relief bottle of formula or breast milk twice a week, once in the evening so you can go out with your husband, and once during the day so you can have a few hours to yourself. Your baby will soon realize and accept that milk comes in other flavors and with different nipples than your own.

SEX AND THE BREAST-FEEDING MOTHER

While you are producing breast milk, the mucous membrane of the vagina is dry, fragile, and supersensitive. So not only do you have the sore episiotomy when you have your first postpartum sexual encounter, but you also get a sore vagina. That is normal, and a little KY jelly will help. It's a water-soluble, odorless, innocuous lubricant that you will probably need to use the whole time you are nursing, as the high level of progesterone that accompanies breast-feeding prevents your body from lubricating the way it usually does, no matter how much foreplay you engage in.

And what about those stories of the women who got pregnant three months after they delivered? It can happen. First of all, you have no idea what point you're at in the menstrual cycle because most women do not menstruate during the time they breast-feed. Second, you may be one of the 80 percent of breast-feeding women who ovulate. You have only a *20* percent chance of *not* getting pregnant, and you are playing Russian roulette if you count on breast-feeding for contraception—there are many "living proofs" of just how many women lose this bet. The pill won't do, either, as it cuts down on your milk supply. Ask your doctor about contraception while nursing.

> *"Breast-feeding the baby was fantastic. I loved the closeness with the baby. I'm going to try and continue when I go back to work. I feel sad we're not going to have so many intimate moments together. I find it absolutely amazing that I could be the sole nourishment for my child and that she thrives!"*

WHEN TO WEAN

I think you should breast-feed for at least six weeks, preferably longer. You need at least three weeks to get used to it and feel comfortable with it, a few weeks to enjoy it, and at least a week to wean. Most women breast-feed for three to nine months, but you want to do what's best for your baby. Some babies wean themselves, usually as they learn to crawl and savor their independence. Rather than feel rejected, be glad he's secure and confident enough to want to be on his own.

You should be able to wean gently enough so that you are not uncomfortable, doing it gradually over a seven- to ten-day period or longer. If your baby is young enough that he still needs to suck, you will need to wean him onto a bottle. In that case, you would begin by giving a substitute bottle at the midmorning feeding for two to three days. Then add a substitute bottle at the late afternoon feeding for another two to three days. Soon you will probably need to offer a supplemental bottle after you nurse. Once weaning is under way, your milk supply will begin to diminish. Some mothers continue to nurse early in the morning and late at night, more as a cozy time together than a nutritious meal.

If you nurse for six to nine months, you may be able to wean your baby directly to the cup and solid foods. (Solids are usually introduced at three to six months.)

> *"Breast-feeding my babies was a delight—and it was the one thing after birth that I alone could give them. Their 'nearness to my heart' was confirmed, and I knew I was giving them all I could to provide a good healthy start in life emotionally as well as physically (especially for my daughter, who was born two months premature)."*

Sometimes it's hard for a mother to give up breast-feeding: weaning signifies the end of the unique closeness she's had with her little baby. Yet the process is inevitable. If you are tempted to hold on to the all-too-fleeting time of snuggling that newborn up to your breast, you need only look to the larger picture of your relationship. Encouraging him to grow while heaping him with love is going to lay a secure and happy foundation for his own independence. Nature seems to provide the cues, in this respect, and weaning is but the first of many, many forward steps. As you gain the hindsight of a parent, you will realize that every phase has its own magic—it's often hard to give *any* of them up. But you do, knowing that as the stages pass, that special closeness you feel is only to remain and grow—just as surely and steadily as will that child you hug in your arms.

Twenty Great Hints for Making Breast-feeding Enjoyable

- Begin each feeding with the breast last used. To remind you which it will be, attach a small safety pin to your bra strap, on the side at which you will start the next feeding.

- If uterine cramping seems unbearable before milk production begins, ask for pain medication to take about 30 minutes before nursing.

- Drink three quarts of fluid daily (four in very hot weather) while you are nursing. Order extra juices in the hospital and replenish your bedside water container when it's empty. Constipation is a sign that your body is not getting enough liquids.

- Continue taking vitamin supplements throughout your entire breast-feeding period.

- If your nipples begin to feel sore, give them a lanolin-and-heat treatment: substitute more protective lanolin for Massé cream, then angle a reading lamp about a foot away from your nipples for ten to fifteen minutes after each feeding during the day. If the nipples are extremely sore or do not respond to heat treatments, use a nipple shield and limit nursing time to 5 to 7 minutes per breast until healing occurs. (Sore nipples are not usually a problem beyond the early days of breast-feeding.)

- If your nipples are not sore, do not be concerned about them. Bruises or small blood blisters can develop that need no attention, and you needn't look for trouble.

- If painful letdown occurs during the first 10 to 20 seconds of nursing time, use transition breathing until it subsides. This phenomenon disappears spontaneously about four weeks into breast-feeding, after the initial adjustment period.

- Don't panic if your milk does not flow the second the baby latches on, even if he cries in frustration. Keep him on, the milk will come. To encourage the letdown reflex, cup your free hand under the breast with the thumb above the nipple, and stroke down on the upper part of the breast, toward the nipple. Slow letdown seems to right itself during the first four weeks when breast-feeding is established.

- Observe your baby carefully. If he nurses beautifully for 30 seconds, lets go, gasps for air, and wants to nurse again, your breast tissue may be smothering him. With your forefinger, gently depress the breast tissue under his nose so there's a breathing space or, if you are lying down, angle his body close to you to keep his nose free.

- If your milk flows so rapidly that your baby sputters, coughs, and gags, try to slow it down as he nurses. Make a "V for victory" sign with two fingers, place them on either side of the nipple and press back slightly on the milk sacs under the areola. Let go once the baby's sucking is rhythmic and relaxed.

- Encourage the poky eater to feed more efficiently: rather than let him nap a little and nurse a little, if he seems to be falling asleep, take him off the breast, change his diaper, play with him, wipe his face with a wet washcloth—whatever works to make him stay awake long enough to have a good feeding.

- If your baby is fretful an hour after feeding, do not assume that he is hungry. Always check the simple causes of discomfort first: reposition him, burp him, change his diaper, swaddle him, see whether he's too warm or too cold, or just cuddle him before offering the breast again. Try to wait at least 2½ hours before the beginning of one feeding to the beginning of the next, preferably longer.

- Put the scales away and try not to worry about providing enough milk; your body adjusts its milk supply to meet the baby's needs. Once your milk is established (about three weeks into breast-feeding), if your baby is urinating frequently, sleeping two and a half to three hours between feedings, gaining weight at an acceptable rate (according to your pediatrician), you can be sure he's well nourished.

- Watch for "growth spurts," the first of which occurs at 10 to 14 days of age, with fussy afternoon or evening feedings and a baby who always seems famished. Your milk supply is not lessening, it's the baby's demand that's increasing. Get more rest, drink more fluids, and nurse more frequently to bring your supply up to the level the baby now demands. Try not to use relief bottles and supplements during this time (about three days) or it will take even longer for your milk supply to increase.

- Get enough rest. Breast milk diminishes temporarily when you are overtired or upset. It's much more important to nap when your baby's napping than to use the time catching up on errands and chores.

- Continue the same well-balanced diet you enjoyed during pregnancy. A mere 250 to 350 calories more than your prepregnant quota is all that is required—that's one fruited yogurt. Do not arbitrarily delete certain foods from your diet, but watch for the baby's reactions to what you eat. Some babies are sensitive to gas-forming foods such as broccoli, onions, cabbage, and beans; other are not bothered by them at all. A piece of fresh fruit or chocolate should be fine, but a whole basket of fresh raspberries or the top layer of a Whitman's Sampler will probably give baby—and mother—a bout of diarrhea. Test foods out. An hour or two after breast-feeding, if you think there's a correlation between a gassy, uncomfortable baby and a specific food you ate that day test it again two hours before nursing and then if the same response occurs, eliminate it.

- Tender, red, lumpy areas in the breast usually signal a clogged duct. To open it up and prevent a possible breast infection, ten minutes before the next feeding apply a heating pad, hot water bottle, or hot, wet towel to the breast and massage gently toward the nipple. The baby's sucking should empty the duct, but if the symptoms do not disappear after two feedings, call your doctor or breast-feeding support group (see below) to discuss other relief measures.

- If you experience breast soreness and you get a fever, you may be developing a breast infection, or mastitis. Do not stop breast-feeding. The baby cannot get this infection, and in fact, nursing is an important part of treatment. Call your obstetrician. He will probably recommend an antibiotic that is safe for breast-feeding babies.

- For breast-feeding support groups, contact your Lamaze instructor, the nurse in your obstetrician's or pediatrician's office, or the local chapter of the La Leche League, a nationwide group that's listed in the telephone book. Be sure the person you speak to is sympathetic to your concerns and your life-style. If not, contact another.

- Let your husband handle some areas of the baby's routine care—bathing him, for example—during the first weeks at home. Dad and the baby need time to enjoy each other's exclusive company, too.

24

The Bottle-feeding Alternative

*I*f you have decided to bottle-feed your baby, the first order of business is to encourage your body to stop producing breast milk. You can do this by wearing a snug bra (one cup size smaller than what you usually wear) during the first week after delivery. During engorgement (page 296), in addition to wearing the bra, you may need to apply ice packs to both breasts and take aspirin for discomfort.

Heat and manual expression may seem like a good idea to relieve the full, tight sensation of breasts filled with milk, but this will only stimulate them to produce *more* milk. Without the stimulation of breast-feeding, the body will begin to reabsorb the colostrum and early milk. The complete reabsorption process can take as long as four to six weeks, so do not be alarmed if some lumpiness remains in your breasts until then or if you notice some dried breast milk or leakage on your nipples during this time.

Formula preparations on the market today all try to imitate breast milk as closely as possible. Since they are derived from cow's milk, which has a larger curd than human milk, bottle-fed babies usually sleep longer between feedings because the curds take longer to digest. Caloric, fat, and protein content is basically the same as that of breast milk, although they take a slightly different form.

You may want to survey the formulas available on the market to decide what is best for you and your baby. The more convenient the product, the more expensive it will be—the price of a bottle of formula that is sterilized and "ready to go" is five or six times the cost of preparing your own.

Discuss sterilization and choices of formula with your pediatrician, and make enough formula to last twenty-four hours. Formula powder or concentrate is substantially less expensive than ready-to-use formula.

Never reuse formula that was left over from a prior feeding. Throw it away.

After each feeding, wash the bottle immediately. If formula is allowed to sit overnight, a crusty ring forms in the bottle and it's difficult to scrub out.

Since most babies do not mind cold formula, you may want to give it to him right from the start. The two A.M. feeding is certainly easier to handle when the bottle can go right from the refrigerator to the baby. If you do decide to warm it up first, an inexpensive one-bottle warmer is nice to keep handy: you can plug it in anywhere, and in five minutes it will take the chill off a refrigerated bottle. If you plan to use it at night, however, you must anticipate the feeding by those few minutes so that you are not trying to warm the bottle while your baby screams from hunger. When that happens, it's better to give him the milk cold.

For bottle-feeding to be a happy experience, it's important that you (and anyone else who feeds him) hold and cuddle your baby

> *"I chose not to breast-feed. All the books I've ever read really emphasize breast-feeding and I felt almost guilty for not doing it. But I felt uncomfortable about doing it and never had a problem with using bottles. Today's technology makes bottle-feeding quite simple compared to what my mother went through preparing formula. I also like the freedom of bottles, and resented the way the books kept implying that by not breast-feeding I was denying my baby in some way. I don't see that he's lacking anything."*

while he eats. The formula nourishes his body; a warm, loving embrace nourishes his psyche!

Burp the baby halfway through and at the end of each feeding (see page 295 for details).

When your baby is old enough to manage holding a bottle on his own, do not be tempted to put him to bed with it. He may love his own competence and you may love the convenience, but if he falls asleep without finishing the formula, some of it sits in his mouth and can cause the teeth, even *before* they cut through the gums, to decay. I've seen instances of such "baby-bottle caries" in three- and four-year-olds. It usually involves the front teeth and they come in so decayed that the only effective treatment is extraction and a little set of false teeth! If your baby needs something to suck to drift off to sleep, use a pacifier or a small bottle of plain water.

"Breast-feeding was incredibly draining and time-consuming. Maybe my diet was inadequate, certainly I didn't get enough sleep, but I was constantly exhausted. So it was a tremendous relief when I switched to bottle-feeding alone for my son and daughter. The bottle gives mobility; you can pop it in the stroller and go places; you can feed the baby in Woolworth's or Saks, on a bus or in a park, without being 'discreet.' The feelings of women who don't want to breast-feed (or can't) should be respected. They have more energy to give to their babies, which more than compensates for any possible nutritional disparity, and their husbands are free to participate as much as they care to in this aspect of nurturing the baby."

Some babies develop an allergic reaction to cow's milk, usually apparent as a rash or gastric distress, in which case a change to a soy-based formula will probably be recommended by your pediatrician. Ask for his or her guidance in choosing the soy formula that's best for your baby.

One of the great advantages of bottle-feeding is that everyone can do it. Fathers love it, grandparents love it, and so will you. There's something about looking into the face of a completely satisfied, contented little baby dropping off to sleep that makes you feel warm inside. It's nice for you to be able to step back and let others who dote on your baby give him a bottle and share this enjoyable experience.

PART FIVE

Now How Do We Keep Him Alive?

Your time in the hospital is over; you are ready to return home with your new baby. The key goes into the lock, the front door opens, and you step into your safe, familiar surroundings. Everything is exactly as you left it, but home is also very different, with the prospect of caring for that little bundle in your arms. Baby, mother, and, yes, father have made it safely to the shores of parenthood, and what a precious moment this is! The reality of being a family and all that it entails has not yet sunk in. For now, nothing is more important than the great hug you and your husband share, encircling the baby and savoring the relief, love, and happiness that wash away the ordeal of childbirth.

The early weeks of parenting present new joys, challenges, and if you are open to them, some amusing moments as well. Some couples find handling the job easier than they expected; some find it more difficult; others are overwhelmed. But the majority of new parents experience a little of each. How you cope depends not only on your attitude but also, in large part, on the temperament and personality of that little baby cradled in your arms. While there is no advance training program for being a parent, it is reassuring to know that there are skills and suggestions that can help you through the early weeks. You will find these "survival tactics" and a survey of baby equipment in the next three chapters, highlighted by choice comments and words of wisdom from new parents very much like yourselves.

25

Settling In at Home

GETTING HOME

Most hospitals supply your baby with everything he needs while he's there; you need concern yourself only with a little going-home outfit, which your husband can bring in with him. Since there probably won't be a horde of photographers waiting to snap pictures as you leave the hospital, there's no need to dress your newborn up in regal robes for his first appearance in public. Save that for later.

Basic underwear will consist of a disposable diaper and a short-sleeved, wraparound undershirt with snaps (newborns do not like to have clothes slipped over their heads). Next comes a terry-cloth stretch suit, with short sleeves and legs in hot weather, long sleeves and legs in cool weather. (Whatever clothing you choose, remember that absorbency is critical because newborns tend to leak from every orifice but the ears.)

For outerwear, dress your baby as you would dress yourself for the season. I have seen newborns going home in 85-degree weather in so many layers of clothing that they cannot bend their arms or legs, and I've gotten frantic calls from new mothers who ask, "My baby has been urinating up to his neck! Is that normal?" What's normal is that he is hot and sweaty and is unable to say, "Mom, it's 85 degrees—get me out of this snowsuit!" While your baby lived in a constant 98.6-degree climate for nine months in your body, his internal thermostat adjusts quickly after birth and he then feels and responds to heat and cold just as you do. Since you're still "running hot" because of your hormone levels, just look out a window. If most passersby are not wearing hats or sweaters, your baby probably won't need them either, regardless of what you may be told.

A twenty-inch-square cloth diaper is an essential accessory to the going-home outfit. As soon as you have him beautifully dressed and step into the elevator, he'll undoubtedly spit up all over everything, and the man behind you won't have anything to offer for mopping it up. (You should have a dozen or so cloth diapers at home, too, washed, folded, and ready for action.)

> *"When we called to start the diaper service I remember thinking they must have been wrong when they said we'd get eighty diapers a week. How could we possibly use that many? Then hoping they'd get here early Friday because at noon on Thursday there were only half a dozen left and they were going fast."*

On departure, many hospitals give each newborn a daily-care kit, including a thermometer, baby toiletries, and disposable diapers. Ask the nurse about these; the tendency is to leave behind what actually is meant for you to keep. Some hospitals also supply a six-pack or so of formula "nursettes"; take it even if you are a breast-feeding "purist" and think you'll never need it.

Your husband should take most of your things home the day before you are scheduled to be discharged. If you have all your toiletries, flowers, gifts, hospital kits, and a baby to juggle, you'll find that even two of you are quite overloaded the day you leave.

As you leave the hospital, it is a thoughtful (though certainly not obligatory) gesture to present a small token of gratitude to the nursing staff collectively and/or to any individuals who have been especially helpful during your stay. Have your husband bring in a big box of chocolates or cookies, for example, and give it personally, or add a thank-you note and leave your gift at the nurse's station.

THE BABY'S WARDROBE

Newborn-baby clothes are irresistible; many a new arrival receives enough of a wardrobe in gifts alone to make it through the first six months. Top-quality clothes for newborns are expensive, however, so if you are inclined to keep to a budget, buy only a few absolute basics. Since most new babies outgrow all their clothes in one season, it's a good idea to return duplicate items you receive as gifts as soon as possible and not even take new clothes out of the box until you are sure your baby will wear them. Returning infants' clothing is standard practice and it's nice to have a store credit waiting for later purchases. (Note: When you buy clothes for the baby, remember that those with a high cotton count will shrink after going through the washer and dryer and you should size accordingly.)

Today's most practical wardrobe for a newborn consists of all-terry stretch suits. If you always wondered why there was such a price difference among stretch suits, feel the terry cloth and you'll know right away. The less expensive ones are usually of inferior quality with one-tenth the number of loops per square inch— much less absorbent than the good ones. For this practical wardrobe item, you'll only regret "bargains."

Babies are perfectly comfortable wearing terry-cloth suits twenty-four hours a day and need not be changed into "afternoon kimonos" or "evening nightgowns." If you simply cannot resist a splurge here and there, think twice when sizing those expensive European brands: "*trois ans*" may be just right for a French three-year-old promenading on the Champs-Élysées, but this same article of clothing may well be too small for the American baby who is *trois semaines!* Furthermore, it seems as if European babies are toilet-trained at birth, or at least the makers of their clothes think so; they rarely come with snap crotches and to change a diaper you must take them completely off.

A basic wardrobe for a newborn should include: 6 terry stretch suits, 6 short-sleeved cotton wraparound snap undershirts (3 each in the three-month size and six-month size), and 3 cotton receiving blankets.

Baby towels and washcloths are popular shower gifts and if you receive a set of them, go ahead and open it (that hooded towel corner over your baby's little head makes an irresistible picture and the small, thin washcloths actually are better than your regular ones for cleaning baby thoroughly but gently), but you might think twice about buying these sets yourself. They're expensive, the baby outgrows them in no time, and a big fluffy Turkish towel is just as cozy.

BABY EQUIPMENT, READY AND WAITING

It's helpful to plan ahead at the end of your pregnancy and begin to organize all the basic "equipment" you'll need when the baby comes home. Ask friends, listen to your childbirth instructor and class discussions, shop around and try to determine which items are best suited for you and your life-style. *Everything imaginable* is available, a good portion of which you don't need, will never use, and should not spend your money on. You can make some purchases later, if the need arises.

I am a great believer in secondhand baby equipment, and if you are thinking, Certainly not for our little darling—only the newest and the best will do! think again! Baby equipment is rarely worn out, it's just quickly outgrown. The large items (cribs, bureaus, and so on) are the most expensive and you'll be saving a substantial amount of money if you take what friends offer (or loan) and shop for bargains.

The crib should be full size unless you've been given a Portacrib. It should have a firm, good-quality mattress and sides with slats so the baby has a view. In their crib, newborns need visual distractions and are pleased as can be if they can examine the wallpaper or light switch for ten minutes and then turn their head the other way to see what you're doing. Once he's able to roll over in the crib, you can add padded bumpers.

Bedding. Peel off all stickers from the mattress (they get gooey) and make the crib up starting with a flannelized rubber sheet. Even if the mattress comes encased in plastic, it needs this extra waterproof layer to prevent deterioration, which can happen quickly with constant wetting.

For ventilation and a soft surface, a crib bed pad comes next, perhaps with contoured corners or anchor straps, and on top of that, a colorfully printed contour-fitted crib sheet. If the saleswoman at the fine department store in your area has told you that only a solid-colored flannel jersey sheet is permissible "due to the fragile nature of a newborn's skin," graciously ignore her sales pitch. Not only do these sheets "run" (like a nylon stocking— one little snag leaves a permanent gap from top to bottom), but they come only in solid pastels. As creamy and delicious as they look in the package, they show every stain from the first moment the baby spits up on them. You can't prevent the spit-up, but you can camouflage it with colorfully printed sheets. If the saleslady persists with the idea that newborns have very sensitive skin and can tolerate only jersey fabric, the fact is that while they *do* have sensitive skin, most of them are very happy on easy-care, regular sheets.

> "I worried all through my pregnancy and so I don't really remember any great moments. For me, the high point was coming home from the hospital and placing our perfect little baby in the bassinette in her room, sun-drenched and filled with all those little clothes and toys that had been waiting so long for her arrival. My husband and I just stood there, overwhelmed by the peace and joy of the moment, the certainty of having made it at last onto the shores of parenthood. We were a family and everything was all right. It was a moment of such closeness and happiness that I will never forget it."

On top of your baby, plan to use a colorful cotton quilt if the weather is cool. It's cozy, washable (hides stains), and the baby can't suffocate under it.

If you assume you'll do laundry every other day, your supplies can be kept to a minimum. Including an unscheduled change of bedding (when the baby soaks the bed in the middle of the night), total bedding should include at least:

- 3 flannelized rubber sheets, 27" × 54" (one for lap pads, see box)

- 2 crib mattress pads

- 4 contoured printed crib sheets (2 for the crib and 2 for the changing table)

- 2 cotton quilts

- 1 set of crib bumpers

HOW TO MAKE LAP PADS

With pinking shears, cut a flannelized rubber sheet into six squares that can be used as lap pads. Diapers leak easily and when your well-dressed guests hold the baby, they will greatly appreciate your sliding a lap pad between their clothes and that little bottom. Lap pads are also great for travel. You may not mind your bedspread getting a little damp as you change a diaper, but chances are your friends, especially childless ones, will feel differently when you need their bed for this chore. Just unfold the little square, do a quick diaper change on it, and put it away.

A crib mobile is essential. When you need five minutes to take a shower, it's the mobile, distracting the baby as he lies safely in his crib, that will allow you the time. Shop for the most colorful, longest-running musical mobile on the market, preferably with faces (animals, clowns, whatever). I missed the boat on my first choice. I bought a mobile with three fleecy white, benign little sheep floating from nylon threads—"so pure and clean," as the saleswoman had pointed out. It *seemed* that the baby liked it, at least until a friend arrived with the gaudiest, tackiest mobile I had ever seen. It had a hot-pink plastic pig, bright-orange cow, turquoise sheep, and a garish green goat and played an obscure melody that to this day remains unidentified. My friend insisted that we set it up over the crib right away, and while I agreed politely I had every intention of getting rid of the thing after she'd left. Then came the big surprise. As he caught sight of those gaudy animals, my baby became so excited that we thought he'd fly out of his crib. His eyes sparkled, a smile covered his face, and his little arms and legs waved and kicked in time to the music—he *loved* it! Similar mobiles are now more cleverly designed with the plastic pig angled down so your child can look right into its happy face rather than at its feet.

What visually stimulates a baby is a fascinating area of study. Researchers have found that when presented with a choice of staring at a face (even if it is distorted) or an object (no matter how dazzling) a baby always prefers the face. Primitive Indian tribes must have known this about their newborns—their artifacts include simple plaques with two eyes painted on, nothing more, that could be strapped onto a baby carrier, right up near the baby's eyes.

The newborn preference for where an object is located has also been researched. In one study, when babies as young as three months took long deep sucks on a sucking device they'd been given, a picture of a face would move closer to them; a short, quick suck would cause the picture to retreat an inch or so. The babies were quick to learn the system and tried, usually quite successfully, to keep the picture about twelve inches away, where they could focus on it most comfortably. If by mistake they gave a long deep suck and the picture came closer, say, six inches away, they almost immediately gave two or three short little sucks to make it retreat! Then their lips would quiver as they tried to hold back the almost involuntary mechanism of sucking, in order to keep that object one foot away. If you hold your baby in your arms at breast level, his little eyes almost never leave yours; and of course, if you measure this distance from your face to the baby's, you'll find that it is just what he prefers—almost exactly twelve inches!

So take advantage of all this research and position the mobile about a foot away from your newborn's face so that he can really appreciate it.

Changing tables seem to be made for the woman who stands 5 feet 2 inches tall. If you are any taller, consider using a bureau top for changing the baby. Not only is it easier on your back, but later on, after the diaper-changing stage is over, it can continue being used as a practical piece of furniture for an older child. If you buy a bureau for this purpose, most stores will custom make a quilted, plastic-covered pad to fit the top surface—all you need do is supply a brown paper pattern so the pad will match the space exactly. Add a crib sheet and lap pad (page 322) and you're all set.

If you're told that you must have a conventional changing table with a protective one-inch edge or a belt, forget it. Even a two-week-old baby would have no trouble maneuvering over that edge, and it's virtually impossible to change a baby who is belted to the table! Obviously, you *never* leave your baby unattended on the table, not even for a second to get a fresh water supply—if you even have to turn away slightly, hold your hand at the baby's belly just in case—but belts and edges are not the answer.

Changing paraphernalia can be set along the back edge or, if you're using a bureau, placed in the top drawer. If there's a shelf over the changing table, make sure there's nothing on it that could drop on the baby.

Just as the mobile is useful over a crib, so a *mirror* next to the changing table can help to provide distraction for your baby during a diaper change. Stick-on mirrored squares (from any hardware or home-decorating store) can go right on the wall next to the baby's face. Even a two- or three-week-old can become happily involved in seeing himself while you change his messy diaper without his "helping hands."

Diapers and diaper pail. Whether you plan to use disposable or cloth diapers, you'll need a diaper pail, lined with a plastic bag.

The lid should be tight-fitting, preferably with a flap so you can drop dirty diapers in with ease and keep them well concealed.

If there is a diaper service in your area you might consider using cloth. They are more absorbent than disposables and less expensive, although disposables are essential for traveling.

A rocking chair with comfortable arm support is not essential, but it can be very helpful when that little newborn has been up at one and three and then insists on staying awake after a brief five A.M. feeding. Rocking him and your own exhausted, aggravated psyche will do wonders for both of you, especially if the back is high enough for you to rest your head.

An infant seat is a must. Bouncing infant seats have replaced the hard-backed, immobile styles as babies learn very quickly to wiggle their legs and feet to rock themselves. You too will quickly learn that jiggling the edge of the seat with one of your feet when the baby fusses at dinnertime may at least allow you time to eat. The bouncing seats usually consist of a wire metal frame with a canvas cover; even a day-old baby can be nestled in securely under the seat belt.

Car seats are required by law in most states. If you have a car and plan to bring the baby home in it, this is an important item to select ahead of time. Make sure the model you choose has been dynamically tested by the Federal Bureau of Transportation. If you're buying a new seat, look for one that converts to a toddler seat, elevating the baby to a position where he can look out the window—staring at the armrest on the door for five hours can get pretty boring. It should also have "wings" to support the baby's head as he naps and a one-step belt-securing system for efficiency.

A sling or "tie-on" baby carrier was aptly described by one mother (Anna Quindlen, writing in *The New York Times*) as such a major advancement in baby equipment it's a wonder the inventor has not been nominated for a Nobel prize. The sling carrier makes going out with your baby in the first few months very easy, and it gives you two free hands while snuggling him close to your warm body. If he fusses at first in the carrier, once you start moving he'll be happy as a clam and usually sound asleep (or quietly observing the scenery) in minutes. Contrary to the unwanted advice you may receive on the street, using this piece of baby equipment will *not* harm your baby's back, cause him to smother, or dislocate his hips!

> *"Never in my wildest dreams did I ever think taking care of a baby could keep me busy all day (and sometimes all night). If you're not playing with him when he's awake, or feeding him, then you're making formula, doing laundry, writing thank-you notes, doing errands for more supplies, maybe sneaking in twenty minutes to read the newspaper so you can keep track of what's going on in the rest of the world."*

A fold-up **umbrella stroller** is the lightest, most convenient stroller available, and it's a must if your life-style requires a good deal of walking or if you frequently use public transportation. Newborns can go right into the stroller in the "recline" position, with "towel sausages" on either side of him to prevent him from slouching over. (You don't want him completely flat; there's a chance that he could slip out the back when you tilt the stroller up to mount the curb.) Be sure you buy a stroller with handles that are at a comfortable height for both you and your husband to use. It's not bothersome if the handles are too high, but it gives you an awful backache to push a stroller that's too short.

Ease in opening and closing can only be truly measured if you try to do it with one hand, since in the other hand you will be holding a baby, a changing bag full of baby equipment, your pocketbook, and your bus fare. In busy midtown Manhattan you would have to be in dire straits before anyone would help a struggling mother—they may watch you, time you, see if you miss the bus altogether, but assistance is rarely forthcoming! So unless you are willing to lay your baby down on the sidewalk amid the bustling crowds, you must be able to deftly maneuver the stroller with one hand.

WHAT TO LOOK FOR IN A STROLLER

Firm back support with upright and recline positions
Tough ball-bearing rubber wheels to survive pavement or gravel wear and tear
Comfortable handle height, with "extender" handles if needed
Ease in opening and closing
Wings for head support as the baby nods off to sleep
Secure seat belt to be worn at all times

BABY'S HEALTH "SUPPORT SYSTEM"

Selecting a Pediatrician

This is an important decision for all new parents, and you should try to make it before the baby arrives. You will depend on your pediatrician's judgment and advice about feedings, weight gain, sleep patterns, toilet training, temper tantrums, and a host of other matters that involve the health and well-being of your offspring for the next ten to twelve years. You'll eventually be a decorated veteran of parenthood but now, unfamiliar with the newborn and toddler phases, you need a pediatrician's accessibility, patience, and understanding, as well as professional competence.

Ask your obstetrician and friends whom they recommend, and then if it's possible, set up and interview with the prospective pediatricians. If you move to a new area where you do not know anyone, call the best hospital in town and ask for the head nurse in the pediatric unit. Ask her whom she uses for her own children. While she may be obligated to recommend several of the new residents out of the program, the pediatrician she has chosen for her own children is bound to be terrific. She's observed all the doctors in action and probably made her choice based on professional performance.

I chose a pediatrician some said was too curt. One friend criticized his reaction when her husband told him he'd dropped the telephone on the baby's head. Dr. Smith asked, "Base or receiver?" and when the response was "receiver," he said, "That's okay, just don't drop the telephone base on him." To me, that was the perfect response for most parents who desperately need medical reassurance in layman's terms and showed a sense of humor, and we were pleased to use him as our pediatrician.

A sense of humor can do wonders when you're a parent, and Dr. Smith helped me to develop mine. It's such a relief when you are in a panic to hear the calm voice of reason from someone who's seen it all. One mother tells the story of having the entire house child-proofed—or so she thought until the day when her toddler's head got stuck between the stair banister posts in the hallway. In desperation she called her pediatrician to describe what had happened, how she'd tried everything and still the baby was *stuck*. The doctor listened in silence and then, in calm, sober tones, gave his expert advice, "Mrs. H., if butter behind the baby's ears doesn't work, do you know how to use a handsaw?" (You can imagine what she envisioned.) "Saw through the post just under the handrail, push it over to one side, and you'll be able to get the baby out." Of course it worked perfectly.

When you interview a pediatrician, ask him about telephone hours, opinions on pacifiers, on "spoiling" children, on working mothers (if you work), and whatever else might give you a clue to his attitude and competence. There are no set answers, but by listening you'll begin to feel whether this pediatrician is right for you. Find out what hospitals he uses in emergencies or if your child needs hospitalization. Ideally, your pediatrician's office should be in your neighborhood or at least a convenient distance from your home. Home visits today are not an issue, for if you have a very sick child, you will want to take him to the emergency room of a good hospital where any tests necessary for accurate diagnosis can be done.

Most pediatricians like to be called shortly after you deliver. They usually come to see the baby while you are still in the hospital (even if they are not affiliated with your hospital, "courtesy privileges" are usually easily arranged) or in their office a few days after you've been discharged if they can't get to the hospital, to spend some time discussing general baby care with you. Write down your questions so you don't forget them, and if possible have your baby with you when he comes to talk to you so he can show you things about the baby that you may wonder about—or things you never even noticed.

FIRST-AID EQUIPMENT FOR A BABY

Assemble these items at home before your baby arrives so you won't be combing the yellow pages to find a drugstore that's open in the middle of the night when your baby first gets sick:
- a rectal thermometer
- liquid acetaminophen, to use only as recommended by your pediatrician to reduce a fever
- glycerin pediatric suppositories, used only at the recommendation of your pediatrician, for constipation (not uncommon when the baby adjusts to solid foods)
- a vaporizer
- a good baby-care and health reference book

"FIRST-AID" TIPS

Placing a vaporizer next to the head of the baby's crib when he has a cold will help break up congestion. Vaporizers are more effective than humidifiers; they introduce more moisture into the air. Hot and cold vaporizers are equally effective, but the cold ones are probably safer to use around a curious toddler. If it makes the room cold and clammy, a hot-water vaporizer may be more pleasant. In either case, clean and rinse them thoroughly between each use.

A good reference book is essential, especially when you are anxiously waiting for your pediatrician to return your call, your baby's fever is 104, and you want to know what you can be doing to help reduce it while you wait. (As a parent, you also need to become a "paramedic"!)

As careful as you may try to be about preparing for emergencies and baby-proofing your home, I think every parent should take advantage of what the local hospital may have to offer in the way of a general first-aid course or teaching skills to parents for emergency situations. Both parents should take the course. You may never need to use cardiopulmonary resuscitation, or the Heimlich maneuver to dislodge a small object that's choking your baby, but at least you'll be prepared for it.

LIST OF EMERGENCY PHONE NUMBERS

At the end of your pregnancy, make up a list of telephone numbers that might be needed by a babysitter and post them next to each phone. Be sure to include:

Your office
Your husband's office
Pediatrician
Police
Fire
Ambulance
Poison control
Neighbor(s)
The nearest 24-hour pharmacy

26

Early Parenting—
A Fine Madness

I remember a Lamaze class father telephoning me just after he had brought his wife and new baby home from the hospital. I could hear the baby crying in the background. "We've made it, Fritzi," the father said, "but there's one thing we need know. *Now* how do we keep him alive?"

This is just what many new parents ask themselves when they get home with their baby. Faced with the awesome reality of being in charge of the welfare, the very *life* of that helpless little baby crying in your arms for no apparent reason, you fight the wave of panic that wells up inside.

Fortunately your baby does not know he's a first baby to someone. Nature has given him strong vocal cords and an insistent cry that is very surely going to set your teeth on edge. This is his only means of communication with you and he's going to use it to signal you for every need: when he's hungry, needs to be burped, is wet or uncomfortable. At first you won't know what he wants. That's the hard part. In no time, however, you'll hear the difference in the *way* he cries, and be able to judge what it is he needs.

EARLY BABY CARE

During your hospital stay, you will have learned from the nurses most of the baby-care basics you'll need when you get home—skill will come with practice. The baby's first needs are very simple: food, sleep, and cozy shelter.

Breast-feeding and bottle-feeding are covered in chapters 23 and 24, along with some suggestions about "burping" specific for each feeding method. Most new babies eat six or seven times in twenty-four hours, and they need to be burped during and at the end of each feeding.

Swaddling, wrapping that little body snugly in a cotton receiving blanket, from underarms down with arms out, usually makes newborns feel secure and happy, a reminder of what it was like back in the uterus. You needn't worry about swaddling for too long, however. As they adjust to the wide-open spaces, most babies enjoy kicking and moving around and will soon maneuver themselves out of the receiving blanket. Most babies find a drawstring kimono (a little nightgown with a drawstring in the bottom hem) inhibiting.

Sleeping. Put your newborn to sleep on his tummy, even if the cord has not yet fallen off, or on his side, so that if he spits up he cannot choke. At birth babies sleep soundly whenever they are tired, regardless of distractions and noise. If you watch them in the hospital nursery, you'll see ten crying bundles and one little fellow blissfully sleeping as if he were floating alone on a cloud. Babies who have the rambunctious activity of siblings to contend with also seem oblivious to noise and just sleep when they're tired. It's that first baby who rapidly loses his ability to tune noises out and sleep—his environment at home is usually too controlled. As he sleeps, if you tiptoe around, keep lights dim and noises down, chances are you'll have programmed your baby to wake up at the drop of a pin. Instead, let him drift off to sleep to normal household noises—the washer or dryer running, a radio on, the vacuum, dishes being washed.

Bathing. Babies are usually bathed once a day. If you've received one of those large plastic tubs as a gift, I would suggest you return it. It's difficult to get it in and out from under the faucet and if you lean down over it in the big tub, your back will be uncomfortable. Instead, if your kitchen is warm and cozy, I recommend putting a large baby sponge into the kitchen sink, placing the baby's bottom on it so he's semireclining and cannot slip, and bathing him there. The sponge is a soft support and generally the kitchen sink is ideal: large enough for a newborn, with a nice dish-rack space nearby for baby equipment, and possibly a sprayer to rinse off his shampoo. If someone tells you that "you can't wash your baby where you wash your spinach"—why not? Just wash out the sink between baths if you think there's a problem.

I recommend that fathers be the baby-bathers. If you save this pleasurable event for the end of the day, when Dad comes home from work, it gives him a chance to enjoy a one-to-one activity with the baby, while you enjoy some solitude. As you bathe your baby, gentlemen, remember to thoroughly cleanse between all those little folds of skin, under the arms, on and between the thighs, and so on, and don't forget to soap behind those little ears!

Shampooing and cradle cap: Shampoo your baby's head twice weekly with a mild shampoo, even if he's bald as a cue ball. This stimulates the scalp and helps prevent "cradle cap," a dry, crusty condition often seen on top of babies heads. Cradle cap frequently occurs when parents are afraid to massage the skin over the fontanelles, or "soft spots," on the baby's head. Although the anterior fontanelle does not close completely until your baby is about one year old and the tiny posterior fontanelle closes at three months, both are protected by a tough, fibrous tissue coating, so massaging, shampooing, and brushing or combing can do no harm. If your baby develops cradle cap, you need to give the scalp a good massage and shampoo to get rid of it. If it persists, coal-base tar shampoos are effective.

It's not uncommon for some babies to have "all-over body

dandruff." If your pediatrician confirms that general dry skin is your baby's condition, try using a cold-cream soap or Neutrogena, which can work to get rid of it.

Laundry tips. The skin of most newborns is more resistant to irritation than you might think. Unless it's a handmade, all-wool sweater, or some precious little outfit that requires hand washing or special care, most baby clothes (check labels) can be added to your normal machine load and washed with the regular family detergent. If your baby is sensitive to certain detergents, you'll know it immediately after you've put a freshly washed undershirt on him: his skin will look pink and slightly irritated. This rarely occurs, but if it does, try changing to a milder detergent before you start washing everything by hand.

LAUNDRY HINT

Both spilled formula and formula spit-up leave a permanent stain if they're allowed to dry on fabric. To avoid this, fill a plastic basin with water and a prewash solution, add soiled clothes or sheets before the milk stain can set, and soak them until the next machine load.

NEW-FAMILY SURVIVAL SKILLS

Most parents describe the early days and weeks with a newborn as "bitter and sweet"—an assessment that seems to hold up regardless of how many children there are in the family. With a first baby, however, those night feedings and the state of general exhaustion seem particularly endless because, of course, you've got nothing to relate them to.

The sweet moments—the smell (which for me was more delightful than freshly cut grass) and feel of that completely depen-

> *"I think the first few days at home with the new baby were the most exhilarating. After the first hesitance over the child's seeming fragility the wonder of her perfection set in. When I would hold her at night (trying to get her to sleep) and she stared at me, it seemed a miracle that she exists. It is still hard for me to believe that I am at least partially the creator of a new being, a godlike function which is awesome, terrifying, and exciting."*

dent, scrumptious little newborn; the sight of his little face during sleep—these are tangible joys. But what makes early parenting so difficult? Six weeks after delivery, what makes new parents roll their eyes as they admit that they had *no idea* how hard those first few weeks would be?

I think the answer lies in the day-to-day realities of caring for a newborn—and the fact that you can never imagine what they will be like beforehand. Understandably, you are so busy focusing on getting through the birth that you figure that whatever lies beyond will be handled later. "Later" arrives soon enough. Parenthood is suddenly upon you and (regardless of how you shouldered your high-powered career) the demands of this job surpass everything else. Not only is it physically exhausting—twenty-four hours of being on duty without time out to take a shower—but it is also mentally exhausting. You give completely of yourself, heap this baby with love and attention you never knew you had within you, nurture him through your every pore—and get *nothing back.* This, I believe, is the crux of why you feel the way you do during those "bitter" moments. Most adults are used to getting good salaries for a job well done, being "stroked" with compliments for their work. Our egos thrive on it, our strength is renewed by it. With positive feedback, even when we're exhausted, we take on the next project willingly. Those first few weeks of parenting are a whole new ball game. With all that work, the boss—a mere baby!—just seems to demand more. And what is there to show for being on duty for twenty-four hours with only four hours of sleep, inadequate nutrition, and no bath? Throw-up on the shoulder!

With a new baby, many areas of your life that once seemed well in control suddenly become unpredictable. If you were always punctual, now you are never on time for anything. Just as you are finally almost out the door, the baby produces the largest poop ever, and you have to wash him down and change all of his clothes at once.

Would you ever have thought something so small and helpless would require such a huge amount of work? At the end of her pregnancy, one mother received as a gift the entire Saks Fifth Avenue layette—a dozen of everything Saks has to offer—and when it arrived she and her husband thought it awfully extravagant. Wouldn't one or two undershirts, a box of diapers, and two stretch suits be enough? After the first full day of caring for her baby alone at home, what with all the pooping, spitting up, wetting, in short the normal newborn catastrophe, this mother had used nearly every piece of clothing on her baby—during one day!

The situation does improve, fortunately, sooner than you would expect. Once again, Nature is very clever. She knows you are essential to the child-rearing job and about six weeks after birth, just when you are about to lose your sanity entirely, she gives you a little "perk" to balance out the demands of that little infant—the first glimmer of a toothless smile. With that smile of recognition, that vote of confidence, that token of appreciation, you are suddenly transformed, with more motivation to do the job well than any salary bonus could ever give you.

Advice. Everyone is ready to give you "just a little" free advice. If you enjoy getting as many opinions as you can on every baby-related subject, and then assessing them in light of all the child development books you have read, that's great. If, on the other hand, you and your husband have established your own child-rearing philosophy and really do not welcome a lot of unsolicited advice, stop the discussion before it even begins. If you want to pick your baby up when he cries and a well-meaning relative admonishes against it, stating firmly that you'll "spoil" the baby, reply matter-of-factly that Dr. Smith, your pediatrician, has told you to pick the baby up *every time* he cries! Or if you would rather not have anyone handling the baby, just say, "I'm sorry, but Dr.

Smith said no one but my husband and I can hold the baby until he's six weeks old." Or whatever.

> *"I was once very organized and methodical about being on time for things and keeping things straight. That has all changed. Being on time for anything is a thing of the past. Otherwise, not much else has changed unless you take into consideration that sometimes we would rather stay home and play with the baby than go out. He goes out with us a lot; he has not proved to be the social anchor we were warned he would be. It may be because we have no hesitance to pop him into his Snugli to take him with us."*

Sometimes it's hard to keep sight of the fact it's *your* baby. One father called me from his office when his baby was a week old to discuss a matter of great concern. It seems that when he would arrive home from work in the evening, eager to get his hands on his little newborn whom he'd missed all day, their "battle-ax" of a baby nurse informed him that he couldn't touch the baby until his body had warmed up. The weather was below freezing, and the nurse told him the warm-up process required one hour. The poor man was completely exasperated. He somehow felt that what this woman was saying had to be wrong, but how dare he question her, with her twenty-eight years of experience! *He* was right, she was wrong; only an amphibian, whose skin assumes the temperature of the surrounding air, would require a long "warm-up time." This bright, well-educated new father had been so intimidated that he lost faith in his own common sense. If ever a similar situation arises, trust your own judgment, or call your Lamaze teacher, pediatrician, whomever—until you recognize the voice of reason, loud and clear.

Whether to have help at home during those early weeks is an issue many new parents try to sort out before the baby is born. I think the best person to give you a hand during the first week or two after you deliver is your mother, sister, or a close friend. It should be someone you get along with beautifully who will not only help with the baby but, even more important, willingly clean the apartment, cook meals, walk the dog, do laundry, if that's what's needed, and won't get on your nerves. Extreme fatigue and hormonal upheaval may at times leave you feeling tearful and overwhelmed—that someone should help to raise your spirits. Other choices might be a neighbor or a cleaning lady who could lend a hand for part of each day during the first week or two. When I asked my wonderful cleaning lady if she'd do this, she replied, "But I have to go to Mrs. Jones on Monday, Mrs. Green on Tuesday . . ." so with her permission I explained my situation to the other ladies she worked for and they agreed to let me have her for that one week. It worked beautifully because she knew our routine, was a terrific help around the house, and with her own two daughters in their twenties, was delighted to get her hands on a little newborn.

You and your husband will have to sort out your feelings on the subject, but having some help can be a great boost.

Professional baby nurses can be terrific, but they sometimes rule the baby to the extent that you end up cooking and cleaning up after them. Tending the baby is by far the best job—so if there's a choice, you take the baby and get someone else in there to do the chores.

Once your initial helper has left, if it's possible for your husband to take some time off from work, this would be the best time of all.

Sleeping through the night. Many baby nurses insist they have the secret for making a baby sleep "through the night." Listen to what they say, but don't hold your breath when you try it. Usually it's best for everyone if you trust your own instincts about the baby's night needs.

The phrase "sleeping through the night" has different interpretations depending on whether there is a baby in the house. Without children in the picture, sleeping through the night represents a solid block of sleep time every night, from midnight to eight A.M., for example. Once you become a parent, if you get a block of six hours of sleep one night, you will have rated it a very successful "full night" of sleep. When another new mother states, "My baby has been sleeping through the night since he was two weeks old!" you will need to clarify what she means. Eleven P.M. to seven A.M.? I would doubt it. One A.M. to five A.M., with the baby then up for the morning? This is probably more like it.

> *"Changes? I haven't slept for the last four and a half months. But somehow it doesn't matter."*

I know a wonderful father who *was* able to break his baby of those nightly sleep interruptions very early. Two days after delivery, his wife had to have her gall bladder removed and needed another week in the hospital to recuperate. Her husband took a week's vacation so he could take care of the baby himself. After he'd been home a few days, I called and asked how things were going.

"Everything's going fine," he said.

"How about the night feedings?" I asked.

"Night feedings? What night feedings?"

"You know, the one A.M. and four A.M. feedings!"

"Oh, we don't have any of those," he replied. "I put Nicholas down each night at twelve and close the door. At six-thirty I go in and get him and feed him. He's a great little guy and *so* hungry in the morning!"

No doubt he was hungry in the morning! Chances are, he was up at one A.M. and four A.M. (or somewhere close to those hours), but after crying for a while, he probably just went back to sleep, figuring, "There's no sense in tiring myself out with this, nobody's coming in so I'd better just go back to sleep."

I'm not recommending that you try to condition your baby this way; most babies do need to be fed on demand, probably every three hours or so and that includes nights. But it does show that babies can survive and adapt to all kinds of schedules. Certainly coming home seven days after major surgery to a newborn who really did sleep through the night was a pleasant surprise for the mother, and when the family came to their Lamaze class reunion, all of them were doing beautifully!

While your baby may not "sleep through the night" at first, you can encourage him to stretch out those night feedings. First, if at all possible, put your baby's crib somewhere other than your bedroom. Babies have very strange breathing patterns, and if you watch them you will notice a whole range of "normal" sounds that go something like "puff, blow, snort, snort, gasp, nothing . . ." It's the "nothing" after all that noisy breathing that will drive you crazy if he's too close to your bed. Yes, he's tiny and he needs you, but that's why Nature has given him such a good, hearty cry to call you when he's hungry or in distress. Don't confuse these sounds with the little whimpers or crying sounds that some newborns make, either. If you're too close to the crib, when you hear those little sounds you'll probably jump out of bed from a dead sleep, gather him up in your arms, and whip out the breast or bottle to be sure he doesn't start to cry vigorously and awaken your husband. In fact, he was only going to make a few noises, roll over, and fall back into a deep sleep for two more hours! When you hear him, it is better to wait a few minutes to see what's what. If he's really ready to eat, he will cry loudly and with persistence—you'll hear him.

It's an old wives' tale that if you can stretch feeding times to every six hours during the day, the baby will go six hours at night. However, there is some truth to the idea that the more daytime feedings you give him, the fewer you'll have during the night. You can encourage this by trying to keep him awake as much as possible during the day. You'll see your own baby's sleep patterns early, but if he's like most babies, he'll prefer to sleep during the day. That's because he's still the "nocturnal animal" he was in the uterus, used to being rocked to sleep by your daytime activities and awake when they ceased at night. If your newborn sleeps more than three and a half hours at a stretch during the day, and you're tempted to think you have been blessed with Wonderbaby, who sleeps day and night, you'll probably find that after that great five-hour afternoon nap Wonderbaby is up every two hours that night—like clockwork! So if he does sleep more than three hours during the day, get him up, feed him, and play with him. (Again, even if you plan "nothing more" than mothering in those first weeks, home, you'll be pleasantly surprised when your baby really does start to stretch out his time between those night feedings. And he will.)

Can you spoil a newborn? This is a question that comes up a good deal, and the answer depends on what you mean by "spoil." Generally, spoiling is considered to be doing something for a child that he is capable of doing for himself. Since newborns cannot do a thing for themselves, it seems to me that it would be stretching things to say he's being spoiled when his early needs— being dressed, held, fed, et cetera—are met promptly.

But let's say your baby at three months old has been sleeping consistently each night from twelve P.M. to six A.M., and one night at three A.M. he awakens screaming. Of course you should go in to see what the problem is—perhaps he is sick or has hurt himself in some way. However, let's say that when you look down into his crib he stops crying immediately, gives you a big smile, and stretches out his arms. Relieved that he is all right, you may be tempted to scoop him up, nurse him a little, and play together in the wee hours. If you do, you're making a big mistake. Tomorrow night, same time, he will act out the same scenario and expect you to reappear. Instead, I suggest you reach down into the crib, pat him gently on the back to assure him that he's safe (it could have been a bad dream that woke him up), firmly explain that it's nighttime and he must go back to sleep until morning (he may not understand your words but he'll understand your firm, quiet tones), and then turn and leave his room. If he begins to fuss or cry again, you know he's not sick or hurt and doesn't need to be fed, changed, or rocked. He may cry for as long as five or ten minutes, but I would still resist going back in. Otherwise, he'll begin to see a pattern in the game that he's created. Any baby would certainly prefer having you all to himself from two to three A.M., but you will have to convince him that this lovely plan is just not acceptable.

Colic. Do not despair if someone makes the annoying remark that "there's no such thing as a colicky baby, just a colicky mother!" implying that it really was a condition brought on by a new mother's apprehensions. When my second child had colic my pediatrician said to me, "We know breast-fed babies are *never* colicky, and we *know* second babies are *never* colicky, so just put him on the phone and I'll tell him!"

Colic, it's believed, is caused by an immature digestive tract that leaves you with a baby who seems inconsolably miserable. Even after you have fed, burped, changed, and rocked him, he's still screaming. It spontaneously disappears at about three months, but three months is a long time to live with a baby who is constantly unhappy and crying.

If your baby has colic, there are a few things you can do to try to help soothe him. A hot water bottle, filled partway with warm water and positioned under his tummy, may be comforting.

A spot of fennel-seed tea, which is a mild stomach relaxant, will not harm him and may also bring some comfort.

FENNEL TEA FOR A COLICKY BABY

Boil 1 teaspoon fennel seeds with 8 ounces of water for five minutes.

Strain, add 1 tablespoon sugar, shake well to dissolve sugar, and store in the refrigerator for up to one week.

When the baby is colicky, take 1 ounce from the master bottle, add 1 ounce hot water to warm it up, and let him drink it.

Talk to your pediatrician about other remedies that he might recommend. Caring for a colicky baby is frustrating and exhausting, and you may find yourself resentful that you are never able to make your baby happy. If your baby has colic, it's important to schedule relief time often, for your own sanity.

The Arsenic Hour. It's no coincidence that all babies choose to scream between the hours of six and eight P.M. Everyone is exhausted. There's a backlog of chores to be done, dinner to get ready, the need to accomplish *something* before your husband comes home—and of course through it all the baby is screaming. Due to fatigue, if you are breast-feeding, this is the time of day your milk supply may be a little low. Take heart. If you were to line up almost all other newborn babies across the nation at this time of day, they'd be crying in unison—tired, a little hungry, and sensing that their mother is tense and tired, too.

A wonderful relief measure for the arsenic hour is to put the baby in a baby swing, a four-legged frame that stands on the floor with an infant seat suspended from the cross bar at the top. Whatever model you choose, this piece of equipment is worth every penny. The newborn goes into the seat, a wind-up mechanism starts the swing going back and forth, and suddenly he's docile and happy. Position him where he can watch you making dinner, and keep cranking up that swing. Don't get battery operated, as you do want it to stop swinging after a while so that if it is used during the night, the baby will then sleep quietly until dawn. The one in our house made a tick-tock noise as it rocked; to this day, my husband is convinced that the sound was what quieted our children.

Taking the baby out. I'm fascinated by the statement, "You can't take the baby out until he's six weeks old." Exactly how, then, do you get him home from the hospital? Obviously, you are not going to take your newborn on public transportation at the peak of rush hour; but if the weather is nice and you are eager to get out for a little walk or to visit a friend, you can certainly take the baby along. You won't want to sit in the park if it's below freezing—babies don't know to move their toes or fingers when they get cold, nor can they say, "Let's go home now, Mom"—but certainly a walk to and from your friend's home even in cold weather is fine if you are both dressed properly for the season. Getting outside will do everyone good.

A special space for play. Starting when your baby is a few weeks old, find a pleasant, safe place where your baby can get used to spending a short period of time twice a day; a playpen would be ideal. Be sure there are toys or an interesting wind-up mobile for him to look at as part of the surroundings. Not only does this encourage independent play, it also assures his safety while you do necessary chores nearby: cooking or doing something else that might jeopardize his welfare if he were right at your elbow.

I had a next-door neighbor who believed in "no restraints": she wanted her child to be a "free spirit." After great inner turmoil about whether I was too structured and up-tight, I decided I really didn't want a free spirit living in our apartment, nor would my friends and relatives enjoy having us for a visit with an unrestrained baby. Babies are too young to understand what it means to have respect for belongings of any kind, and rather than having mine crash about unrestrained, it seemed that everyone was happier (baby included) when there was a limit to his early explorations and safe, interesting toys for his distraction. (Be sure to look over all toys before introducing them to your baby to see that they are smooth, safe, and free of small parts that he could swallow. From his hands they'll go right into his mouth, as this is one of the first ways in which babies "explore" an object.)

Pacifiers. You may already have your own opinions on pacifiers, and of course you should do what you think is right for your child and your own situation. If you haven't really thought much about them, let me help you evaluate them in a fair way. First, I believe pacifiers should not be used to "pacify." To me, pacifying a baby means that when he cries, for whatever reason, rather than trying to meet his need you give the baby a pacifier. This sort of plugging him up to stop his crying is no solution. On the other hand, all babies need sucking, some more than others, and if after you have fed him (twenty minutes at each breast if you are breast-feeding) and his little puckered lips are still eager to suck, this would be the time a pacifier, or what might better be called a sucking device, could be used. If a baby has been fed, burped, changed, and is having trouble relaxing and falling off to sleep, again this might be the right time for a pacifier. No one wants to see a four-year-old (or a one-year-old, for that matter) at the playground with a sucking device on a ribbon around his neck, and that doesn't have to happen. From the start, you can limit the use of a pacifier quite easily by letting the baby suck it only in the crib.

Our first baby had a voracious sucking need and we used a pacifier with definite limitations. I was worried about whether it would be difficult for him to give it up, so on Christmas Eve, when he was two and a half, we agreed to leave it for Santa in exchange for all the gifts he would receive the next morning. Although I had been convinced that giving up the pacifier would be a nightmare, Dr. Smith's wonderful words "I promise he won't go to college with a pacifier!" easily came true. With our second child, I thought we would do without the pacifier altogether, so of course, with a similar strong sucking need, my baby immediately found his right forefinger to suck, which not only could I not control but also wrecked his dental formation.

It was back to the pacifier for baby number three, only this one had no interest in it at all. If you do decide to use a "sucking device," choose one that is an "orthodontic exerciser" designed with dental formation in mind.

Visitors. Although I hope no hospital staff can hear me say this, I would suggest that you have as many visitors in the hospital as possible so there will be fewer at home. You must, of course, abide by hospital rules, but if there is a maximum number of visitors permitted, invite the maximum. I say this because in the hospital, visiting hours are pleasantly strict, say, three P.M. to four-thirty P.M. Everyone *must* leave at four-thirty and a guard will come by to firmly remind stragglers. Furthermore, you needn't play hostess in the hospital: you can't offer your guests a cup of tea and a brownie because, fortunately, there's no kitchen available to you. At home, the visiting situation is quite different. Your guests come early, stay indefinitely, expect a cup of tea and a brownie, and love to hold the baby—but only until he's fussy; then they turn him back to you. If you don't know how to diplomatically discourage visitors from landing on your doorstep, blame me or your pediatrician. "The nurse [or doctor] said no visitors until the baby is three weeks old." Or three months— whatever you want to say.

Pets. If you've been concerned about how your pet will handle the addition of a newborn baby, relax. I think it will be a lot less traumatic for everyone than you may have imagined. Let your dog or cat sniff all around the baby equipment as you set it up. Cats often think the crib is a nice new napping spot; fill it with hard objects to persuade him otherwise. A few cat hairs won't kill the baby, in any case, and contrary to warnings you may have had from friends or relatives, cats do not like to sleep on top of the baby's head. Nor has there ever been one who "sucked the breath out of the baby." It's impossible (think about it). And how could even a cat get comfortable sleeping on a baby's head? Besides, a newborn can move his head from side to side and will even use his hands to push something away from his face.

When you first arrive home with the baby, allow your pet to sniff him and even to lick him. Dogs and cats have natural antiseptic in their saliva and it's actually more hygienic to have your baby licked by your pet than kissed by your relatives!

Some cats become territorial and may even urinate around their food bowl, a message that says, "Don't eat my food, baby." But this is very rare, and if your pet shows any territorial behavior, it will be short-lived. By the time you've had your baby at home for a week or two, everyone will have adjusted nicely—and soon it will be the pet who needs protection. Many a cat has been picked up by tail, whiskers, or ears and has lost big tufts of hair to a baby who has not yet learned to be gentle.

If you have cats, one interesting phenomenon you may encounter is a "purring baby." This occurred in my own family and more than once in the hospital pediatric clinic when I was a student nurse. My mother became concerned when my younger sister Scarlett was late to talk and seemed to be making a guttural noise, similar to purring, whenever our two big black cats were around. In time it became obvious that when she was playing or napping in the playpen with Blackberry and Midnight, all three of them were purring loudly in unison. Worried that this might become a substitute for speech, my mother contacted the pediatrician, who said not to worry, that it was not uncommon for babies to purr with their feline friends and speak among humans— an early talent for bilingual speech, you might say.

Pets can serve as wonderful companions for small children. The delight in a four-month-old's face as he holds or pats a kitten or puppy is priceless to observe, as is the mutual respect and loyalty that develops as they grow.

Baby food. Always discuss the introduction of solid foods with your pediatrician. Generally, it is recommended that you hold off introducing baby foods until your baby is three to six months old. Prior to that time, a baby's digestive tract is too immature to absorb the nutrients; what goes in one end passes out the other without being utilized.

Once you become a parent you also become primary food supplier for your child, and it's a good idea to establish your own nutritional standards before solids are introduced. There are good books on the subject, including Sue Castle's *Complete New Guide to Preparing Baby Foods,* which I recommend (see page 376).

During your baby's first year, he needs:

Sleep
Sucking and nourishment
Visual stimulation
Auditory stimulation
Tactile stimulation
Love

27

Time Out for Parents

*I*n those early weeks at home, when caring for the baby eclipses their every thought and activity, new parents often forget about themselves—that they need a little special care, too.

"Baby blues," postpartum depression, is no myth. It's a natural occurrence due to hormonal levels dropping after delivery and it can occur on and off during the first few months after birth. If you are breast-feeding, the drop will be more gradual and not complete until you have discontinued breast-feeding altogether. If you are usually anxious or depressed just before your menstrual periods, after birth your bad moods will be magnified one hundred percent. One minute you're elated, happy to cuddle that little sleeping infant, the next minute overwhelmed by the total, never-ending responsibility of parenting, depressed that your past life is gone, and unsure whether you will be a "good mother." Or maybe you just feel like crying for no apparent reason at all. Baby blues seem to peak on the fourth day after delivery, often the day you plan to leave the hospital. Fatigue magnifies the condition, so when you feel tearful, take a nap—things usually will fall back into perspective with rest. Talk things over with friends who have young children—it helps to know that your situation is not unique.

Gentlemen, it's hard to know how to deal with a wife who is

> *"After we were home a couple of days, to our amazement, Andrew went to sleep right when we were ready to eat dinner. We were overjoyed at this opportunity to eat without interruption, since the food smelled great and we were both hungry. I put the food on the table and lit a candle, just as I had always done before Andrew was born. We sat down to our meal, but instead of eating we sat there with tears in our eyes. It felt like it was just the two of us. We missed each other and our frequent intimate moments. We both wondered if Andrew was worth the loss we felt. Then we went to Andrew's room. We held each other as we watched him sleep and we knew he was worth the changes we were going through."*

normally so rational and now suddenly begins to cry and can't tell you why. An extra hug will be appreciated, especially when you are at a loss for words to offer help. Try to come home from work early, or line up a sitter so you and she can get out for a couple of hours together. Surprise her by taking a day off from work in the middle of the week if at all possible, and take over baby duties that day.

SEX AFTER CHILDBIRTH

Your doctor will, of course, give you a guideline as to when it is considered medically safe for you to resume having intercourse, usually after all the vaginal discharge has stopped. However, there are a few facts that may be helpful.

Although you may have delivered a large baby, remember that the vagina heals back to a size even smaller than when you were having regular intercourse and therefore you will probably feel a certain amount of discomfort the first few times. There will also be local tenderness due to the final healing stages of the episiotomy incision.

If you have intercourse during the first few weeks after the baby is born, before the lochia has tapered off completely, your husband should use a condom, as your cervix is still slightly open, and the placental site is still healing and draining. A diaphragm (if you normally use one) will need to be refitted by your doctor postpartum.

Most women do not lubricate as usual during the first two to three months after childbirth as hormones are readjusting and this influences lubricant production. Once you resume ovulation, this problem should resolve itself. Until that time, if you feel that it is needed, use some KY jelly (see page 304).

Finding a quiet, peaceful hour during the day or night when you can both enjoy each other and make love without interruption can also be difficult. Forget the gourmet meals, cleaning, and dishes and save some time each day for yourselves. You will both need it.

> *"Our marriage is solid. The sex life was slightly diminished but we're conscious about putting and keeping the romance in it. If anything, we're much closer now that we are bonded in Julian."*

Remember that you can become pregnant as early as a few weeks after giving birth. Speak to your own doctor about the method of contraception that you are interested in. Birth control pills are 99.9 percent safe against pregnancy but are not recommended if you are breast-feeding. Your doctor will probably have you begin taking the pill after your first normal period. Be sure to alert him to any pertinent past medical history.

The coil or intrauterine device (IUD) is approximately 97 percent safe against pregnancy. It is usually inserted without discomfort when you go for your four-to-six-week postpartum checkup. It is normal for most women to experience heavy menstrual flow for the first few periods after coil insertion. Coils are contraindicated for many women. Check with your doctor.

The diaphragm is approximately 95 percent safe against pregnancy. Usually after childbirth the cervix or neck of the uterus has changed slightly in size; therefore many women require a larger diaphragm.

Contraceptive foam and condoms are approximately 70 percent safe against pregnancy when used together, but are generally discouraged as an effective long-term contraceptive.

Breast-feeding is not an effective method of contraception (see page 304).

> *"Our life-style has slowed down a great deal, but we could not be happier. Luckily, we have a solid, communicating marriage, so when all is crazy we are able to laugh and talk. It is essential to be able to talk all the situations out. Times can be rocky in terms of being organized with the baby, and one must be able to laugh!"*

> *"Having no control over plans and timing is the biggest change to this previously organized person."*

POSTPARTUM SLIMNASTICS

Of course you will want to get back into shape as soon as possible. The sooner you begin, the easier it will be. Get your doctor's approval before you start an exercise program, and don't push yourself. The number of repetitions for each exercise suggested below is arbitrary and you should not overdo it. If you had intense back labor, you may want to concentrate more on the back exercises than the leg exercises, at least at first. Or you may focus on another part of your body that needs toning. Incorporate the exercises you did during pregnancy into your postpartum repertoire.

Waistline

Arcs

Stand with legs placed wide
apart. Bring the arms straight
up over the head, close to the ears,
palms facing. Drop the arms and
torso forward from the waist, allowing the upper
body to swing in a wide arc side to side like a pendulum. Feel
the stretch at the waist and on the inner thigh. When the arms
reach out to the sides, hold that position and really stretch. Repeat
two series of eight swings. Breathe out as you bend down. Breathe
in as you reach out to the side. Remember, breathing is particularly important to increase circulation.

Abdomen

Bicycling

Lie on your back on the floor with
your palms down. Bring your knees all
the way in toward your chest and
stretch your legs out as long and
straight as possible. Keep your toes
pointed. At a moderate speed, rotate
your legs as if you were riding a bicy-
cle, pedaling forward and backward.
Breathe deeply and evenly. Don't work
for speed.

Stomach and Thighs

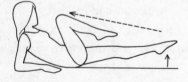

Lie on your back on the floor.
Raise your upper torso to a half-sitting
position, resting your palms and elbows
on the floor. Slowly bring your right

knee to your chest, at the same time lifting your left leg about three inches off the floor and keeping it straight, toes pointed. Now reverse, stretching your right leg out and drawing your left knee to your chest. Continue to alternate slowly. Do two sets of six, resting in between for a few minutes while you breathe in and out deeply.

Isometric Stretch

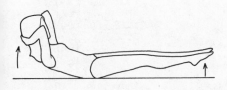

Remain on the floor, on your back, clasp your hands behind the base of your head, and lift your head and torso about twelve inches from the floor. At the same time, lift your legs about three inches, so that only your buttocks are resting on the floor. Stretch your legs with toes pointed. Hold for three counts. Relax, and lie flat. If your stomach muscles tremble, it means they need strengthening. Do this six to eight times after four weeks when your abdominal muscles have begun to knit together down the center of your abdomen.

Hips and Thighs

Scissor Lift

Lie on your right side, right arm extended, with your head resting on your arm. Place the left hand against the floor at the bustline for balance. Slowly raise your left leg to the count of eight. Breathe in as you raise, and exhale slowly as you lower the leg. Change sides and repeat. Do each side three to five times.

Side Leg Lift

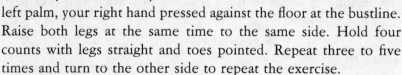

Remain lying on your left side
and rest your cheek on your
left palm, your right hand pressed against the floor at the bustline.
Raise both legs at the same time to the same side. Hold four
counts with legs straight and toes pointed. Repeat three to five
times and turn to the other side to repeat the exercise.

Legs

Strengthening Calf Muscles

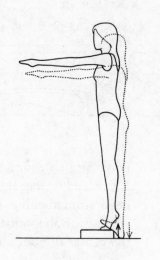

Stand on a thick telephone
book with your heels resting on
the floor and your arms straight
out in front of you. Slowly raise
up so that you are finally on
your tiptoes on the telephone
book. Slowly lower back down
so your heels are on the floor. Repeat
ten times.

Arms and Bosom

Arm Circles

Standing with plenty of room
around you, make a large circle
with each arm, one coming up as
the other is descending. Do ten
rotations with each arm.

"It's a joy being a parent, knowing that that little life is totally dependent on you for love and care. It's also exciting, challenging, and frightening to think that this is only the beginning of a lifelong process. I can only hope that I as a parent will be open enough to bend and change when necessary, to be willing to accept the challenges, and to continue to laugh with my child, as the gift of laughter is a great healer."

RELIEF TIME, OR WHERE ARE YOU, MARY POPPINS

Whether or not you have help during the first week at home, after two weeks it's wise to line up a reliable babysitter, someone to come in one morning or afternoon a week as well as an occasional evening so that you can get out with your husband. A "mature woman" would be the best choice to care for your newborn; it can be your mother or mother-in-law, friend of the family, or someone in your neighborhood whose own children have left the nest. Ask everyone you know for recommendations—you must feel totally confident about leaving your baby alone with this person.

Your gut reaction often seems to be the best guide in selecting a babysitter, but you should be as thorough as you can in the screening process. Schedule an interview to get the prospective sitter talking about babies. Ask what she would do if the baby fell in the park and cut his head badly; or whether she thinks a newborn can be spoiled. Judge the answers for yourself. Is she dressed comfortably, and not as if she's going to a corporate meeting? Is she neat and clean? A simple act such as washing her hands before picking up the baby can give you a clue about her personal habits. As the interview progresses, ask her to hold the baby while you leave the room to go get something. Stay away a few minutes, and when you return, see how she's handling the baby and if she's enjoying holding him. Ask for at least two references and call those people after she leaves. If everything seems favorable, get her in for a morning while you do a few errands in the neighborhood. Do not race off for four hours the first day she comes to work; rather, slowly increase the length of time the baby is in her care. When you feel confident about leaving the baby with her, line her up for one evening two weeks after the day of delivery, for a minimum of three hours.

> *"Sometimes I can't believe I am really a parent and that the baby I am holding really belongs to us and is here to stay. I feel a certain ambivalence—realized recently when I found myself looking out the window and wondering, 'When is the mother coming home?'"*

If you are thinking, Oh, but I can't leave the baby—I'm breast-feeding! this first evening out is the time your baby will get his first substitute, or relief, bottle (for techniques on how to offer it to your baby, see page 300).

> *"We spend enormous amounts of time just watching Alex—watching him smile, cry, wiggle, play naked baby, try to suck his thumb. We sleep less, go to bed earlier, see more of people with children (especially babies) and less of people without children. I don't work now, so it's a big change. The lack of structure and ability to plan anything is hard to get used to and frustrating at times but much less so than it was at first."*

Getting out may seem difficult at first. You may feel guilty leaving that poor, helpless little one with someone else; but once you are out and away, with your husband or alone, you'll begin to recognize the need for short periods of separation as a time for readjusting your focus and revitalizing your system.

> *"Plans are made around naps and feeding. Our marriage has become even stronger. We can't imagine what life would be like without our baby. She is the greatest thing that has happened to us."*

Gentlemen, persuade your wife to get out one evening a week, and be sure she has planned a weekly morning or afternoon away from the baby—not only to maintain a healthy marriage, but also to keep her feeling some self-respect as an independent being.

A final, cynical word about hiring part-time help. This will probably be your first experience with babysitters and it is wise to collect valuables and either lock them up or take them to your local bank safe-deposit box. It also wouldn't hurt to lock up your liquor and "forget" something during some of those early times you have a new babysitter to see if all is well at home. Unfortunately, there are few Mary Poppinses to glide down into the home of new parents today.

If you plan to return to work after your maternity leave, perhaps the part-time sitter you have been using for these early weeks would consider a full-time position.

> *"I've tried working for about three weeks now and have decided to stop. I had a feeling that I'd decide that. We've had to put some personal needs aside. I don't like the feeling of being pulled in too many directions, which I am with work, household maintenance, mother and wife roles."*

> *"I went back to work when Lucia was a little over two months old. At present, my job is and will continue to be a nine-to-five job through May. It's been very workable."*

"I am on a six-month leave of absence from my job as a banker. Before we had the baby, I thought I would try to find a caretaker for the baby so I could continue my career. Now that she is a reality and not an abstract 'baby,' I find it is very difficult to consider leaving her with someone else on any kind of consistent basis."

"Day-to-day life is certainly less spontaneous and we get less time with each other. On the other hand, we cherish our little baby and don't mind the lack of spontaneity. I'm lucky; I can work part-time as opposed to full-time and I love the combination. I do feel the need to get out. It makes the baby all the more precious when I come home."

MOTHER-INFANT GROUPS

I suggest you find a mother-infant group in your area and become actively involved in it. Not only will it provide a support system, it's also fun. Most groups meet weekly (with babies, of course); more often than that may be too much. Since you'll find that the baby completely encompasses your time and energy, it's great to share some of your difficulties and remedies with other women who have exactly the same concerns.

If you decide to keep the group going beyond the infant stage, you'll also see the advantage of early socialization for your child. This may take some refereeing because babies are a long way from learning how to share, but at least in the company of other small children they begin to recognize that other "little" people exist and that they will not always have exactly what they want.

. . .

As the early days of exhaustion and chaos begin to evolve into a semisettled routine of early infancy, remember to cherish even the difficult moments—they rarely repeat themselves and the tiny baby you brought home will be, in only three months, twice his original size and a totally different little person.

> *"It is difficult adjusting to not finishing a task and having things done at a certain time. As far as career, I thought that after a year I would go back to teaching, but I enjoy Meghan so much that I can't imagine leaving her."*

> *"Having a baby certainly makes you examine your priorities. I think I am so much happier now even though I am working less. And I know that when I do work it is for us and not for me. He is the most important thing in our lives right now; all the rest will be there when we choose to go back to it." (Father)*

To me, parenthood is such a dynamic state, so full of wonder, surprises, joy, and difficulties, that it teaches you to be flexible and to continually adjust not only your daily routines but your attitude. What seemed a monumental task today is taken for granted tomorrow.

If a sense of humor was not an intrinsic part of your personality, work on developing one now, at the birth of your first child. It will not only be a necessary survival technique, but it will allow you to laugh at yourself, with baby spit-up on your shoulder, and not really care what other people might think. Share your thoughts with your husband and tell him about your daily escapades with the baby when he comes home from work. Encourage his involvement and see how you flourish, not just as parents but also as a family!

THE VALUE OF VALUES

Mother, O Mother, come shake out your cloth
Empty the dustpan, poison the moth,
Hang out the washing, make the bed,
Sew on a button and butter the bread!
Where is the mother whose house is so shocking?
She's up in the nursery, blissfully rocking.
Dishes are waiting, and bills are past due!
(Lullabye, rockabye, lullabye loo)
The shopping's not done and there's nothing for stew
And out in the yard there's a hullabaloo.
But I'm playing "Kanga" and this is my "Roo,"
(Lullabye, rockabye, lullabye loo)
The cleaning and scrubbing can wait till tomorrow.
But children grow up, as I've learned to my sorrow.
So quiet down, cobwebs! Dust, go to sleep!
I'm nursing my baby and babies don't keep!

—AUTHOR UNKNOWN

Epilogue

Having Another Baby
or Second Time Around

Having a second baby is never a "repeat performance" of the first. For most women, pregnancy the second time around seems to pass twice as quickly, with far less time to dream about the baby that's "in the works." The second pregnancy is more physically challenging than the first (your firstborn makes sure of that!), but more important, because you are now a family and not just a couple, the prospect of a second baby presents a situation that's more emotionally complex: you have a child who knows nothing else than your exclusive devotion and parental love. Fortunately, your love for that child remains the one constant, reliable base of his security, and that's what's going to count the most in making a smooth adjustment after the birth. Acceptance of the situation will take time, of course, but usually the anticipation of the effect of a new baby on your child turns out to be far more problematical than the reality.

Most psychologists recommend holding off the news from your other child (if he or she is only two, three, or four) until your sixth or seventh or even eighth month. Nine months away is too hard to fathom, and cutting down the "waiting time" seems to minimize some negative fantasies of what a new baby sister or brother will be like. Even with your growing size, most children seem oblivious to the pregnancy until the very end, when your lap is gone and the contingency plans for the anticipated birth are discussed. When my little boy gently felt and patted my tummy at the end of the pregnancy, "Ah," he said, running his hand over my protruding belly button. "Mommy, I have found the baby's eyeball!" At this point, we got out Nilsson's terrific book (see Suggested Reading, page 375) to clarify things, and the wonderful pictures of a baby in utero at eight months, pink-faced and sucking his thumb, were so endearing to my son that he couldn't wait for the baby to be born.

If your older child is still in a crib and quite happily so, it might be better to plan to use a bassinette for the new baby to give your child an extra few months to decide that a "big bed" is preferable. Plan to set things up a month or so before your due date to allow for adjustment time, whatever you decide about beds and room situations. If space permits each child to have his own room, great; if not, it's usually better to put the two children together than to separate them. When the baby cries at night, your older child will quickly learn to "tune the baby out," roll over, and go right back to sleep, whereas if the baby sleeps in your room, the older child may feel quite left out.

If your child is two or older, a "sibling class" in the maternity unit of the hospital you are using for the birth is a nice introduction to babies as well as a memorable outing for you both, particularly if it's followed by a lunch together in your child's favorite restaurant. Inquire at your hospital or ask your Lamaze instructor if such a class is available.

Your second pregnancy may be easier or more challenging than the first. In either case, most women find that having been through the experience once before, they have a new level of confidence about the outcome.

Braxton Hicks contractions not only appear much earlier than they did in the first pregnancy, maybe even in the fifth or sixth month, but they are usually more frequent and progressively more uncomfortable. Many women claim to have these quite painful contractions in "mini-bouts" for the last two months of pregnancy. Why you experience so many more of them so early is unknown, but perhaps the fact that your abdominal muscles are less supportive with each birth and the fact that each subsequent baby is usually a little bigger are partly responsible. In any case, when you're hit with one of these contractions, stop, take a deep breath, and relax for a moment until it passes.

The "stitch" in the groin that you may have experienced during your first pregnancy is markedly pronounced this time and may even warrant a slightly slower pace, again probably due to a bigger baby and less abdominal support.

Fatigue may be magnified, with less time to relax or nap. Try to make time for naps—you need the rest.

False labor is more prevalent. Usually 25 percent of women having second babies have several bouts of false labor, versus only 10 percent of women having first babies.

When you pack your Lamaze bag, tuck in a present you can give to your child when he visits you in the hospital—not "from the new baby," which would cause confusion, but from you because you've been away for a few days and have missed him!

Labor itself will be quite different than with the first baby. Although the prospect of *any* very painful hours is not great, most women are pleasantly surprised to experience only one or two horrible hours in labor this time—much different from the usual eight to ten hours the first time around!

Once progression of contractions has been established, stop eating solid foods. You probably have only three to five hours before delivery if your first labor was the normal ten to twelve hours—and you need to get to the hospital.

Use your breathing techniques as reviewed on page 124. Most hospitals or independent Lamaze teachers offer a refresher class as a review session for couples having second or subsequent babies.

If contractions suddenly become very strong as you walk through the admitting office, do not allow the staff to detain your husband for information as they whisk you up to the labor-and-delivery suite. He may very well miss the delivery altogether!

Gentlemen, women can dilate from five to ten centimeters in half an hour. Once your wife is in the labor room, put on your scrub suit when she's about five centimeters dilated, rather than waiting until she's at ten as you did with Baby #1.

As labor progresses and contractions suddenly become extremely intense, you may decide this second labor is more than you bargained for and you want medication right away. This is the typical pattern of second labors, and usually when you make that demand you are only fifteen to twenty minutes from delivery as you enter transition. With a fairly manageable early and active labor, this phase hits hard and fast.

The nurse will undoubtedly reassure you that delivery is close at hand and that you can make it through that last twenty minutes without medication. Trust her experienced judgment, as tempted as you are to give up completely at that moment!

The pushing stage is significantly shorter with the second baby, the urge much more pronounced, for most women. Until you're given the go-ahead to push, it's still important to suppress the urge with the blow technique you used in labor with Baby #1— this time not because of the risk of tearing or having the cervix swell, but because delivery is imminent and preparations for it need to be made.

The birth seems quick and easy as the baby, even though half a pound bigger than the first, slips right out.

Greeting him or her is no less wondrous a moment for you and your husband than it was with your firstborn. Gentlemen, hold fast as he's placed in your arms—he's a mere feather! By comparison your youngster at home seems ready for college!

Placenta expulsion and episiotomy repair are similar to your last delivery, but somehow everything seems to go more smoothly, more easily, probably because your system has been through it all before.

Recovery will probably go much more smoothly this time, and breast-feeding, although your nipples can become sore, is a breeze in comparison to the first time around.

If possible, have your first child visit you in the hospital, not only to reassure him but also because you miss your little constant companion. Find out how long you are going to be there and consider your child's personality. A visit is usually most beneficial if it is short and takes place on the day before you leave the hospital, so that when he must go home a reassuring "See you tomorrow when you come to take us home!" makes his good-bye easy.

When you leave the hospital, have your husband carry the baby so you can be with your older child. Once you arrive home, he may express an interest in holding the baby. Sit him on the bed or sofa in case he drops the baby and show him how to support the head. Undress the baby so he can look him over. After this first meeting, tell him, "You may hold the baby any time as long as you get Daddy or Mommy first."

Your child deserves your undivided attention when you first arrive home; the baby's presence should be as unintrusive as possible. Beyond the initial period, however, the more "baby care" the older sibling is offered, the more accepting he or she usually tends to be about the whole situation: with his involvement you become allies in taking care of the helpless little newborn. Some children want "a baby of their own," perhaps to compete with their mother's new situation—an easy request to meet and a nice outing together to the nearest toy store for a doll of his or her choice. Look for a child-sized carrier (Snugli makes them!), stroller, or carriage to round out the picture, and encourage this need to emulate your every move; it's a very healthy outlet for your child, and entertaining as well.

Of course, when the baby is fretful and crying, demanding the mother's attention, juggling the needs of a newborn with those of an older sibling is a challenge. A clever strategy that worked for one mother was to point out to her child how miserable that baby was: "Look at him, he can't talk, he has no teeth, he can't even hold anything [all things the older child took pride in mastering], he is just plain miserable." The jealousy over the baby's getting Mom's attention seemed to dissolve every time.

Another mother found that her little three-year-old daughter could manage every other interruption by the baby but seemed to have a very difficult time watching him breast-feed. She cried and tugged at her mother, miserable that the baby had taken over this cozy spot, and said she would like to try nursing. Her mother offered her some breast milk in a cup, which she found far less tasty than her usual cold apple-juice snack. Another mother said, "Want to try?" Of course the child was delighted with the idea, but when the moment of truth arrived, she started to giggle with her mom, it seemed so funny and strange! Pretty soon you become adept at feeding your newborn with your arm around your older child as you read a favorite story.

It is quite common for your older child to want to come into your room when you undress. This is due to his need to see that you are still in one piece. Even though he may never have noticed your enlarging belly, he does now notice that it has shrunk and that the new baby has somehow escaped out of your body. Let him look you over. If you have had a Caesarean, it is quite easy to explain how the baby got out; if you delivered vaginally, and he asks how it got out, don't be too vague about the process. If you say "the baby came out below," a three-year-old may think that means a bowel movement and, to be sure not to have another baby enter the family, vow never to have another bowel movement himself. It would be better to give an explanation such as, "There is a special hole next to the b.m. hole [or whatever term he knows] that gets larger when the baby is born and then smaller again." If his next question is "How did it get in there?" again, don't be too vague. He is asking for basic reproductive information. If the seed concept is your answer, do not be surprised by a response such as "Dad, when you planted my seed in Mom was my picture on the packet?"

It's normal to see some form of regression in your older child, and your beautifully toilet-trained three-year-old may start wetting his pants. Do not overreact. Try to plan some outings with him that he would enjoy.

One mother found herself saying to her older child, "You'll have to wait . . ." many times a day, so to even out the disparity, when they were about to leave for an outing, she would say to the newborn, "You will have to wait, we are going out now!" and her older child would heartily second the motion!

If your older child becomes angry easily, he may push or even hit the new baby. Be firm and make him realize that although he may not always like the baby, he cannot hurt him. Perhaps a hammering toy would allow him to express his anger in another way. Finally, it is not uncommon to hear an older child say, after a few days at home with a newborn, "I think we have had this baby long enough. Let's take him back to the hospital now!"

Someone once compared the introduction of a new sibling to

a husband coming home one evening and saying "Tomorrow I'm going to bring home a new wife, because you have been such a terrific first one!" Perhaps there is an element of truth in this that causes some confusion in the mind of a three-year-old. Obviously, the more natural and open you are to the needs of your child, heaping on him the same hugs and kisses, playing the same fun games and returning to as much of your old routine as possible, the more accepting your child will be. It takes an enormous amount of work for parents at first to help incorporate that new baby into the family, but the rewards are soon evident: siblings entertain each other from day one, forming a bond of loyalty that far outdistances their daily struggles as they engage in healthy competition. Soon it feels as if you've *always* had a second child—and you don't regret a minute of it.

Glossary of Obstetrical Terms

Abortion (miscarriage): either spontaneous or induced delivery of the fetus before twenty-six weeks' gestation

Afterpains: Uncomfortable or painful contractions of the uterus, felt by the mother as the uterus heals and returns to its normal size; more common after each subsequent childbirth and when breast-feeding

Amniocentesis: Removal of a small amount of amniotic fluid with a long thin needle for genetic and chemical evaluation to determine the well-being and sex of the unborn baby

Amniotic sac: see "Bag of waters"

Analgesic agent: Medication that reduces pain

Anesthetic agent: Medication that relieves pain

Apgar score: An evaluation of the baby during the first one to five minutes after birth, determined by the baby's color, muscle tone, heart rate, grimace, and cry

Back labor: When uterine contractions are felt in the lower back area, usually due to a baby presenting in a posterior position

Bag of waters: The membranes containing amniotic fluid, which surrounds the baby in the uterus

Bilirubin: A pigment produced during the breakdown of extra newborn red-blood cells, characterized by a yellow tint to the skin ("jaundice")

Bloody show: Blood-tinged mucus from the cervical opening expelled before and/or during labor

Bradycardia: Slowing of the baby's heart rate to less than 120 beats per minute

Braxton Hicks contractions: Intermittent, usually painless contractions of the uterus toward the end of pregnancy; "practice contractions"

Breech: The presenting part of the baby during labor when it is the buttocks or one or both feet

Caesarean birth: Delivery of the baby by incision through the abdomen and the wall of the uterus

Caput: The appearance of the baby's head at the vaginal opening

Cervix: The lower portion, or neck, of the uterus

Colostrum: A yellow fluid in the breast that is made during pregnancy and serves as the initial and complete nutrient for a breast-fed baby until true milk production begins on the third or fourth day

Crowning: Appearance of the largest part of the baby's head at the vaginal opening

Cystitis: A bladder infection usually characterized by the need to urinate frequently and burning on urination

Demerol: An analgesic injection frequently administered during labor to aid in relaxation and to help reduce pain

Dilation: Widening of the cervical opening to permit the baby's head to pass through

Dipping: When the baby's head or buttocks are between floating and engagement

Eclampsia: An unusual medical problem in pregnancy characterized by severe elevated blood pressure

Ectopic (tubular) pregnancy: A pregnancy that begins to grow in the Fallopian tube and will usually rupture through the tube if not removed

E.D.C.: Expected date of confinement (birth); due date

Edema: Swelling due to fluid retention, usually in ankles, feet, and hands

Effacement: Gradual thinning of the cervix before and during labor from zero to 100 percent

Embryo: The fertilized egg, up to eight weeks of age

Endometrium: The lining of the uterus

Endorphin: Natural analgesic produced by the body

Engagement: When the largest measurement of the baby's head or buttocks descends well into the pelvis, usually two to six weeks before birth in women having first babies, and in early labor in women having second or third babies

Engorgement (breast): Enlargement and swelling of the breasts when milk production begins, which may occur on the third or fourth day after delivery and usually subsides within twenty-four to forty-eight hours

Epidural anesthesia: A local anesthetic injected outside the dura, or protective membrane of the spinal cord, to eliminate pain during labor

Episiotomy: A small incision made to enlarge the vaginal opening to facilitate birth

F.H.R.: Fetal heart rate, 120 to 160 beats per minute

Fetus: The unborn baby from the eighth week of gestation to delivery

Floating: The position of the baby in the uterus before the baby's head or buttocks engage, or settle down into the pelvis

Forceps: Instruments used to aid in the delivery of the baby's head

Fundus: The upper portion of the uterus

Gestation: The period from conception to delivery, about thirty-eight weeks.

Hyperventilation: A feeling of light-headedness or tingling and cramping in fingers or toes when there is a sudden drop in CO_2 level in the body

Induction: The initiation of labor through artificial means, usually by the administration of Pitocin

Involution: The healing of the uterus back to its prepregnant state over a six-week period

Lanugo: A downy hair that covers the fetus and may be visible at birth over forehead, neck, and shoulders

Lochia: The discharge of blood, mucus, and tissue from the uterus through the vagina, after the birth of the baby, which gradually lessens in color and amount over a two-to-three-week period after childbirth

Meconium: A newborn's first black, tarry bowel movement

Molding: The pushing together and/or overlapping of a baby's skullbones during labor to facilitate birth

Monitor: A mechanical device used to observe uterine contractions or the baby's heartbeat to ascertain proper functioning

Mucous plug: A plug of mucus which blocks the cervix during pregnancy, referred to as show when expelled, usually at the onset of labor

Multigravida: A woman who has had one or more previous pregnancies

Multipara: A woman who has had one or more deliveries

Occiput posterior: Vertex presentation when the back of the baby's head presses against the mother's spine; often causes back labor

Oxytocin: A natural hormone secreted into the mother's bloodstream to initiate and maintain labor

Pelvic floor: A sling of muscles which supports the pelvic organs and through which the fetus must pass during delivery

Pelvimetry: An X-ray evaluation of the pelvis to assist in determining its capacity for delivery

Perineum: The region between the vagina and the rectum where the episiotomy is made at the time of delivery

Phases of labor: Differentiation in contractions in the first stage of labor: Phase I, "early"; Phase II, "active"; Phase III, "transition"

Pitocin: Synthetic oxytocin, given intravenously to induce or speed up labor

Placenta: A circular, flat, vascular structure which nourishes the baby throughout pregnancy, usually attached to the upper portion of the uterus or fundus, and expelled following the baby's birth

Postmature: A baby who is overdue, usually exhibiting dry, peeling skin and long fingernails

Premature labor: Onset of labor after twenty-eight weeks of pregnancy but before thirty-seven

Presentation: The part of the baby that enters the pelvis first

Primagravida: A woman who is pregnant with her first child

Quickening: The first time the mother feels the baby move

Sacrum: The bone at the base of the spinal column that also forms the back of the pelvis

Show: A blob of mucus with streaks of blood discharged from the cervix and vagina just prior to the onset of labor

Sonogram: The pictorial outline of anatomic structures through the use of ultrasound radiology to determine the size of the baby and the position of the placenta

Sphincter: A muscle surrounding and closing an opening

Stages of labor: One: from the onset of labor to the complete dilation of the cervix to ten centimeters; two: from ten centimeters through the birth of the baby; three: expulsion of the placenta

Station: The measurement of descent of the baby through the birth canal during labor, from −4 centimeters to +4 centimeters

Striae: Silvery lines that appear on abdomen, breasts, and thighs, caused by stretching of the skin during pregnancy

Tachycardia: An abnormally fast heart rate in the fetus or newborn, usually over 160 beats per minute

Teratogenic: Something that could cause damage to the unborn baby

Toxemia: A complication of pregnancy of unknown cause usually occurring in the last three months of pregnancy, characterized by a severe increase in blood pressure

Transition: The last two to three centimeters of cervical dilation (from eight to ten centimeters) before pushing, Phase III of the first stage of labor; usually the most painful part of labor

Uterine inertia: Weak or ineffective uterine contractions

Vacuum extraction: Delivering the baby with the assistance of a small suction cup to turn or rotate the head as needed, often used in place of forceps

Vernix: The layer of cheeselike material covering the skin of the baby in the uterus to prevent waterlogging from amniotic fluid

Vertex: The presenting part of the baby is the head, which occurs in 95% of labors.

Vulva: External female genitalia, including the labia and clitoris

Suggested Reading

The following books may be helpful if you wish to read more about topics covered in this book:

ON PREGNANCY, LABOR, AND DELIVERY:

Bing, Elisabeth. *Six Practical Lessons for an Easier Childbirth.* New York: Bantam Books, 1980.

Eisenberg, Arlene, et al. *What to Expect When You're Expecting.* New York: Workman Publishing Co., 1984.

Hausknecht, Richard, and Joan Heilman. *Having a Caesarean Baby.* New York: E. P. Dutton, 1983.

Karmel, Marjorie. *Thank You, Dr. Lamaze.* New York: Harper and Row, 1983.

Kitzinger, Sheila. *The Complete Book of Pregnancy and Childbirth.* New York: Alfred A. Knopf, 1986.

Noble, Elizabeth. *Essential Exercises for the Childbearing Year.* New York: Houghton Mifflin Company, 1982.

ON FETAL DEVELOPMENT:

Flanagan, Geraldine Lux. *The First Nine Months of Life*. New York: Simon & Schuster, 1982.
Nilsson, Lennart. *A Child Is Born*. New York: Dell, 1986.

ON MOTHER AND INFANT NUTRITION:

Castle, Sue. *The Complete New Guide to Preparing Baby Foods*. New York: Bantam Books, 1983.
Heslin, Joanne, and Annette Natow. *No-Nonsense Nutrition for Your Baby's First Year*. New York: Bantam Books, 1979.

ON BREAST-FEEDING:

Eiger, Marvin, and Sally W. Olds. *The Complete Book of Breast-feeding*. New York: Workman Publishing Co., 1986, *or* Bantam Books, 1986.

ON BABY DEVELOPMENT AND CHILD CARE:

Brazelton, T. Berry. *Infants and Mothers: Differences in Development*. New York: Dell, 1986.
Caplan, Frank, ed. *The First Twelve Months of Life*. New York: Bantam Books, 1978.

Dodson, Fitzhugh. *How to Parent.* New York: New American Library, 1983.

Fraiberg, Selma H. *The Magic Years.* New York: Charles Scribner's Sons, 1984.

Leach, Penelope. *Your Baby and Child.* New York: Alfred A. Knopf, 1978.

ON MISCARRIAGE AND LOSING A BABY:

Berezin, Nancy. *After a Loss in Pregnancy.* New York: Simon & Schuster, 1982.

Borg, Susan O., and Judith Lasker. *When Pregnancy Fails.* Boston: Beacon Press, 1981.

Resources

International Childbirth Education Association (ICEA)
P. O. Box 20048
Minneapolis, Minnesota 55420
1-800-624-4934
Fulfills orders for books concerning various methods of childbirth education.

American Society for Psychoprophylaxis in Obstetrics, Inc. (ASPO-Lamaze)
1840 Wilson Boulevard, Suite 204
Arlington, Virginia 22201
1-800-368-4404
An organization consisting of professional physicians and family members who promote an optimal childbirth and early parenting experience.

American College of Nurse Midwives
1522 K Street N.W., Suite 1120
Washington, D.C. 20005
202-347-5445
   This is the professional association of certified nurse-midwives in the United States.

National Organization of Mother of Twins Clubs
12404 Princess Jeanne N.E.
Albuquerque, New Mexico 87112
505-275-0955
   Offers support for parents of twins.

Cesareans Support, Education, and Concern Organization (C/SEC)
22 Forest Road
Framingham, Massachusetts 01701
617-877-8266
   Provides support and information to parents and professionals on Caesarean childbirth, Caesarean prevention, and vaginal birth after Caesarean.

The Triplet Connection
P. O. Box 99571
Stockton, California 95209
209-474-0885
   Information and support network for families that have triplets, quadruplets, or larger multiples.

TO OBTAIN GLAZED DRIED FRUITS:

Treat Boutique
200 East 86th Street
New York, New York 10028
212-737-6619
   Write for ordering information and prices.

BREAST-FEEDING NEEDS AND INFORMATION:

La Leche League
9616 Minneapolis Avenue
Franklin Park, Illinois 60131
312-455-7730
    This breast-feeding support group has chapters across the country; check your local telephone directory before calling the main headquarters listed here.

Mary Jane Company
5510 Cleon Avenue
North Hollywood, California 91609
213-877-7166
818-763-7315
    Good selection of nursing bras. Write for catalogue.

Happy Family Products
12300 Venice Boulevard
Los Angeles, California 90066
    Nursing bras and reusable nursing pads. Write for catalogue.

FOR EARLY TOOTH-DECAY PREVENTION:

Nursing Bottle Mouth or Baby Bottle Tooth Decay
American Dental Association
211 East Chicago Avenue
Chicago, Illinois 60611
ATTN: BPI
    Write for information.

WHEN SPECIAL PROBLEMS ARISE:

Cystic Fibrosis Foundation
1655 Tullie Circle N.E., Suite 111
Atlanta, Georgia 30329
404-325-6973

National Foundation for Jewish Genetic Diseases
45 Sutton Place South
New York, New York 10022
212-371-1030

National Tay-Sachs and Allied Diseases Association
92 Washington Avenue
Cedarhurst, New York 11516
516-569-4300

National Foundation for Sudden Infant Death Syndrome
330 North Charles Street
Baltimore, Maryland 21201

Center for the Prevention of Sudden Infant Death Syndrome
2 Metro Plaza
Landover, Maryland 20785
301-459-3388

Index

ABOUT THE AUTHORS

Fritzi Farber Kallop is one of America's most experienced and well-loved childbirth educators. She has an R.N. and B.S. from The New York Hospital–Cornell Medical Center and was certified by and held an office with the American Society for Psychoprophylaxis in Obstetrics. She has worked with over 5,000 couples as a staff nurse, assisting them in labor and delivery for over thirteen years. In her popular New York City Lamaze classes her wit, wisdom, and insight provide thousands of couples with the excellent preparation needed to handle pregnancy, childbirth, and early parenthood, clearing up misconceptions and bringing the experience of having a baby into focus. She lives in New York City with her husband and three children.

Julie Houston has had a long career in book publishing. With thirteen years' experience as an acquiring editor in the trade divisions of two of New York City's major hardcover publishing firms, she has for the last seven years combined her work as a free-lance writer and editor with raising a family. She lives with her husband and two small children in Park Slope, Brooklyn.